REMEMBERING

Father Flye

A Century of Friendships

WILLIAM I. HAMPTON
FOREWORD BY ARTHUR BEN CHITTY

Father Flye in 1940

REMEMBERING

Father
Flye

A Century
of Friendships

WILLIAM I. HAMPTON
FOREWORD BY ARTHUR BEN CHITTY

IONE PRESS
2001

Remembering Father Flye: A Century of Friendships/by William I. Hampton

Copyright William I. Hampton 2000

Ione Press Inc.
P.O. Box 3271
Sewanee, TN 37375

ISBN 0-9666674-5-X

Library of Congress Number 2001131059

First printing
10 9 8 7 6 5 4 3 2 1

2001

Cover: Father Flye in the classroom at St. Andrew's, circa 1926

Photo credits:
Bennett Collection: 23, 97,106
Boorman Collection: cover, 3, 12, 13, 14, 58, 78, 130, 206, 229, 239
Chattanooga Times: 32, 163
Chubb Collection: ii
Robert Costa: 190, 196
Father Flye Collection: 80, 83, 84, 162, 180, 201
Norris Houghton: 205
Kevin Kennedy: 235, 245
Brian McDowell: 132, 133, 150, 198
Order of the Holy Cross: 27, 28, 29, 30, 31, 35, 36, 42, 47, 55, 107, 108, 109, 112, 113, 114, 116, 117, 118, 123, 126, 127, 151, 204
Polk County: 4
St. Andrew's School: 48, 119, 135, 148, 152, 153, 157, 223, 233
John Steiger: 207
University of the South: 24, 25, 26, 100
Vanderbilt University: 103
Kathleen Yokley: 45

To
All The Caring Teachers

To Teach Is To Touch A Life Forever

CONTENTS

Foreword ix
Preface xi

1 The Flyes—The Great Freeze—
  Yale—Grace—Milledgeville 1
2 The Early Years at St. Andrew's School 21
3 Ed Yokley—Oliver Hodge—Ed Hubbell—
  Claude Wright—Dale Doss 40
4 The Bungalow—Views on the World—
  Reminiscences—A Microcosm 57
5 The Teacher—The Man 76
6 DuBose—EQB Club—Close Friends—
  High Jinks 95
7 The Bishop's Anger—Dark Journals—The King's
  Beard 111
8 James Agee and David McDowell 129
9 Football—Toilet Troubadours—
  Student Hazing 146
10 Father Flye's Teaching Philosophy—
  Birdwood—Poetry and Prose 160
11 New York City Memories 177
12 Robert Costa and Frederick Santee 189
13 Grace Houghton Flye 200
14 After St. Andrew's 219
15 Twilight and Eulogies 234

Acknowledgments 248
Index 250

FOREWORD

My wife, Betty Nick, and I knew Father Flye personally, so we were keenly interested when Bill Hampton asked us to review his manuscript. It was a labor of love. Both of us learned riveting facts about Father Flye that we didn't know before.

Remembering Father Flye has the pathos, humor, suspense and controversy equal to any screenwriter's fancy. This book has incredible anecdotes. Dale Doss's memory of Father Flye gave him the strength to endure while he was a prisoner of war. Oliver Hodge had been expelled from St. Andrew's School when Father Flye persuaded the Headmaster to reconsider. Bill Hampton has uncovered many accounts in which Father Flye turned a boy's life around for the better.

There is the melancholy story of David McDowell. Most readers will be surprised to learn he was the primary force behind the literary fame of James Agee.

Father Flye's wife, Grace, was well-known on the Mountain as a portrait painter, but her personal life was enigmatic. This book chronicles her illnesses and eventual seclusion.

The book also explores Father Flye's idea of having his own school; his relationship with the Order of the Holy Cross; his compassion for the homeless in Greenwich Village; his many friends, ranging from poets to stevedores. Our personal observation was that Father Flye never met a child who did not respond eagerly to his friendliness.

This book has nostalgic recollections and photographs that capture the history of St. Andrew's the way it really was. To experience the essence of great teaching, one need only read about Father Flye as interpreted by Bill Hampton.

Arthur Ben Chitty
Historiographer, University of the South
Fulford Cottage
100 South Carolina Avenue
Sewanee, Tennessee 37375

PREFACE

I arrived at St. Andrew's School when I was 13 years old, perhaps destined to end up in prison or prematurely dead, but the school saved my life. My attitude changed and I left the school a winner. I give Father Flye much of the credit. For reasons I still cannot explain, the soft-spoken priest took an interest in me. Thank God he did.

To say Father Flye played an important role in my life is putting it mildly. He was the "Dad" I never had—and I adored him.

Father Flye selected books from his enormous personal library for me to read. Through him I came to know Edgar Allan Poe, Robert Louis Stevenson, Ernest Hemingway, James Joyce, and other writers. I have been an avid reader since that time.

My private times with Father Flye at St. Andrew's were not always earthshaking, but they were important to me. We discussed a variety of subjects, ranging from ancient philosophy to the absurd. For example, we once talked about why ghosts invariably appear alone (we never solved that riddle). The bottom line is that he introduced me to the love of learning. My memories of him are precious.

During my senior year at St. Andrew's School (1950-51), Father Flye and I listened together to the Evening News Roundup on the CBS Radio Network. He had installed an antenna on the roof of his campus house, but the radio signal often faded or was obscured by static, so it was a hit-and-miss situation. Nevertheless, I looked forward to the daily ritual, because it was a privilege to be alone with him.

His house was filled with dark shadows and overrun with books, magazines, and old newspapers. It had a distinct musty smell. It was an enchanting place. While listening to the radio with Father Flye, I became addicted to keeping up with current events. This led to my becoming a radio newscaster.

One of Father Flye's heroes was Edward R. Murrow, who became famous for his radio reports from London during the 1940 blitz . Years later I met Murrow in Paris and I sent a telegram to Father Flye with the news of my lucky encounter. Father Flye wrote back, demanding that I repeat every word Murrow said.

After I graduated from St. Andrew's, I maintained casual contact with Father Flye through short letters and Christmas cards. Between 1951 and 1972, I visited him four times in New York City. It was a joy to see him. He had a wonderful habit of pushing his chair up close, and I felt he was hanging on every word I said. His witty poetry always left me smiling.

In late 1993, I drove onto the St. Andrew's-Sewanee School campus for the first time in 42 years. I was shocked when I learned the school had years earlier merged with Sewanee Academy (Sewanee Military Academy in my era), and the school had become co-educational. This change took some getting used to.

A nagging reality evolved during my subsequent visits to the school. Other than a small plaque in the Lady Chapel, there was nothing at the school honoring Father Flye. He had taught at St. Andrew's for nearly four decades, he was famous for his association with the writer James Agee, but the priest's name was nowhere to be found. In addition, I saw none of Grace Flye's portraits on the campus, yet she was probably the most renowned artist in the Mountain's history.

The idea that the Flyes could be forgotten was unthinkable to me, so I decided to write my recollections of the history teacher and his wife. As I began to talk with people who knew them, I realized there was a larger story that should be told. What began as a private look back in time became a trip through uncharted waters.

Six years of research took me to New York City; Berryville, Virginia; Miami, Haines City, Winter Park and Orlando, Florida; Milledgeville, Georgia; Little Rock, Arkansas; Wichita, Kansas; Omaha, Nebraska; Chattanooga, Nashville, Sewanee, Monteagle and Tracy City, Tennessee; Green Valley, Arizona; and West Park, New York. I conducted interviews in all these locations. I talked with people by telephone across the United States, as well as in Italy and England. The project also required searching through archives at Vanderbilt University and the University of the South.

I interviewed almost 150 people. Undoubtedly, many others should have been questioned. But who knows how many individuals Father Flye knew over his long life? In any event, in early 2000 I decided to organize the information I had, and finish the manuscript. I had fulfilled my original goal.

It is important to note that this book only touches on a fraction of the information accumulated. The information on Father Flye is a gold mine for many stories yet to be told, and should be of interest to other authors and historians. Most of the Father Flye material is housed in the Special Collections Archives at Vanderbilt University; other information has been donated to the Archives of duPont Library at the University of the South: Grace Flye's letters; Father Flye's letters and journal notations; recorded interviews; photographs; publications of St. Andrew's School and the Order of the Holy Cross; copies of newspaper articles; and Gil Adkins' unpublished work on the history of St. Andrew's School.

My research took unexpected twists. I was astonished to learn that Father

Flye had a history of rebellion against authority. The story of David McDowell was an eye-opener. The same can be said of the stories of Ed Yokley, Doc Santee, and others. Grace Flye's letters were invaluable. Besides exposing her husband's inner feelings, her way with words was as beautiful as her paintings.

This book is not a biography of Father Flye, nor is it the full history of St. Andrew's School; however, it comes close to being both. I think of this book as a memoir. In many ways, it is an oral history. Whenever possible, an interviewee's own words are used to describe personalities, attitudes and events.

Father Flye and Grace Flye had rich lives, but their lives were not without frustration and bitterness. Readers of these pages will be surprised, perhaps even shocked, but the truth is rarely painless.

The following pages take the reader to Paris, London, Brussels, Florence, and the Bahamas. To Miami, Chicago, Jacksonville, San Francisco, New York City, Milwaukee, Cincinnati, Boston; Elko, Nevada, Bangor, Maine; Wapwallopen, Pennsylvania; and to many places in Florida and Tennessee.

When I think of Father Flye, I'm reminded of these words by Ralph Waldo Emerson:

> To laugh often and much; to win the respect of people and the affection of children; to earn the appreciation of honest critics and endure the betrayal of false friends; to appreciate beauty, to find the best in others; to leave the world a bit better; to know even one life has breathed easier because you have lived. This is to have succeeded.

This book is my personal "thank you" to Father Flye. He should be remembered.

James Harold Flye is gone, but he is not forgotten. His presence remains. Some people believe that if you sit among the stately trees in the quadrangle at St. Andrew's-Sewanee School, and let your imagination wander, especially on a foggy day, you will look across and see him energetically carrying his books, and you will know he is going to have a productive day in his classroom.

James Harold Flye is gone, but he is not forgotten. His presence remains. Some people believe that if you sit in the Rectory garden at St. Luke's Chapel in New York City, and let your imagination wander, you will see his smiling face. You will see this man of faith, with his big expressive hands, giving wise counsel to a needy person.

CHAPTER 1

The Flyes—The Great Freeze—Yale—Grace— Milledgeville

The unexamined life is not worth living.
—PLATO (428?-347 BC)

THIS IS THE STORY of James Harold Flye, a soft-spoken Episcopal priest who had a remarkable capacity for friendship. His life spanned a full century, and few have been revered by so many. About Father Flye, *Washington Post* journalist Colman McCarthy wrote: "In the literature of friendship the name of James Harold Flye has an honored place." University of the South historiographer Arthur Ben Chitty has said: "The world will recall this man of compassion who helped change the lives of so many. Few men had such enormous impact on people, both young and old."

A social chameleon with a common touch, Father Flye was at ease in any setting, from the rural coves of Tennessee to New York's arty Greenwich Village. Some of Father Flye's friends were famous; most were not so well known. Highly intelligent, in the thrall of ideas, he recited thousands of poems from memory. A teacher, poet, author, linguist, historian, and geographer, Father Flye's lifelong commitment was to philology, but he never lost his enthusiasm for life, for people, and for the human potential.

However, he was also stubborn and rebellious, and made errors of judgment that were sometimes disastrous. He was unapologetic about his opinions and the life he led. He wrote: "I am an individualist, and wish as much personal freedom as possible." He was married to Grace Houghton Flye, an accomplished portrait artist. Both were eccentric and their marriage was pecu-

1

liar, but it suited and supported them.

This is not a biography of Father Flye, but rather a portrait of him derived from letters and verbal accounts by people associated with him. Nobody really knew the man, because his life was one of contradictions and many facets. He was viewed differently by his wife, his in-laws, his own family, his friends, his students, church officials, school administrators, and the world at large. Yet he was unforgettable.

□ □ □

James Harold Flye spent his early years in the isolated hamlet of Haines City, Florida, between Tampa and Orlando. His parents, of solid Yankee stock, were pioneers in the development of central Florida. His father, James Tyler Flye, was born September 22, 1841, in Bangor, Maine. He was an ambitious business-man, undeterred by risk. Father Flye's mother, Mary Ann Simpson, was born November 17, 1852, near Bar Harbor, Maine, to a middle-class family that owned part of a quarry supplying paving stones to New England cities. A few of the Simpson clan were wealthy.

James Tyler Flye and Mary Ann Simpson were married in Bucksport, Maine, in 1883, after a friendship of 12 years. He was 42; she was 31. They did not stay long in Maine. James Tyler Flye had plans to go south. In the 1880s railroad tracks were extended to remote parts of central Florida, enabling citrus growers to easily ship oranges and grapefruit to northern markets. By 1886, Florida's citrus production reached one million boxes. The citrus "gold rush" that attracted thousands, including the Flyes, was fueled by newspaper reports about how "men of modest means" could prosper by owning just a few acres of orange or grapefruit trees.

Would-be moguls booked passage to Jacksonville. From there they traveled on paddle-wheel freighters down the St. Johns River to Sanford, north of Orlando. They then traveled over primitive dirt roads and around mosquito- and alligator-inhabited lakes to stake their claims. Newcomers thought, "growing oranges can't be all that hard," but they soon learned that northern newspapers had not reported the whole story.

Clearing the land was slow and back-breaking work. If a planter could afford it, he used oxen, horses or mules to uproot trees and indigenous shrubs. The cleared land still had to be weeded, usually by hand. After the citrus trees were planted, it took at least seven years before a grove produced a viable cash crop. Pickers wearing shoulder bags climbed tall ladders against the thorny "hedge" of a mature tree to reach the fruit. They emptied their bags into small boxes, which were hauled by mule-drawn wagons to a packinghouse. The citrus fruit was then put in ventilated crates to be transported via the railroad to northern markets.

The process took waiting, worrying and sweating. However, the entrepre-

James Tyler Flye

neurs of the 1880s and 1890s knew it was worth it. With the exception of tobacco, citrus produced the greatest return per acre of any crop in the nation. Within several decades of first planting citrus seedlings, a man could be rich. These facts drove the marketplace in 1885. At that time, the menu at the posh Palmer House Hotel in Chicago listed one orange for one dollar. Steak with all the trimmings cost fifty cents. If they could afford it, people gave oranges as Christmas presents. Dentists told their patients to eat oranges and grapefruit to prevent gum disease.

James Tyler Flye read the newspaper accounts about growing oranges in Florida, and decided to jump on the bandwagon. After an investigative trip to Florida, he returned to Maine and convinced his brother, Vondel, and Harmon Stevens, a friend, to pool their resources and go south. They decided to grow oranges near the rail line constructed by tycoon Henry Plant between Tampa and Sanford.

In early 1884, the trio bought land in and around what would later become Haines City, Florida. Draining and clearing the land was tedious: the land was a combination of lakes, swamps, oak and pine forests. Summers brought gnats, mosquitoes, alligators, snakes, and oppressive heat and humidity. Over the next several years, seven families from Maine, working as a unit, built houses for each of the seven family groups. The workmanship was first-rate. James Tyler Flye's house had a wide front porch, hardwood floors and a spectacular chandelier.[1]

The risks for the Bangor transplants were enormous. Four of the seven families had owned fruit orchards in Maine, and they sold them to finance their venture. This was not an endeavor for the weak or lazy. Haines City had no labor pool at that time—black families did not arrive until later—so the Maine pioneers did all the work themselves.

When Mary became pregnant, she returned to Bangor temporarily to give birth to her first child, James Harold Flye, on October 17, 1884. Because his first name was the same as that of his father, he was called Hal by relatives. When Mary returned to Florida in 1885, she moved into a newly built two-story house on Third Street in the center of Haines City.

Flye home in Haines City, Florida, circa 1894. Left to right: Mary, Donald, James Tyler, Barbara, Hal.

James Tyler Flye opened a general merchandise store and operated a livery stable. Almost everything in the store was imported, from tools to grain. Much of the inventory was kept in burlap bags or barrels. Like other general stores of that era, it became a popular meeting place. Checker games, played atop a seed barrel, were a daily ritual. The store smelled of dust, pipe smoke, leather harnesses, wood and ash, feed sacks, lantern oil, and the sweat of hard-working men. The Haines City women went to the store to buy coffee, flour, salt, tea, spices, cloth, needles, and buttons.

Hal's father bought more land, eventually acquiring more than 20 parcels. Some of them were later cleared to become orange groves. He also invested in the collecting of turpentine obtained from the area's abundant pine trees. As he acquired more cash, he bought more property, spending $300 here, $400 there. He eventually had local investments of more than $3,000. In only a few years, James Tyler Flye was known as a prosperous businessman. Meanwhile, Haines City was growing. By 1890, the population exceeded 100.

Hal's brother, Donald, was born in 1890, the first white child born in Haines City. In 1892, in the same house on Third Street, Mary gave birth to a girl who was named Barbara.[2] By then, the town had grown to 500 people. The future looked bright for the local citrus industry—and the Flye family.

It is not uncommon for a woman to give an inordinate amount of attention to her first child, and this is what happened to Hal. Mary was a good mother to all of her children, but her first-born held a special place in her heart. Hal nearly died from diphtheria when he was two years old, and Mary fussed over him, so that

4

relatives considered him to be an overly protected "mama's boy." Leland Chubb, Jr., one of Hal's nephews, said: "There was this resentment that Uncle Hal was grandmother's favorite. He grew up thinking he was special. He wasn't liked that much by my side of the family."

In 1890, at the age of five, Hal was composing poetry. Mary proudly mailed some of her son's poems to relatives in Maine. Hal began school that year in Haines City's one-room schoolhouse. A teacher, Adele Pennington, noticed his photographic memory and eagerness to learn, and Hal became one of her favored pupils. Mary had done an excellent job of preparing him for school, and she told Hal's teacher to "push him hard." Miss Pennington did so, and was tutoring him in Latin when he was just eight years old. One year later, she introduced him to French. Mary was pleased that her oldest child received special attention. Hal's father, on the other hand, was too distracted with his business ventures to give much notice to his oldest son's progress in school.

In a 1980 speech, Father Flye discussed the sequence of events at that time in his life: "My mother and my teacher knew I wouldn't be happy being a farmer. Miss Pennington was a great teacher who introduced me to the background of European civilization, and what that heritage meant. I was fascinated, and read and read. My mother asked our relatives in Maine to send me certain books, instead of other Christmas presents, because better books were hard to find in Haines City. I recall getting a book about the English navigator, Captain James Cook, who discovered Australia. He was the first sea captain who made his crews eat fruit and sauerkraut to prevent scurvy. He was one of my boyhood heroes."

An indication of the strong bond that developed between the "schoolmarm spinster" and Hal is the fact that years later, in 1910, he invited Adele Pennington to attend his graduation from Yale University. During an interview late in his life, Flye said: "Outside of my mother, Miss Pennington was the one who guided me toward getting an education. I have nice memories of studying with her, even during the summers, when I was at an impressionable age."

Adele Pennington also introduced Hal to music, and he became an accomplished harmonica player. He later reminisced: "Grandfather Simpson had sent me a Super Chromonica as a present, and I fell in love with that mouth organ. My teacher showed me how to read sheet music, and gave me an appreciation of how music has influenced people since the dawn of history." His musical talent was to help him survive later on when he was a university student.[3]

Mother Nature put an abrupt halt to Hal's idyllic life in the winter of 1894-1895 with the *Great Freeze*. The Great Freeze was actually two freezes: one on December 29, 1894, and another on February 7, 1895. The days leading up to the freeze gave no hint of what was to come. Christmas Day 1894 saw temperatures in the 80s. But several days later a cold front pushed through the state. Then a hush came and the temperature began to drop. By December 29, pumps were frozen, water pipes had burst, foliage was blackened and dead. The mercury had dipped to 24 degrees.

In Orlando's San Juan Hotel, a favorite meeting place for local businessmen, arguments and fistfights broke out in the lobby as prices fell to "no sale" on citrus products. Commission merchants frantically tried and failed to get out of options. At 9 a.m. on December 29, a dapper older man wearing a black frock coat and Stetson hat walked up to a thermometer that had been nailed on the hotel's front door. He groaned aloud, "Oh, my God!" and in front of shocked onlookers, shot himself.

For the next three days an icy spell fell across a silent, frozen world. Despair inside the San Juan Hotel was almost palpable. Outside the hotel, row after row of citrus trees were dying. As the season's crop hung limp, most growers gave up. The bulk were mom-and-pop enterprises. They sold their land at great loss, or moved away leaving behind foreclosed mortgages. Others were forced to sell at a loss. Land values fell like a rock. In 1895, seven out of Orange County's eight banks failed. Across central Florida, from Lakeland to Malabar, Daytona Beach to Tampa, packinghouses were boarded shut.

Some trees did survive the first stage of the great freeze. January 1895 brought warmer and wet weather and the hardier trees began to produce new growth. Woody tissue, located just under the bark, began to fill with sap as the damaged trees began to recover. The sap flow made the trees especially vulnerable to the second freeze. On February 7, 1895, the mercury fell to 17 degrees, and the morning air was filled with what sounded like gunfire as sap froze and blew out tree bark. The only orange trees left of any value were those with extremely large root systems. Ninety-five percent of the orange trees were killed that winter. The Florida citrus industry did not recover for another 15 years.

Before the Great Freeze, Hal had a slow-paced carefree childhood. He had enjoyed sitting on a pickle barrel at his father's general store, sucking on sugarcane, soaking up the intoxicating smells of feed grain and coffee. At the store he listened to the men who gathered there to talk politics, play checkers, and carve wooden figures. He heard stories about the Civil War from veterans of the conflict. He studied the Seminole Indians who came to the store to buy Bull Durham tobacco and roll-your-own paper. He always recalled his father's store with fondness.

The Great Freeze irrevocably altered the lives of the Flye family. Vondel Flye's groves were completely destroyed. He sold them at 5 cents on the dollar. When he left Haines City to start over in Texas, he said that he would have given his 40 acres of orange groves for one acre of an apple orchard in Maine. Vondel never recovered financially. His final years in Texas were painful.

Everyone in Haines City was suddenly poor. No one had cash. The dreams of a few years earlier had become bitter ashes. Within a few months, self-employed land owners were looking for work, and any kind of job would do. Many of the local men went to work for a Haines City entrepreneur who sold palm fronds to churches for the Lenten season. He had a patented green mixture to dye the fronds, and nearly everyone in town made green crosses and dyed fronds after the disaster. It remained a thriving business in Haines City for years.

James Tyler Flye was too proud to do such work; after all, he was a community leader of high standing. However, something had to be done, and quickly. James Tyler closed his general store, and chose Miami as the place to begin again. Another Maine transplant, Claude Towers, who had a cache of $500, went with him.

Mary's relatives in Maine were dismayed by her husband's move to Miami; some of them thought he was abandoning his family. James Tyler had told Mary he would "get settled," and then send passage money for her and the children. He gave her $300 of $1,000 from the sale of pine trees on their Haines City property. The remaining $700 was his "nest egg" for south Florida. James Tyler Flye and Claude Towers checked into the Miami's Parham Hotel in April 1895, with plans to open another general merchandise store.

Mary was left with three children to raise, little money, and depleted citrus groves. True to form, her husband's initial letters were filled with glowing promises of the great future Miami held for them; her letters to him were ones of financial worry. Flye and Towers opened a store on Biscayne Boulevard in Miami, but the going was tough. James Tyler Flye sent money to his wife, but it was never enough. Humiliated, facing property taxes, Mary was finally forced to ask relatives in Maine for money. The well-to-do Simpsons offered to pay for her and the children to relocate back to Maine, but they would not pay Mary's property taxes in Florida.

In 1896, tycoon Henry Flagler extended his railroad line to Miami, and the financial outlook in the small town immediately improved. James Tyler Flye could now order supplies and receive them in a matter of days. For the first time, letters from Mary's husband contained sizable amounts of cash. He had written to her earlier about a large house he wanted to rent. Plans were made for Mary and the children to move to Miami in December of 1899. Mary was ecstatic with anticipation.

However, in October 1899, a yellow fever epidemic hit Miami. Both Claude Towers and James Tyler Flye died within days. Hal's father was 59 years old. Mary went to Miami to retrieve her husband's body, but the area was under a quarantine and she was forced to stay indefinitely. Years later, Hal Flye described the letters he received from his mother at that time: "There were little holes through the envelopes, where the letters had been fumigated. This was in 1899, before people knew that yellow fever was transmitted by mosquitoes."

At age 47, Mary was a widow facing a bleak future. Back at Haines City, she took in boarders, including transient laborers. Hal, 15 and rail-thin, was now the man of the house. Fate had robbed him of his adolescence. He helped his mother, doing household chores and taking what jobs he could find. One of them was working for a Tampa furniture maker who used Spanish moss as a cushioning material. Hal's job was to collect moss from the local oak trees, and spread it out to dry in shallow trenches. The moss was then bundled and taken to the rail line for shipment to Tampa. It was hard work and paid little. Hal became convinced that a formal education was necessary for his future.

Meantime, Mary Flye was becoming more desperate. She had property, but there were taxes to be paid. She sold one parcel of 40 acres for only $68. Each year she sold more land just to meet her tax obligations. In 1901, with a small inheritance she received from her father's death, she relocated to Winter Park, Florida. She rented a little house and went to work at the Winter Park library. In 1903 she bought a house in Winter Park for $750. Wild peacocks roamed the neighborhood, and breezes from several lakes made the house comfortable. Mary again took in boarders, charging them $5 per week. She wrote in a letter that she did not want to take back Miss Lena Brown, a teacher, the next year, because "the woman eats too much." With her boarding house income plus her job at the library, she had a life of genteel poverty.

Meanwhile, Hal took college preparatory classes at Rollins College in Winter Park, and taught American history at the seventh-grade level in nearby Orlando. In those days, Florida school systems hired high school graduates who seemed to be literate. Hal Flye rode the trolley to work in Orlando, then returned to Winter Park to spend evenings at Rollins as a student. Young Hal had no social life—nothing was going to stop him from getting his college degree.

Father Flye later described his delays in getting to a university: "I had taken the Yale entrance exam at Rollins College, and passed those parts dealing with Latin, Greek, one modern language, algebra, geometry, English. But I couldn't go north; I didn't have enough money. A friend of my mother had suggested I teach school, and save my paychecks. The pay was $50 a month. I had earlier taken the Florida exam for teaching elementary school subjects, so it wasn't hard for me to find a position. I taught several years at little country schools and enjoyed the experience. I had saved $600 by the time I entered Yale."

In June 1905, with the fares supplied by relatives, Mary took the younger children on a trip back to Boston. Twenty-year-old Hal wrote his mother long letters, urging her to take his brother and sister to the museums and library. He wrote: "You must take Don and Barbara to the Boston church I wrote about. And when you go to the Library, notice the faces of the spirit of the Harbinger of Light in the large painting at the main staircase. You should study the Prophets closely and the Quest of the Holy Grail. See the painting of the Dogma of the Redemption. There are old and curious things in that room."

In another 1905 letter to his mother, who was still visiting near Boston: "I earned a big $2.25 for my work clearing the Parsonage lot, which added to the $.50 for taking care of the reading room, and 5 cents for biscuits I made for Mrs.

Grafstedt. Since the grocery bill was $1.00, I had a balance of $1.80. I'm doing better than Thoreau. Speaking of him, you must visit Thoreau's home in Concord." On August 3, 1905, he chided his mother: "Have you been to Trinity Church? It is open every day, and what about the Art Museum? You have not written anything about it. It is open free on Saturdays. You might stay another week at least. Then there is Harvard. I will feel bad if you leave Boston without getting your eyes examined. It will cost less than it would here, for you would have to pay for the rail fare to Tampa or St. Augustine and back. Think what it means. You must have it done before long. You know your glasses do not fit, and to wear ill-fitting glasses strains the eyes still more. If economy must be practiced, let it be on something else."

Flye wrote to his younger brother, Donald, on July 25, 1905: "I sincerely hope you and Barbara are having a great time. Of course, you enjoyed the ocean steamer trip. I'm sorry you didn't see more of Charleston. Maybe you'll get to see Forts Sumter and Moultrie in the harbor on your way back. Were you up and about as you entered the New York harbor? The scenery as the boat comes in is most beautiful.

"What did you think of the Boston Terminal Depot? Near there is a brass tablet that marks the spot where the Boston Tea Party happened. I want you and Barbara to see as much as possible. Things about the Public Library keep occurring to me. Which of the paintings at the staircase do you like best? The one showing Plato teaching his disciples is beautiful. I can see him now, as he stands with his hands raised in earnest discourse on a high theme, while clear in the distance gleams the Acropolis. Study the series on the Quest of the Holy Grail.

"You may want to get some things for your bicycle before you leave Boston. One of the ball bearings is out on your wheel. And then there is a need for a rubber tube for your pump. I know you are interested in machinery, Don, so be sure to go visit the Institute of Technology. Be a good boy, Don, in every way. Look out for mother and see that she has a good time and goes to see the interesting places I have mentioned. Do not forget what I have told you, and stand up for what is right."

Hal's letters show an intimate knowledge of Boston, one that hardly could have been gleaned from only books. It is not surprising that he liked Boston. The areas around Beacon Street, Cambridge and Concord were the nation's centers of morality, culture and, to some extent, progress. William D. Howells, novelist and critic, paid tribute to the city in an article he wrote in 1902: "Boston, capital of the nation which is losing itself in America, qualifies the thinking of the country at large. The nation's grander causes were first befriended there."

Boston was also the center of an intellectual revolt. The complacent and comfortable upper class institutes (such as Harvard) were attacked in newspaper articles as bastions for out-of-date social snobs. It was a period of new idealisms, among them labor unions and feminism, born in the shadow of Faneuil Hall.

Hal's trips to Boston were electrifying adventures.

Hal enrolled in Yale in October 1906, and stayed north during the school year and the summers. On the New Haven campus, he began a serious study of theology. Hal was beginning to form some rigid ideas about religion. In his junior year, he wrote that the university president should be fired for allowing a Unitarian minister to speak at Yale. He wrote: "Unitarians are bogus. They don't believe in anything."

Mary wrote her son at Yale on September 22, 1907: "Get as much pleasure as you can from your own surroundings and hold fast to your faith. Mr. Marsh preached today on the faith of Paul under all circumstances. The way seems hazy sometimes, but I believe light will shine through some way. You need not pay me the $66 now. I will extend your loan until you are in better shape financially. I can get along till October when I can draw out some. I will send to the Bartow Bank and have them send me a check for around $80."

Hal was a serious student, with no interest in sports or fraternities. His concerns were getting better grades and supporting himself financially. He washed dishes, waited on tables, sold pots and pans door-to-door, and played his harmonica for tips at the New Haven train station. Adele Pennington wrote him in 1907: "Your mother has told me of your schedule. Avoid being side-tracked with college foolishness. Don't forget why you are there."

During his years in New Haven, Flye developed his lifelong habit of keeping abreast of current news. As he once put it: "I went daily to the Yale library to read about what was happening around the world. The *New York Times* was very helpful." He wrote in 1907: "The world is developing and there are growing pains. An apple is meant to be mellow and sweet, but the immature apple is not. Since the world is in an unripe stage, there is acidity. This evil is incident to the production of a more perfect state."

Hal visited Europe during the summer of 1908, arranging free passage from Boston to Liverpool by taking care of several hundred cattle on shipboard. He later called it an "odorous" experience. He bicycled throughout England and northern France. He later wrote about the province of Lorraine where he saw bullet holes from the 1870-71 Franco-Prussian War. His knowledge of French served him well during that trip. He visited Anglican churches in England and Roman Catholic churches in France and studied their rosters of clergymen going back thousands of years. He was awed by the church's continuity from Biblical times to the present. During the 1908 European trip, he began his lifelong hobby of collecting ancient coins.

In 1910 Flye graduated from Yale with a bachelor's degree in history, and began to teach at a high school in Columbus, Georgia. His stay there was short, because he had decided to obtain a master's degree in history at the University of Virginia. While he was in Charlottesville, he felt a call to the priesthood. After a great deal of reading and study, he zealously embraced the Church of England.

Father Flye once told the *New Yorker* magazine: "When I left Yale, I was committed to education. I had no idea of ever becoming a clergyman. But, over years, I combined my convictions about the heritage of civilization with the historical continuity of the Anglo-Catholic Church. I discovered I had a vocation."

After graduating from the University of Virginia in 1912, he enrolled in the General Theological Seminary in New York City. Among the students he met there were men who later became monks with the Order of the Holy Cross. They enjoyed the "high church" pomp of the Roman Catholic Church, even though they were clergymen of the Protestant Episcopal Church. Hal's meeting the future monks at the seminary would have a profound impact on his life.

Mary Simpson Flye had misgivings about Hal becoming an Episcopal priest. She was a life-long member of the Congregational Church, and had a no-frills view of religion. Congregational places of worship were unadorned and simple. The pastor was the spiritual leader as long as the congregation wanted him there. If his approach did not square with those of the majority, he was forced to go elsewhere. The congregation set its own standard for church services; no hierarchy came between them and their spiritual choices. Many of the congregations did not celebrate Lent except to change the linen on the altar.

This was the faith James Harold Flye was born into; however, he wanted a church with historical continuity, pomp, and ceremony. His mother never understood this, but for appearances, she adjusted. Mary Flye's biggest concern came in 1915 when she heard of her son's wedding plans—she thought her future daughter-in-law was scatterbrained, and certainly not the intellectual equal of her scholarly son.

❏ ❏ ❏

Grace Eleanor Houghton was born on September 16, 1875, in Mansfield, Ohio. The Houghton lineage in America extended back to the 17th century, when two Houghton cousins migrated from England to Massachusetts and Ohio. The eastern branch of the family went into publishing in Boston and into glassware manufacturing in Corning, New York. Grace's parents were part of the midwestern branch of the family, not as wealthy as their eastern relatives.

Grace's father was Albert Charles Houghton, who had served in the Civil War with the 2nd Ohio Cavalry. He was severely wounded, and dissuaded Army doctors from amputating his left arm, but it was essentially useless for the rest of his life. After the war, he received a disability pension, and was called "the Major" by his family and friends. His post-war activities varied: he was a lawyer, land developer, newspaper editor, and orator.

Grace's mother was Amy Twitchell of Brimfield, Ohio. The Twitchells were farmers and small-town business owners in Ohio and Indiana. The scattered family kept in touch via "round robin" letters, bundles passed on to each house-

The Houghton family in 1903. Left to right: Charles, Grace, Amy, Henry, Albert.

hold. Generally speaking, they were people who had enough money to indulge in traveling, and could afford to send their children to college. Grace had two brothers. The elder, Charles, became a lumber dealer in Indianapolis. The younger, Henry, was a physician and the medical administrator of the Union Medical College in China.

Grace's artistic talents were recognized early. When she was four years old, she was drawing charcoal sketches. By the time she was 12, she was painting oil portraits of her family and friends. Her teenage summers were spent at midwestern art museums where she sat for hours analyzing other artists' work. The Major doted on Grace, and went to extremes to indulge her whims. She was his spoiled pet.

In 1898, when Grace was 23, she attended LaSalle Academy in Newton, Massachusetts. She was active in the Foreign Missionary Society at school, and played a minor role in the school's production of *The Merchant of Venice*. From 1901 to 1905, she was at the Art Academy of Cincinnati, where she took advanced classes in painting. One of her mentors was the artist Frank Duveneck, who strongly influenced her evolving style.

The Major financed a trip to Italy for Grace in November 1906, so she could study at major museums. She had her own studio in Florence and was chaperoned by her mother's sister, Myra Twitchell. Their stay in Italy ended in 1908 with the news that her mother had died of a heart attack. After her grief lessened, Grace began to imagine herself in the role of gracious hostess for her father. She wrote to

Grace Houghton in 1896 (left) and in 1903.

him about the two of them opening grand salons in New York and Washington, D.C. Her buoyance did not last long. In 1910 she received a shattering letter from her father—the Major wrote that he would soon marry Myra.

The news put Grace in a state of hysteria. She was bedridden for weeks, but her affection for her aunt Myra and a desire for her father's happiness prevailed. She wrote them a welcoming, gracious note, and a short time later, the Major and Myra informed Grace that she would have her own studio at 104 West 90th Street in New York City. She was thrilled.

For the next several years, Grace flitted from spot to spot, her life aimless except for the desire to paint portraits. Her letters were always bubbly, dominated by a naivete, filled with pet names for everyone. Her mother had left her an inheritance, managed by her father, and she tried to live on just the income, but she kept dipping into the principal. The Major always sent his daughter "a little something to tide you over."

Grace's life at this time consisted of a succession of trips to Florida, North Carolina, Ohio, New York and Massachusetts, with no sign of her settling down to get married. In her letters she claimed she had ardent beaus, but her status as a spinster seemed permanent. Relatives thought the prospect of her ever finding a spouse was almost nil. Grace was born just 10 years after the end of the Civil War, and American society in those days held firm ideas about a woman's place. Spinsters were seen as women who were dreadfully crippled. A middle and upper-class woman was raised from birth to be a perfect wife. If a woman failed to marry she was a misfit. Desperation set in when a woman reached 30 without a commitment from a suitable man, and Grace passed 30 with no prospects in sight. Men never beat a path to Grace's door. She had protruding front teeth, and her flights of fancy were interpreted as childish behavior.

However, in February 1915, family members began to get dizzying letters from Grace. There had been a marvelous new turn in her life, and her letters were filled with giddy hints of changes to come. In a letter meant to be read by everyone, on March 2, 1915, Grace announced she was getting married. Her family thought it was a miracle, and a collective sign of relief was heard

Oil portraits by Grace Flye. Left to right: A. C. Houghton ("the Major"), Amy Twitchell Houghton , and Myra Houghton.

from Ohio to Massachusetts.

Husband-to-be was James Harold Flye, who would soon be an Episcopal priest. She had first met him in Winter Park, prior to his studies at the General Seminary in New York. They had courted during his seminary days there, and they had seen each other frequently in Winter Park. They planned to be married in either June or July.

In a 1980 interview, Father Flye described how he met Grace: "I was able to do some studying in Winter Park to get advanced standing. My mother had some dear friends in Winter Park, and one of the families from Ohio brought their daughter, Grace, with them that year. She decided to stay in Winter Park that summer, and we saw each other quite a bit. Over the next several months, she and I concluded that we should marry. I came up to New York, to spend two years in the seminary. Grace was also in New York much of that time, staying at her Manhattan art studio. The things we had in common included our love of poetry and the overall beauty of life, and we married in Florida after I graduated from the seminary."

In April 1915, Grace sent her father a 40-page letter, part of which read: "I will marry Mr. Hal. I can paint in my studio. I want a man of my own. I want to run away after all the hardship you have been through. I had made up my mind after I'd been in New York awhile that I couldn't keep up professionally more than a brief period each year. I cannot paint in Ohio the year round. Much as I wanted to and made up my mind to. I cannot work that way. I am too theatrical. I have made my professional stage. I have made my debut.

"It would kill me to give it up. I want to handle it the way I have to. I decided I'd finish my copies and go on a farm. A common farm where I could do work. It is the proper way. You will say didn't I know Mr. Hal wanted to marry me. Yes, of course. Others want to also. I love many others that way. Robert Newbegin I was keenest about. You are all my audience and those I paint are the ones on my stage. I want a common domestic life.

"I have to follow that road. It is my fate and what makes me more a character and will be my greatest enthusiasm. The whole house will reflect our temperament. We are all artists. I crave atmosphere all my own the way my mother did. No doubt you can see my mother in me, seeing a loving side aching for change.

"My own money I will leave in your hands, not take it. Mr. Hal won't be settled in his appointment for a time. I want to get all my copies I planned done with. And I wish to see that the studio is finished absolutely and the library made entrancing and the dining room decorated. I have it absolutely worked out in my mind even to the Carot for the drawing room and a small Vermeer.

"I want none of mother's furniture or things. They are best where they are. Mr. Hal can take care of me other ways. To eat and to sleep. And I can run around his house. If I have a child he can get a colored mammy to care for it. Mr. Johannsen told me that Jean McClane Johannsen painted up to the hour when her child was born and never did so brilliantly. Could you come visit Mr. Hal also? You will wonder what Mr. Hal will like about all this. He does like it. A professional person is a more keenly alive person. One can in a shorter time press a hundred-fold more life and color into ones surroundings and into others. It is my firm belief that every person on the globe should have a profession and in the millennium we will all have every profession. That is what it means when it says in the Bible we will all play harps. It only means we will all have time to express ourselves.

"This land of Orange blossoms and draped trees in Florida soothes me momentarily. You will say why did I change and want to marry Mr. Hal. Well I found out he was like the country to me— close to earth and near to nature. He rests me. The way my mother did. He has the same disposition she did. Sweet like the good earth itself.

"After I was in New York awhile I told him to go away and never see me. It was the same to me as when my mother died. The whole world went grey. I wrote him to come back. I couldn't move. I was all dead. I couldn't say goodby to him and he came and it was as if my mother came back to life, and it was on the day she died seven years before, I think. It was the twelfth of February. It is the only date I've noticed since she died. It is as if I woke up and found her in heaven. He makes me glad the same way she did. She told me before I went to Europe that she wanted me to be married sometime. I couldn't see it then and now I can.

"Mr. Hal said he never loved anyone except me this way. And I always say to him that I love many this way. This I found after my mother died. Mr. Hal listens to me the way my mother did. Interested in me on account of my being another sort of disposition. What I say sinks into him smoothly. I want to be first and foremost a portrait painter. It is my language in which I interpret the universal principles. What I have to say to the world. It is my test on which I dilate.

"Marriage isn't marriage to my mind as to others. To artists and composers marriage is impersonal isn't it? One marries ones own thoughts. Still I want to be married like a country girl in church in a white dress. Mr. Hal is awfully high church. He will be a Priest and will be called Father and wear a cape. He is scholarly with that quality my mother was. He is strong in constitution. I wish I could see my cat, my dingy white cat. Mr. Hal is going to write to you too. Please say something nice to my cat Mister Hotun. I always loved Mr. Hal one way. He is like my mother to me. A million kisses to everyone."[4]

Grace and Hal were married on July 15, 1915, at All Saints Episcopal Church in Winter Park, Florida. She wore a white wedding dress. She was 40; he was 30.

On December 21, 1915, James Harold Flye was ordained a priest by the Episcopal Bishop of Atlanta, and became the Curate at St. Stephen's Church in Milledgeville, Georgia. The Flyes began their life together in Milledgeville with a pattern that was to continue for the next 39 years. He left the everyday concerns of the household up to Grace. He did not pack a box, hire a workman, or make repairs. His mind was filled with reading, writing, ministry, and preaching.

Their home was the Rectory, located next to the church in the center of the historic town. Milledgeville had been the capitol of Georgia and, during the Civil War, Union troops had deliberately burned almost every building in Milledgeville to the ground. St. Stephen's Church was spared, because the soldiers needed a place to keep their horses. The church was used as a livery stable. Permanent hoof marks were left on the church's wooden floor. General William Tecumseh Sherman's "march to the sea" through Georgia in 1864 had left a residue of bitterness.

On August 8, 1916, about a year after the Flyes had arrived in Milledgeville, Grace wrote her father: "Even though I'm new at being a pastor's wife, I will try to answer questions you posed about Hal's preparations for his obligations on Sunday. Hal's sermons are important to him. He feels people must hear his words in a clear manner, for, as he said, the whole congregation only sees him once a week. When they see him during the week it is usually a case of when something goes terribly wrong, and they need a foundation of faith which is already in place. He chooses a passage from scripture and then tries to develop it into a morality lesson. Hal's message of faith is not stern; no, it is one of love. He emphasizes God's true nature: redemption, mercy, charity."

Flye had not been in Milledgeville long when he was faced with a problem that had not been discussed at the seminary. An older couple came to see him and explained their son had died, but they did not want their Baptist minister to officiate at his burial. The preacher and their son had not liked each other, and they were worried about what the Baptist minister would say. Would Father Flye conduct their son's funeral service? A novice, Flye was not sure he had the clerical authority, so he immediately sent a telegram to the Bishop in Atlanta, asking for advice. The Bishop wired back: "You have my permission to bury as many Baptists as you wish."

Grace was not the usual pastor's wife. She thought of the Rectory as *her* house.

In her letters, she wrote of the Rectory in Milledgeville in the same way she had spoken of her studio in New York City. She arranged things the way she wanted. The idea of entertaining in "her house" for a parish function was beyond her comprehension. If she was doing a portrait and her subject was posing, it was unthinkable to her that she should stop to make tea and host a discussion group. She was an artist, not a housewife. She sewed some of Father Flye's clerical clothes and during her first year in Milledgeville, she made a creche for Advent, but as time passed her interest in church affairs waned. She would be a cheerleader for her husband's work on Sundays and Holy Days, but her interest in day-to-day church matters was superficial.

Grace was best remembered at Milledgeville for an incident that took place on a bitterly cold Sunday morning in February 1917. The congregation had gathered around a wood-burning stove at the church's main entrance. Meanwhile, Father Flye stood at the lectern, 50 feet away, giving his sermon. Grace was the only person sitting in the normal pew area. Father Flye was oblivious to the fact that his words were not clearly heard by those gathered around the stove. Suddenly Grace stood up. Loudly, she accused the startled churchgoers of irreverence for not paying closer attention to what her husband was saying, and then she sat down. There was a moment of silence. Father Flye continued his sermon, as if nothing had happened. The churchgoers slowly left the church via the front door. Except for Grace, Flye had no audience for the rest of his homily. Seventy years later, this episode was still talked about in Milledgeville.

In 1995, the pastor at St. Stephen's Episcopal Church in Milledgeville, A. Edward Sellers, said: "It is impossible to know everything that went on in those days, but my speculation shouldn't be too far off the mark. This was a small church in those days with a congregation that could not have numbered more than 35. If you offended the wrong people or just a few families, your tenure here would be very hard. This was a low church parish. They were used to Morning Prayer with few, if any, vestments. Father Flye came here with ideas of high church services, and this was more ritual than they were used to, or wanted. This would cause a deep rift. Going back to the Reformation, the Protestant attitude about anything Roman Catholic, especially the church services, has been severe."

Father Sellers continued: "In addition, the church here in Milledgeville had been vacant for extended periods of time, and this let the laymen leadership exert greater control. The laymen would have great difficulty giving that power up when any new priest arrived. Knowing this, one can only wonder how Father Flye lasted here as long as he did. Incidentally, for 13 months of his Milledgeville tenure, he also conducted monthly services at the nearby state penitentiary."

Father Flye was ill-suited to be a parish priest. He hated the administrative duties of a pastor's job. He had a noticeable lack of concern about financial details. He liked people, in general, but abhorred dealing with dullards who were influential in the parish's upkeep. He was good at providing personal spiritual guidance, but he lacked other skills necessary to be a successful pastor.

In 1916 Mary Simpson Flye made a trip to Milledgeville at Christmas. Father Flye's mother had kept her family together through hardships in Haines City and Winter Park. But, sturdy as she was, she became an early victim of the influenza epidemic that took millions of lives worldwide in 1917 and 1918. Mary died in Milledgeville on January 14, 1917, at age 65. Father Flye was devastated. Grace wrote her father: "Hal is suffering so much. I worry about his state of mind." After an Episcopal funeral service in Milledgeville, Mary was buried in Winter Park. Barbara inherited Mary's home in Winter Park. After Donald returned from his Army duties in France, he took over what land was left in Haines City. He later became the mayor of Haines City. James Harold Flye received nothing from his mother's estate; his exclusion remains a mystery.

Shortly after the United States entered World War I in 1917, Father Flye wrote in a letter to the Major: "It is interesting that a nation's future is saved by the young, while its past is saved by the old." On February 16, 1918, he again wrote the Major. The contents of this letter were prescient: "It is hard to estimate the actual situation. What a pitiful thing is the collapse of Russia. It makes me ill to think of what treachery has wrought there. What extraordinary times these are. I feel sure that later on there is to come an outburst in the far east, China and Japan involved, and people will be studying the Orient as they are now studying the movements in Europe. I don't think the close of this war is going to end trouble and selfishness and suffering for this world. Economic and social troubles are coming to this and other countries. There are tendencies in the moral, industrial and religious spheres which could only mean ferment."[5]

By 1918, Father Flye had begun to search for a job elsewhere. Grace wrote her father: "Hal is ready, as I am, to leave. He is really keen on a parish in Washington, D. C., because of the vast Library of Congress there. He is really anxious to go, no longer satisfied with this tiny field, though he dearly loves these people."

During a 1980 interview, Father Flye reminisced about leaving Milledgeville: "The situation was not good, so I applied at numerous places. I almost went to a parish on the Mexican border at Del Rio, Texas. But in March of 1918 I got a letter from an Order of the Holy Cross priest at a school in Tennessee. I first met him in seminary class in New York City. He knew I had teaching experience, and he asked if I would consider teaching at St. Andrew's School. I went to look things over in April."

Grace was enthusiastic about the prospect of a change. On April 19, 1918, she wrote: "Hal comes back Saturday from St. Andrew's. I can scarcely wait to hear his final decision. Won't it be wonderful if he can have a whole summer off? Father Harrison made a great impression here, and everybody is talking about him. The town people are carried away with him, and the church people adore him. He also made a great impression on Hal. He might pick St. Andrew's based on Father Harrison's enthusiasm."

Grace wrote her father a short time later: "I'm thrilled we are going to St. Andrew's. I will have a big house to begin painting again. Father Harrison says we will get $25 for food a month, or we can eat meals at the dining room. Isn't it wonderful?"

Father Flye wrote the Major and Myra: "Grace and I both feel that going there is a good move and that we shall enjoy the year there. I shall have masses and occasional preaching, and shall teach history and some English in the high school department. The high school and grammar grades are kept quite separate. I will have sufficient access to books to do some studying and reading on my own account. This will be only a temporary place; I plan to get back into strictly parish work after one year."

In June, 1918, Grace left to visit relatives in Ohio. Father Flye, meanwhile, went to visit family members at Ellsworth, Maine. The Flyes met at St. Andrew's School in September, 1918, at the beginning of the school term. They were entering unknown territory—little did they know that Grace would live there for the rest of her life, or that Father Flye would teach there for the next 36 years.

[1] Summers in Florida have historically been marred by crushing heat and humidity. In 1906, an engineer in Charlotte, North Carolina, coined the term "air conditioning." The Florida Theater in St. Petersburg opened with full air conditioning in 1926. It was not until 1951 that an inexpensive window-unit air conditioner became available. As late as the mid-1950s, only about one in ten Florida homes had any form of air conditioning.

[2]THE FLYE FAMILY TREE

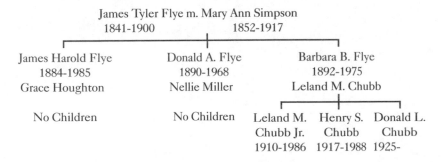

James Tyler Flye m. Mary Ann Simpson
1841-1900   1852-1917

James Harold Flye	Donald A. Flye	Barbara B. Flye
1884-1985	1890-1968	1892-1975
Grace Houghton	Nellie Miller	Leland M. Chubb
No Children	No Children	Leland M. Henry S. Donald L.
		Chubb Jr. Chubb Chubb
		1910-1986 1917-1988 1925-

[3] An undated note in Father Flye's handwriting reads: "These are some of the songs I played on my harmonica at the New Haven train station. Red Wing—Hiawatha—Good Old Summer Time—Blue Bell—Austrian Hymn—Marseillaise—Spanish Cavalier—Oh, Susanna—Beautiful Lady—Vive L'amour—Soldier's Chorus—Beautiful Ohio—Over The Waves—Auld Lang Syne—

Nelly Gray—Dark Eyes—Kiribiribin—Satisfied—Long, Long Trail—Merry Widow Waltz."

[4] Grace's rambling state of mind is shown in this long letter to her father. She skips from one lofty idea to another, then dips into the mundane. Perhaps likening her future spouse to her mother was an indication than her marriage would be different.

[5] In this letter, Flye predicted the Japanese incursion into China that took place 17 years later.

CHAPTER 2

The Early Years at St. Andrew's School

Better build schoolrooms for the boy, than cells for the man.
—ELIZA COOK (1818-1889)

*S*TRETCHING NORTHEAST from the Alabama-Tennessee border, the Cumberland Plateau reaches into seven Tennessee counties. Four of them—Franklin, Grundy, Coffee, Marion—converge near an area of the plateau called "the Mountain" by local residents, especially those between Sewanee and Tracy City, Tennessee. The location is sometimes called Sewanee Mountain or Monteagle Mountain. The traditional designation— the Mountain—is used here.[1]

St. Andrew's School (which has today evolved into St. Andrew's-Sewanee School) was located on the Mountain in Franklin County, 2 miles east of the town of Sewanee, and 3 miles west of the town of Monteagle.

Former St. Andrew's pupils from different periods of time will not have the same recollections of the school. The earliest years were primitive, but the same could not be said about the later years. What was true in 1920 was not true in 1950. The school began as a vocational school, but evolved into a college preparatory institution. The history of St. Andrew's was never static. Changes always took place, some quickly and some at a glacial pace.

Two men handled the school's administration. The Headmaster (like the Principal of a public school) managed the curricula, student body and faculty. The Prior was the overseer of the monastery, responsible for the school's spiritual life. He was also in charge of finances. Obligations often overlapped. At times one person served as Prior and Headmaster simultaneously.

The Order of the Holy Cross monks who served at St. Andrew's had taken vows of poverty, chastity and obedience; however, the image of a totally silent monk doing chores at an abbey does not describe these men. They were not cloistered men who chose a life of silent isolation. They were active as teachers, preachers and, for the most part, they were socially gregarious. St. Andrew's was one of the few places in the country where Episcopal monks were visible to the public. There were two kinds of monks at St. Andrew's—ordained priests called "Father" and laymen members of the Order called "Brother." The better-educated Fathers celebrated mass and heard confessions.

The St. Andrew's faculty had three components: Civilian laymen, non-Order Episcopal priests (some married; some unmarried), and the Order monks.

The Order of the Holy Cross administered St. Andrew's for 75 years (1905-1980). The school's survival was always tenuous. This was especially true during the Great Depression. After the school merged with Sewanee Academy in 1981, the school was known as St. Andrew's-Sewanee School. Technically, St. Andrew's ceased to exist in 1981.

□ □ □

The Mountain's summit is about 2,100 feet above sea level, about 1,000 feet higher than the surrounding valleys. The difference in altitude gives the Mountain lower temperatures—Sewanee can be 10 degrees colder than Cowan, 6 miles away. This coolness is a welcome contrast to the wilting summer heat of the valley floor. Folklore says: "The summer creeps up the side of the Mountain 50 feet a day." For the well-to-do, escaping the summer heat and infectious diseases that frequently struck southern cities made the Mountain a popular resort area as early as the 1880s.

Monteagle was put on the map in 1882 when Episcopal, Lutheran, Presbyterian and Methodist leaders jointly founded a campground and convention site that was called "The Monteagle Sunday School Assembly." Local residents shortened the name to "The Assembly," and the site became famous as the Chautauqua of the South.[2]

The Mountain is heavily forested with a mixture of deciduous and evergreen trees. Flowering plants such as dogwood, mountain laurel, iris, redbud and wild azalea are plentiful. The smell of pine needles is intoxicating. One can stand at the edge of the escarpment and watch thunderstorms with lightning flashes occurring below. Deer, wild turkeys, squirrels and rabbits are as plentiful as the birds that have always been part of the Mountain's appeal. However, nature can be capricious during the winter, when fog shrouds the Mountain for days on end.

Until the 1930s, the most comfortable way to reach St. Andrew's was to use the Nashville, Chattanooga and St. Louis Railroad system to Cowan, then get aboard the "Mountain Goat," a local coal mine train, and proceed 9 miles up the side of the mountain, past Sewanee to Gipson's Switch, a "flag stop" located less

Railroad work crew in Monteagle, 1921

than one mile south of the campus. When the Flyes arrived at St. Andrew's in 1918, their train ride from Chattanooga to Gipson's Switch took three hours.

Passengers riding the "Mountain Goat" often had their clothes soiled by soot, but for many years the train was the preferred way to travel to the top of the Mountain.

Several highways have long spanned the Mountain. The struggle to maintain these roads played a significant part in the area's history. Over the years they changed from dirt roads to washboard logs to gravel and then to asphalt or concrete. Until Interstate 24 was completed in the 1960s, the two highways crossing the Mountain were State Highways 64 (Chattanooga to Memphis) and 41 (Chattanooga to Nashville). They intersected at Monteagle.[3]

In the 1930s a drive from Sewanee to Nashville meant going through many towns, a stop-and-go exercise taking up to three hours; the same trip today takes 90 minutes. With improved roads and modern communications, the plateau is no longer isolated. However, when Father Flye began teaching at St. Andrew's, poor roads quarantined the area. David Lockmiller was 13 years old and a student at St. Andrew's in 1919: "Car travel was risky at best. You had to drive very slowly to avoid the stumps and ruts. Winter storms and road travel were a bad combination. During the winter, you were better off staying put." The remoteness of the Mountain never depressed the Flyes. Except for an occasional visit to see her relatives in central Florida, Grace had no desire to travel. Her personal needs were fulfilled. As early as 1921, Father Flye cured his cabin fever with summer duties, serving as vacation relief for other priests, at Episcopal churches in midwestern and northern cities.

□ □ □

In November of 1884, a 30-year-old Episcopal priest, James Huntington, knelt in a convent chapel in New York City and pledged: "To devote myself body, soul and spirit to the service of God in the religious life as a member of the Order of the Holy Cross, and to that end to take upon me of my own free will the vows of religious poverty, chastity and obedience."

After ministering to the poor in crowded tenements in New York City for a decade, the Order's survival appeared dim. There were only three members in the Order by 1895, and there was little prospect for any growth. After several more years the tiny contingent moved to a house in Westminster, Maryland. Their arrival was viewed with suspicion by the Bishop of Maryland, who thought they were "too flamboyant." He denied them the right to preach beyond their half-acre premises. Nevertheless, the Order's message was popular with nearby residents, and its nine-room house was crowded on Sunday mornings.

The Rev. William S. Claiborne

In 1898, the French steamship Burgoyne sank off the coast of Newfoundland and more than 1,000 passengers drowned. On the fatality list was Reverend W. G. Webster, who had bequeathed $3,000 to the Order of the Holy Cross. The Order quickly used the money to buy property at West Park, New York. Now, finally, the Order had enough land to build a monastery. The West Park structure was the first Anglican monastery to be constructed anywhere in the world since 1534.

In the meantime, an Episcopal priest in Tennessee, William Sterling Claiborne, had embarked on an ambitious mission. While working in six southern states on a railroad crew, he had seen the region's need for traditional and religious schooling. Years later as a seminary student, he became involved in missionary work in the Sewanee area. On July 1, 1900, he was put in charge of Otey Memorial Parish in Sewanee. Claiborne was a dynamic man, a visionary, and a skilled orator. With his heavy baritone voice, he reminded parishioners of an Old Testament prophet. More than anyone's, his influence brought education to the less-privileged mountain children, who lived in remote coves where there were no roads. These "covites," young casualties of geography, did not live within walking distance of existing schools.[4]

❑ ❑ ❑

Sewanee Military Academy, date unknown

The University of the South in Sewanee was founded in 1857 by ten dioceses of the Episcopal church. A domain of 10,000 acres was secured. The Civil War interrupted the founders' plans, and it was not until 1868 that the university's doors were open to nine students. From this humble beginning, the university, called "Sewanee" by local people, became the intellectual center of the Mountain.

The university's preparatory department became the Sewanee Grammar School in 1870. It became the Sewanee Grammar Academy in 1902, and in 1908 was named the Sewanee Military Academy. The school was demilitarized and became the Sewanee Academy in 1971. Always a boarding school for boys, it was scholastically and financially out-of-reach for poor families.

St. Mary's-on-the-Mountain, an Episcopal convent near Sewanee, opened a training school for girls in 1896. Most of the girls were boarding students. The curriculum was limited "…to train mountain girls as seamstresses, laundresses, cooks, nurses, [and] a simple English education to teach them the care of a house."

St. Mary's closed from lack of funding in 1899. Father Claiborne, determined that the school be continued, started raising money, and the school reopened in 1902. St. Mary's Preparatory School for Girls had an exceptional history. Accreditation came in 1930, the first commencement the following year. St. Mary's closed at the end of the 1967-1968 school year. Sixty-eight St. Mary's girls transferred to the previously all-male Sewanee Military Academy. A smaller number transferred to St. Andrew's.

After the reopening of St. Mary's in 1902, Claiborne decided what was needed next was a boys' boarding school. He made a down payment on the Robert Colmore farm, 2 miles east of Sewanee. The farm had 15 acres of cultivated land plus 60 acres of forest. Then he put his oratorical skills to good use. For the next

St. Mary's School, 1908

three months, he traveled through four eastern states asking for money to begin a school for "needy mountain boys." He had phenomenal success. For example, a widow in Pennsylvania donated $500. When his tour was over, the priest had collected $12,500.

He called his new school the St. Andrew's Industrial and Training School for Boys. There was a two-story house on the Colmore Farm, but it was not large enough to serve as both classroom and dormitory. The energetic cleric needed help. The Order of the Holy Cross knew of Claiborne's pioneering efforts near Sewanee, so the stage was set for the men from West Park to get involved. After two reconnaissance trips to the Mountain, the decision was made—the Order of the Holy Cross was going to bring its brand of religion and rudimentary education to a remote part of Tennessee. The decision would have a profound impact. The Order had only six men, but their faith would have the force of an army. Sewanee would soon have four Episcopal private schools (the university and three high schools), co-existing almost next door to each other.

Harold Kennedy, a 1939 St. Andrew's graduate, wrote in his college thesis: "People of the Appalachian Mountains are said to be the oldest stock continuing permanently in one place to be found anywhere in the United States. They are descendants of the more adventurous elements of Colonists who centuries ago pushed into the interior, and founded their backwoods commonwealths among and beyond the big ranges of the Alleghenies. Few people anywhere have more stalwart virtues. Rough-handed in fight, brave and loyal, there is underneath a

Colmore House, circa 1909

stern exterior an unseen gentleness and refinement. It was among these people that St. Andrew's made its appearance."

□ □ □

On September 21, 1905, the Order took control of the school. Its name was quickly shortened to St. Andrew's School. Classes began with only a handful of boys. Aware that the boys' parents were poor, but would not accept charity, the new Headmaster charged only $4.50 per month. That fee was soon lowered to $2 per month. Eleven students were enrolled by March of 1906.

The boys did the work of the school, including carrying wood and water, cleaning up the kitchen, helping prepare meals, and doing odd chores at the school's farm which provided white and sweet potatoes and feed for the cattle and swine. The duties were not thought of as inordinate by the boys; they came from families where all members had to do their share. For example, one 13-year old boy had been plowing in fields since he was eight years old. At sundown each day, the school had mandatory foot washing for barefoot boys.

According to a Holy Cross publication, in December 1906 two boys walked

Isolated mountain home, circa 1910

from Tracy City to apply for admission. One cleric, Sturges Allen, was astonished that they had survived the trip without adequate footwear in the winter weather. Both boys were welcomed and given a bath before they went to bed. The next morning they were gone. They left word they did not want to stay in a place where people were "softened by pipe water."

The generosity of the mountain boys was sometimes as great as their poverty. On Christmas Eve in 1906 a visiting priest jokingly remarked he had no present under the Christmas tree. One young student, about 10 years old, overheard the remark and offered the priest his most precious possession, a licorice stick.

One observer, Edwin S. Utley, wrote in 1906: "This endeavor to teach even the most simple subjects is a great task, when one takes into consideration the fact that all of the occupants must first be taught what school means, for their lives have been spent in an almost lawless freedom."

This handbill was issued in October 1907: "School will reopen Tuesday, October 1. Terms—School is free. Board and washing is $2.00 a month. Clothing will not be given to the boys, but will be sold to them at cost price. Apply early as only 15 boys will be taken. Fr. Hughson, O.H.C."

The priests knew practical skills were important. A school advertisement illustrated the school's ambition at the time: "Instruction in all the Common School branches. Carpenter work; Basket and Chair Making; Music; Physical Culture; Printing; use of Tools; Scientific Poultry Raising and Horticulture." Reading, penmanship, English and "social etiquette" were also offered. By the fall of 1908, 30 boys were enrolled.

In 1911, tuition was raised to $24. Local parents helped the school as best they could, offering fruit, berries, apples, acorns, corn, beans, turkeys, squirrels, and deer. In December 1912 an anonymous donor left 13 newly slain rabbits at the school's entrance with this note: "Kiled [sic] for boys to eat."

Harold Kennedy described two case histories circa 1910: "There was ten year old Billy. His mother took him out of St. Andrew's because he could earn fifty cents a day in Alabama cotton mills. Take the case of Jack, sixteen years old with years of work in coal mines, stooped over, frail, resembling a person twice his age."

Articles published in the Holy Cross Magazine depicted a grim picture of

St. Andrew's farm, circa 1915

those early days. In 1913: "For several years those boys who entered St. Andrew's neither knew the alphabet nor had even said prayers." In 1914: "Some of the students come from mountain cabins that are overcrowded, without sufficient heat, dark, squalid, causing the tuberculosis rate to be high. Their parents have no desire for cleanliness, such as washing hands. Dangers of bacteria are beyond their understanding."

Between 1908 and 1914, on average, boys stayed at St. Andrew's for only two years. The major reason for the turnover was that the school was put on a 12-month basis in 1908. One hour of the summer term day was devoted to studies; the rest of the day the younger students were committed to garden work. The older boys worked on the farm or in the furniture-making shop. Mountain families were willing to send their boys to school in the winter, but summer meant "there was work to be done here at home." The older a boy was, the more valuable he was as a worker. The summer program was never popular and was dropped in 1914.

As early as 1910, Franklin County had approached the Order to see if St. Andrew's would accept day students. Beginning in 1915, the school enrolled day students who went home after class each day.

Adjustment to the new school was a problem; homesickness was endemic. A boy's home might have been a squalid log cabin, but he missed his family. He was used to sleeping with his brothers in a communal bed, under a "feather down" quilt, with plenty of body heat to keep him warm. At St. Andrew's he went to his bed wearing pajamas with only a blanket. Just learning to sleep alone was a big adjustment.

In October 1911 a polluted well caused a typhoid outbreak at the school. One student, Jackson Rollins, 18, died. One dozen boys and two priests were quarantined by local authorities. After a convalescence in Florida, both clergymen resumed their duties at St. Andrew's.

At that time, many of the boys had gum disease and rotting teeth. Most mountain boys came from a home environment where using a toothbrush was unknown. A notation from 1912 showed that St. Andrew's students were forced to brush twice daily, using salt or baking soda as an abrasive. Oil of cloves was

Monk leveling St. Andrew's tennis courts, circa 1920

commonly used as a pain-killer for toothaches. A priest wrote in 1912 that the older St. Andrew's boys rarely opened their mouths, because of their self-consciousness about missing teeth.

The dedication of the school's chapel took place in 1914. Episcopal parishioners in Philadelphia played a key role in the building of the chapel. Five hundred dollars was donated by the city's St. Mark's Church; an additional $5,570 came from elsewhere across the country. The chapel's architect, Horace Sellers, had hoped to emulate the Presidio in Monterey, California, but money restraints blocked his efforts. Still, Sellers designed an impressive house of worship.

The St. Andrew's chapel became noted for its elegance. It had almost life-size portraits of St. Andrew, St. Michael, St. Stephen, St. Peter, St. Dominic, St. Jerome, St. Thomas Aquinas, St. John the Baptist, St. Katharine of Alexandria, St. Francis of Assisi, and St. Lucy. Fourteen Stations of the Cross plaques hung on the chapel walls. The pastel depictions of Jesus's crucifixion were imposing. A life-sized crucifix was located at the baptismal font near the entrance to the chapel. Located near the main altar was the tiny Lady Chapel, used for morning mass and confessionals. A huge painting of the Madonna hung over the Lady Chapel altar, and the Lady Chapel statues were placed on pedestals.

The Nave seated 150 people. The pews had wicker chairs made in the school's workshop in 1917, held firmly in place by long wooden slats attached to the backs of the chairs. The chairs were functional, but never comfortable. In the 1960s they were replaced by traditional wooden benches.

Construction of the School Building began in 1916, with older students doing much of the labor. The building's basement had a blacksmith shop. On the first floor was a manual training shop, a chemistry laboratory, and three classrooms. An auditorium and other classrooms were located on the second floor. The entire third floor was a gymnasium. The cost of the School Building construction was $12,500.

The first out-of-state pupils enrolled in 1910. Enrollment that year was 35 boys from Tennessee and 11 from Alabama. Boys from northern and western states did not arrive until 1931, when enrollment reached 155. During Father

St. Andrew's boys, 1922

Flye's 36-year tenure at St. Andrew's, the student body normally numbered between 100 to 150 boys.

The high school department was initiated in 1913, and a few years later the school issued its first diploma to Allious C. Reid. He later returned as a teacher, then served as Headmaster from 1932-1938. Before the 1920s, a few graduates did go to college, but high school accreditation was not obtained until 1932.

St. Andrew's enrolled a few girls during the early years; the first was Gertrude Collins in 1907. The first female to earn a St. Andrew's diploma was Mary Helen Goodwin, in 1921. Mary lived with her parents at the school, where her father taught manual arts. Mary's portrait was painted by Grace Flye in 1919.

On December 27, 1921, The *Chattanooga Times* published a story about St. Andrew's, in which Father Flye was quoted extensively: "Many come to the door who can't find room to enter owing to inadequate dormitory space. The day school is open to them, but many live where trails are long and steep, and their cabin homes are too far up or down the mountainside to permit walking in bad weather. We have one boy, James Evans, who is at West Point, making a fine record. There is another student, Fletcher Skidmore, who is making a fine scholastic showing at Sewanee."

The campus expanded as the years passed, to include a chapel, a dining hall, a school building, a three-story administration building and several dormitories. In the center of the campus was a quadrangle with pine trees. In the southwestern section of the property was an athletic field with a circling cinder track. The northeastern part of the grounds was dominated by the monastery. The school's farm and dairy were to the west. The main entrance had a large sandstone marker.[5]

Fires plagued the school's history. Over the years, the monastery, the dining hall and several dormitories were destroyed by fire. Overloaded wiring (electricity had arrived in 1915) was usually blamed. Following a St. Andrew's dormitory fire in 1930, the DuBose School in nearby Monteagle donated 36 beds, and the University of the South gave 100 blankets.[6]

Starting in 1926, a pupil had to complete 16 credits in College Preparatory or General Studies in order to graduate.

St. Andrew's manual arts class, 1922

College Preparatory	General Studies
4 English	4 English
3 Mathematics	2 Mathematics
2 Advanced Science	1 Science
2 Foreign Languages	2 Manual Arts
1 American History	1 American History
1 Church History	1 Church History
3 Electives	5 Electives

St. Andrew's adhered to an axiom similar to that of a British boarding school in the 19th century: study, work, discipline, and Christian ethics. Students lived by a hard-and-fast schedule from 6:30 a.m. until 9:30 p.m. on weekdays. The routine consisted of worship and classes followed by work or sports. Every weekday morning at 6:15 a mass was held for the boys who cared to participate. Attendance was compulsory for the weekday chapel services at 8 a.m., the Sunday morning Mass and Sermon, plus the Benediction at 7:30 Sunday evening.[7]

Despite the daily agenda, boys found time for childhood games of their era: marbles, jumping jacks, mumble-peg and dodge ball. They flew kites, ran races and wrestled. Checkers and pitching horse shoes were popular. Claude Smith was a 1922 student: "We played 'paper chase.' We filled a sack with bits of torn-up newspaper; if we went in a straight line, we didn't have to drop any. But if we turned a corner, we would drop a few pieces of paper so pursuers would know which way we had gone. It was like hide-and-seek. Our games were simple by today's standards, but we were happy."

There was never a time when every student had his tuition fully paid. Costs were kept low through a self-help system in which staff and students did the day-to-day maintenance. This self-reliance, started in 1905, prevailed throughout the school's history. David Lockmiller, a 1919 student, recalled: "We had daily chores. We swept out hallways and made our own beds. There were boys who washed or dried dishes, and everyone took turns waiting on tables. Older boys had the heavier jobs."

Students received a modest weekly stipend. As late as the 1950s it was only $1.50 a week, but admission to the movie theater in Sewanee was then only 12 cents. Candy bars could be purchased for a penny each. Young entrepreneurs at St. Andrew's always found ways to earn extra cash—ranging from managing the school's commissary to having a hidden still for the making of a hybrid "moonshine."

During the first two decades of its existence the school did not have a structured designation for classes. A 10-year-old might sit next to a towering teenager in English class, for example. In the late 1920s, the students were segregated into Class Forms. A freshman was in the Third Form; a senior in the Sixth Form. St. Andrew's had an excellent teacher-student ratio: about 10 to one. A positive factor for the faculty was that housing and food were free.

A "prefect system" was introduced in 1919. Prefects were seniors who supervised the underclassmen. Demerits were given for minor offenses, ranging from chewing gum to being late to class. The punishment was usually doing extra chores: raking leaves, polishing silverware, cleaning gutters, dusting furniture, shoveling snow. If a boy had a Red Mark—six demerits in one week—his penalty ranged from doing heavy labor to being grounded over weekends or corporal punishment. Penalties varied with the boy's age and offense. Cheating, lying, or stealing were not tolerated.

David Lockmiller remembered a 1919 episode: "This one boy had a Red Mark and was ordered to dig up a tree stump. He had to use a shovel, an axe and a crowbar. We saw him work on that stump for several hours every day, and it took him at least a month to end the job. None of us wanted to get stuck doing anything like that."

Corporal punishment for younger boys usually meant their outstretched palms were hit with a ruler. Older students, guilty of more serious offenses, had a "butt warming" with a leather strap or wooden paddle. But physical punishment was seldom used; its threat normally kept boys in line.

For most of its history, St. Andrew's students lived in one or two-story dormitories. In most cases, two to four underclassmen lived in a room with bunk beds, a closet, a table and chairs. The walls were usually bare. Living space was at a premium. Each boy had a foot locker where he kept personal belongings. Dormitories were inspected on Saturday. The boy or boys responsible for a bad inspection ran a gauntlet belt whacking; this kept failed inspections to a minimum. There was a strict 9:30 p.m. lights-out curfew.

Every week night underclassmen who were not doing well in their classwork were required to attend a 2-hour Study Hall. Absolute silence was imposed. Textbooks were the only reading material allowed in the room.

Seniors were not bound to "lights out" or to many of the other regulations. By the time a teenager reached the Sixth Form he had paid his dues. Beginning in the 1930s, seniors had a Studio for fun evenings of playing Bridge, Hearts, Canasta, listening to records, sipping coffee or cocoa, playing table tennis, throwing darts. It was a place where the St. Andrew's seniors could let their hair down, but decorum was enforced. Seniors were expected to wear coats and ties, and behave like gentlemen. By the late 1940s, the Studio had a kitchenette and a piano. The Studio was a place where visiting adults talked with Sixth Formers about college, traveling, serving in the military, the opposite sex. In its own fashion, St. Andrew's tried to prepare seniors for the outside world.

The school's meals were prepared by women who lived near the campus. Cooking was done on a huge woodburning stove. The food was usually plain, but nourishing. From dawn until evening, these women were busy in the kitchen. They had no respite during the summer months, because that time was spent canning fruits and vegetables, which were usually kept in Mason jars. The kitchen's woodburning stove was converted to gas in the 1960s.

A small crew of local men did the school's carpentry, plumbing, masonry, and electrical repairs. These same men operated the school's farm and dairy. Cows, chickens, pigs, goats and mules required daily attention. The farm and dairy were discontinued in the 1940s.

The cooks and handymen were as much a part of the official family at St. Andrew's as were the students and faculty. Their loyalty to the school was strong. A number of their children graduated and stayed to become second-generation employees. Their contributions to the school were invaluable.

The monastery was an imposing three-story building. The monks slept in small individual rooms. The monastery had a kitchenette, but the monks usually ate food brought to them from the school's main kitchen. Meals were eaten at long wooden tables, and during meals a monk read from scripture. Otherwise, silence was imposed and communication was restricted to written notes. The monastery was a place for reflection and spiritual renewal. Five monks were the normal monastery roster, but visiting clerics and secular men on weekend retreat sometimes boosted the number of men staying there. St. Michael's monastery had the capacity to sleep 40.

The Great Depression hit the school hard. St. Andrew's had to swap labor for food in the fall of 1931 and spring of 1932, when students were sent to local farms to stack hay, shuck corn, pick beans, and feed livestock. In return, the school was given part of the food harvest. The school was $60,000 in debt in 1932.

St. Andrew's was broadsided in the 1930s by another problem. Local coun-

Monastery at St. Andrew's School

ties, with state funding, began offering free bus transportation to public school children. The Mountain's roads had been greatly improved by then, and local boys began to take advantage of the free education at public schools. The student body at St. Andrew's was being depleted at an alarming rate. A frantic call went out to Episcopal churches everywhere: the school needed more students.

Arthur Ben Chitty, historiographer at the University of the South, recalled: "To be competitive with other private schools, St. Andrew's had to advertise its improved curriculum and spiritual purpose. If the school had not acted so quickly it would have closed down many years ago.

"I knew Father Flye had been unhappy with the way things had been going. He had been disgusted with having to teach boys who were not motivated. For years he had been irritated with the school's insistence that boys had to take required courses for which they had no aptitude. He thought this only produced a feeling of inadequacy. He told me: 'God didn't intend that everybody be good in math.'

"So, strange as it may sound, Father Flye was pleased about the crisis. He felt that an improved scholastic playing field would help. However, what he didn't know was the nature of challenges around the corner. The mountain boys were replaced with city boys who saw the place as a prison. Boys from broken homes and orphanages, mostly streetwise and tough. Not all of the new boarders could adjust. There were invariably a few runaways who couldn't handle the rough-

Palm Sunday at St. Andrew's, 1931

and-tumble environment. Boys had to have a stoicism to survive the St. Andrew's experience."

Dr. Chitty continued: "It was very rough for a divorced woman or widow to get by financially. St. Andrew's was an answer to her prayers. She had tears in her eyes as she put her boy on a bus to come up to the Mountain, but in 90 percent of the cases, the school turned the boy around and the story had a happy ending.

"After the mid-1930s, St. Andrew's would never be the same again. From then on, it would have its share of throwaway boys, juvenile delinquents. They were not an easy bunch to teach. Regardless, the school did a wonderful job. That was the great thing about St. Andrew's. Against tremendous odds, the school turned out fine young men.

"The school initially had a reputation of being one for dumb hillbillies, followed by the slander in the 1930s that St. Andrew's was a reform school for jailbirds. These were terribly inaccurate generalities. Father Flye was teaching Latin, including Cicero, to bright boys as far back as the 1920s. One of his students, Oliver Hodge, spoke fluent French, got a master's degree in Romance Languages, and later worked for the American government in France. The school never blew its own horn. There was one St. Andrew's boy who was a Rhodes Scholar, but there wasn't any publicity about it. The school never had any public relations."

A review of the 1951 St. Andrew's Yearbook sheds light on the standard duties of the school's faculty in those days: the Rev. William Turkington, Science and Music History; the Rev. Joseph Huske, English and Sociology; the Rev. Bonnell Spencer, Church History and Dramatics; William Bayle, Mathematics. Arthur Mann, English and Latin. Ms. Georgie Brown, Spanish and Mathematics. Eugene Towles, Science and Geography; the Rev. James Flye, History and Latin III.

Mr. Towles was the football, boxing and track coach. Mr. Tate and Father Huske were assistant football coaches. Mr. Mann, Father Flye and Paul Lowdenslager (the school's storekeeper) did private tutoring. Mr. Bayle coached tennis. Mr. Alligood coached basketball and baseball.

There were 23 teenagers in the 1951 graduating class. They originally came from 11 states ranging from South Carolina to California. A majority of the class was at the school five years, living together during a formative time in their lives.

The average tuition paid in 1951 was $370; the expenses per student came to $700. The gap was closed by endowments and private contributions.

The Prior in 1951 was Father Bonnell Spencer: "With each family or single parent, we negotiated what they could pay. Most paid less than a full tuition, and I took a few boys at $25 a month. We had a small endowment, and the rest was gotten from friends of the school, to whom we appealed three times a year. The alumni gave the school almost nothing in those days. St. Andrew's provided spiritual guidance and a good secondary education, but it didn't have any school-sponsored class reunions.

"During my years there, the student body was made up of boys mostly from southern states, but there were boys from New Jersey to Colorado. Most came from Episcopal backgrounds, but there were a few boys who never joined the church. We had boys from orphanages in Memphis and New Orleans. Most of these boys needed a home, as well as a school, and were sent to us for those reasons."[8]

The campus population diminished during the summer. Some boys had summer jobs at St. Andrew's, but many of the students had no place to go. Many hit the road to fend for themselves. Their summer jobs were good training for future survival. The Flyes received summer mail from boys who were working as a short-order cook in Paducah, a fishing boat grappler in the Gulf of Mexico, a truck driver with migrants picking melons in Arizona, a plumber's helper in Ohio, a clerk at a grocery store in Memphis. One youngster was a gaffer on a movie set in Utah. The boys returned in September with a feeling of achievement, and had some entertaining stories about their summer adventures. Many of them were rehashed inside the Flye's campus home. The history teacher and his artist wife were always attentive listeners.

There are no major accounts of the school's history; however, what is known clearly shows a picture of dedicated administrators and teachers. Their efforts were heroic. Considering the bleakness of the early days, as well as the challenges along the way, the St. Andrew's story was a miracle in itself. Father Flye was a key architect in the school's legacy. He was a great teacher, but he was equally remembered for two attributes: his kindnesses and his eccentricities. The man's rapport with young people was exceptional. He cast a long shadow.

An irony is that, in the beginning, Father Flye did not plan to stay at St. Andrew's, yet his service was the longest in the school's history. Dr. Frederick Santee once asked him why he had stayed at St. Andrew's so long. His answer was an ancient proverb: "*Ou Dieux vous a seme, il faut savoir fleurir.*" Where God has sown you, one must know how to flower.

The next chapter details how Father Flye's "flowering" brought dividends to some boys who were under his caring umbrella.[9]

❑ ❑ ❑

[1] The issue of what to call the Mountain may never be resolved. Sewanee is an Indian word meaning south or southern, and the area was called Sewanee by the earliest tribes which had migrated south from present-day Ohio and Indiana. In 1857 the Sewanee Mining Company donated 5,000 acres to the Episcopal church for the building of a "University of quality to be called the University of the South." This was aided by gifts of land from about a dozen individuals. Soon after the university's founding, people began to call the area Sewanee or University Place. Grundy County leaders wanted their area to be the plateau's preeminent area and planned to give Tracy City the name of Sewanee; however, university leaders went to postal authorities and cornered the name. Grundy County had lost out in its bid to capture the name Sewanee, yet the coal mines located near Tracy City would be known as the Sewanee Mines for the next 100 years. J. Waring McCrady, a professor at the University, said: "Due to an ignorance of history, truckers began calling this area Monteagle Mountain, and commercial interests started using 'Monteagle Mountain' on brochures in the 1970s. The media followed suit. Our newspaper, The Sewanee Mountain Messenger, has kept the correct name on its front page."

[2] The Chautauqua Movement began in New York in1874 as a training program for Sunday School teachers, but evolved into a traveling lecture series. Well-known orators drew crowds to large tents where the atmosphere resembled a church revival. Lecturers ranged from world explorers to politicians. In the 1930s, motion pictures, radio and the Great Depression reduced the attendance figures. The movement, which had drawn thousands of people to a single event, lost its popularity. Chautauqua meetings still occur, but on a much smaller scale. The Assembly in Monteagle, originally designed to host lectures, is best known today as a place of Victorian cottages. Monteagle was originally called Moffat's Station, for John Moffat who once owned the entire mountaintop except for the university property. According to postal records, the road junction became Monteagle in 1884.

[3] Contemporary motorists can get an idea of driving conditions in years past by driving on Highway 41 between Pelham and Monteagle, a two-lane serpentine with many switchbacks. On the one hand, there were grinding trucks slowly climbing to the summit, while there were descending trucks with squealing brakes. Drivers dreaded using Highway 41, but they had no choice. Winter ice and fog tested a driver's skill and willpower. In those days, larger cities and towns in Tennessee could afford to maintain upgraded road systems, but the state's hilly areas were not so fortunate. The state's inability to conquer the rugged terrain was not unique; all mountainous areas in the nation were historically plagued by engineering difficulties of road building. President Dwight D. Eisenhower was the prime mover in the building of the Interstate Highway System. This huge federally funded project, the largest construction project in modern history, started in the 1950s and ultimately linked remote areas to a fast-moving highway grid system from coast to coast.

[4] Mountain cove dwellers were called "covites," which was a pejorative term describing people who were uneducated. The word is rarely heard today, but it was used often by local residents in the 1920s.

[5] The word "secluded" is used advisedly. Today's motorist driving between Sewanee and Monteagle takes little notice of the school, because the campus is located some distance from the highway. The Headmaster at St. Andrew's-Sewanee School, Rev. William S. Wade, said in a 1998

speech: "I was a university student in Sewanee for years, but I never set foot on St. Andrew's property until I was hired to be Headmaster." Today's campus no longer has a farm, dairy or monastery, and several modern buildings have been added to the complex. From 75 acres in 1905, the school property has been expanded to more than 450 acres.

[6] Fire plagued the campus until the very end. In 1981, shortly after St. Andrew's had merged with Sewanee Academy, a fire leveled St. Michael's Monastery.

[7] Many boys viewed the long chapel services as torturous, because there were no kneeling pads available. Students sneaked towels or shoulder pads (used in women's suits) into the chapel services to protect their painful knees. Traditional kneeling pads and benches were installed in the chapel during the 1960s.

[8] In the beginning of the 20th Century, isolated families living on the Mountain clearly had difficult lives; however, a meaningful perspective is in order: 15 percent of the nation's military draftees in 1943 could neither read nor write; three million American adults had never spent one day in school. President Franklin D. Roosevelt's New Deal did not eliminate poverty in the United States. In 1946, 40 percent of the nation's homes had no bathtub or shower; 35 percent did not have an indoor toilet; 30 percent had no running water.

[9] St. Andrew's had a sister school, Kent School, in Kent, Connecticut, but there was little contact between the two campuses. Kent School was founded by the Order of the Holy Cross in 1906. Numerous regulations at St. Andrew's were first developed at Kent. A number of the Order priests had served at the Connecticut institution before they were transferred to St. Andrew's, and this occasionally caused some resentment. For example, Father Flye wrote in his journal: "Fr. Turkington keeps saying: 'This is the way we did it at Kent.' He is always mentioning Kent as if how they do things there should be chiseled in granite. His remarks about Kent make our boys feel like they are runts of the litter." Academically, Kent was superior to St. Andrew's. It was also wealthier. Close to New York City and other areas of established wealth, Kent School always had a reservoir of well-to-do patrons and students. The two schools were "sisters" in name only. The Order of the Holy Cross severed its relationship with Kent School in 1943. Father Bonnell Spencer, who served at St. Andrew's from 1943 to 1955, wrote: "There were pleasant feelings between Kent and St. Andrew's, with formality, but there were no special contacts. The only boy who started at Kent and later transferred to St. Andrew's was Harold Wilson. His father was a secular priest, and he went to Kent on a scholarship. Harold was unhappy at Kent, because the other boys came from rich families and were snobs. He could not compete with them socially. Kent School was always considered one of the better New England prep schools."

TIME LINES
Sewanee Military Academy 1868-1971
St. Mary's School 1896-1968
St. Andrew's School 1905-1981
Sewanee Academy 1971-1981
St. Andrew's-Sewanee School 1981 -

CHAPTER 3

Ed Yokley—Oliver Hodge— Ed Hubbell— Claude Wright—Dale Doss

Lucky is he who has been able to understand the cause of things.
—VIRGIL (70-19 BC)

S T. ANDREW'S HAD MANY SUCCESS STORIES; the saga of Edward Dallas Yokley was different from all the others, and Father Flye wrote part of the script. Ed Yokley was born August 1, 1912, in a remote log cabin 17 miles from the nearest town at Pleasant Point, Marion County, Tennessee. The two-room cabin was dark, crowded, and unhealthy. It had a dirt floor and a woodburning stove. Any indoor light, what little there was, came from a kerosene lamp. The cabin reeked of body waste collected in chamber pots. A hand-pumped well was located 50 feet north of the cabin; a one-seat privy 50 feet south of it. The log cabin did not have electricity or a telephone, and its inhabitants did not have much contact with the outside world. Ed's parents were illiterate. Their knowledge was thin, limited to word-of-mouth learning. They loved their children, but expected them to carry their own weight. Everybody in the Yokley clan had to contribute in the collective struggle to endure.

At the insistence of his niece, Colleen Racine, in 1994 Ed Yokley recorded his life story. Following is an edited version of what he said:

"My job at the age of five, and my brother at seven, was to help mother clean the house, do the cooking, render the lard, and cook the sausage after hog-killing time. My oldest brother, William, was the family babysitter. My other brothers did farm work and gardening. It was normal for the children to leave home when they became teenagers. Jim, Lee and Carl, for example, left and went to work earlier than most young men. Josephine, Sally, and Elnora left and were soon married. I was the little one in the Yokley family, the youngest of 10 children.

"Pleasant Point was isolated, many miles away from any school. The only time we had church, to speak of, was when a circuit preacher came through and threw up an altar and sermonized. When someone in my family had a bad tooth, my father did the pulling. When nearby people had any sick animals, they notified my dad who would treat their stock. If he had a hog to be castrated or a gelt to be spayed, he used me as a youngster with small hands to manipulate inside after he had cut the hog.

"My mother died when I was 11 years old; she had been sickly for years. We couldn't get a doctor, so midwives delivered my brothers and sisters. After mother died, we moved to Jump Off, between Sewanee and Monteagle. My father, Dallas Yokley, was a logger. At that time on the Mountain, loggers cut down ash trees for the making of baseball bats. The flu epidemic in 1918 killed several men my father worked with.

"After we moved to Jump Off, I was given the job of keeping meat on the family table. William gave me his treasured single-shot .22 caliber rifle plus a box of shells. My father told me to never hunt in populated areas, and to use every shell wisely. He said: 'Ed, I want meat from each shell.' I became an expert sharpshooter. I brought home squirrels, goats, turkeys, deer and rabbits.

"In 1925, at the age of 13, I was walking near the Natural Bridge close to Sewanee, with 27 squirrels hanging from my belt. Two women and their black maid, who had the unusual name of America, appeared out of the bushes, surprising me. I knew, as they did, I was trespassing on someone else's property, but they were very cordial. They asked if they could buy some squirrels. I told them selling wild game was illegal, but I'd be glad to give them several squirrels, if they bought me some .22 shells, and they agreed to do that. My appearance shocked them. There I was, a short, scrubby hillbilly, an aberration in their eyes. Nevertheless, serendipity played a hand. That accidental encounter dramatically changed my life.

"To make a long story short, the two ladies took me under their wings and basically adopted me. Leila Warren and Nina Pearce were sisters, from Senator LeRoy Percy's family in Mississippi, one of the richest families in the Delta. They owned a vacation home in Sewanee, and hired me to be their private chauffeur. I had no experience as a driver, but I somehow managed. My first drive was over an awful log road between Sewanee and Winchester. Roads were atrocious then.

"Their automobile was a Cord, 25 feet long with two jump seats and a canvas top. The seats were genuine leather. The car was luxurious. My job took me to a world I had never seen, only dreamed about. We drove through much of the south over the next five years, an education in itself, and I developed a friend-

Fr. McVeigh Harrison

ship with Ms. Warren and Ms. Pearce. To me they were 'Mother Warren' and 'Aunt Nina.' I came to think of them as substitute aunts. The traveling was beneficial. For the first time, I wore suits and brushed my shoes. Mile after mile, day after day, the three of us would go down the highway and talk about every subject under the sun. The process opened up a new universe to me.

"A significant conversation took place in 1930, when Mother Warren and Aunt Nina suggested I think about my future. The depression was taking its toll and the future didn't look bright for someone like me, a peon. In the lobby of the Peabody Hotel, in downtown Memphis, they suggested I attend St. Andrew's School. They knew the priest who ran the monastery, Father McVeigh Harrison, and they said they would persuade him to let me attend classes. They also assured me I would never have to worry about tuition. My mind was whirling when we left Memphis. Their idea was well-intended, but I was 18 years old and had never set foot inside a classroom. I was an ignoramus and I knew it. Putting me in such an academic setting would be like dumping an aborigine in the middle of New Orleans at high noon. But, by the time we reached Sewanee, I agreed to give it a try. I was numb with anxiety."

In November, 1930, St. Andrew's administrators happily accepted Edward Yokley as a student. Their endorsement was colored by Leila Warren's check for $2,000. The depression had a malignant hold on the country, and the school was desperate for money. The unexpected check was an early Christmas present.

St. Andrew's had to make special adjustments. Instead of attending classes during his first two years, Ed was taught exclusively by a team of tutors: Allious Reid, Brother Dominic, Fathers Webb and Harrison. His main tutor was Father Flye, who took a special interest in Ed's education. Edward Yokley's natural leadership qualities did not go unnoticed. During his first year at St. Andrew's, administrators appointed him the Head Prefect, a title he held for an unprecedented seven years.

Yokley had this to say about the 1930s: "There were some boys who had no family, no place to go during summers. About 15 boys stayed at St. Andrew's year round. They hauled coal for the furnaces, and did chores at the school farm. The football players kept in shape by digging ditches for the school's water system. Summers included extra schooling for some of us.

"Sometimes I would advance two grades in one year. I hit the books hard, and was known as 'Mr. Question' on campus. I had so much catching-up to do. It was tough, of course, but I was encouraged every step of the way. I accomplished in seven years the equivalent of 12 years of education. I also developed socially; one of my greatest satisfactions at St. Andrew's was being elected class president.

"Mr. Reid, the Headmaster, bought me a set of clippers, and I became the school's barber. I cut hair for 25 cents per head, and made a nice buck. Oh, I was quite the businessman. I took over a room in the administration building basement and ran a little commissary. The arrangement was that St. Andrew's would get 10 percent of the profits. It reached the point that I hired my roommate to help me operate the commissary. I also collected clothing for a dry cleaner shop in Sewanee, and got a 10-cent commission for each garment.

"The student body was a close family unit, everyone trying to keep the school from closing. I recall days when all we had to eat for breakfast was cheese over crackers, some coffee and milk. For lunch, pork and beans with pickles. Supper was potatoes with pickles and gravy. For dessert, if we had one, peanut butter and molasses. The school's financial situation was so terrible that bills and salaries weren't paid for months. I recall seeing a Birmingham newspaper article in which Father Parker was asked to capsulize the story of St. Andrew's. Instead of going on about history and such, he answered with one word: survival. During my time at the school there were good and bad students, good and bad teachers, good and bad morale.

"Shortly after I arrived, a University of the South student was hired to manage the study hall. The first night he was on the job someone cut the light off and the poor guy was scared to death, surrounded by bullies who were yelling and beating on his desk. The college boy never came back. Then a teacher was given the study hall job. He brought a BB gun to keep control, but that didn't work. He was high-strung and didn't last long. I was put in charge, and I told Clyde 'Bosh' Medford to rig the light switch where turning it off was impossible. When the first boy went to the bathroom and tried to turn the light off, he received a hard punch. That ended such foolishness in the study hall.

"Another boy I knew, Samuel Motely Anderson, had five stepmothers in his awful childhood. Despite that hellish start, Sam survived the Bataan Death March and retired as a Marine Corps Colonel. He credited St. Andrew's with giving him the starch to survive. His original interest in history had been stirred by Father

Flye, and Sam eventually became an expert in Middle East archaeology."

Beginning in 1936, each St. Andrew's student had to take an IQ test. The school had two separate curricula and the tests determined which courses pupils attended. Ed Yokley scored 130, demonstrating his native intelligence and his educational level by the time he was a high school junior. His case proved that when put in the proper atmosphere, even the craggiest stone can be polished into a valuable gem.

When he first met Ed in late 1930, Father Flye detected a trait he always looked for: intellectual curiosity. When he began tutoring Yokley, the priest had no idea that his abilities would be tested as never before. Years later, Flye reported: "I had been asked by Mr. Reid to tutor Eddy on a one-to-one basis, and this turned out to be the most demanding job in my teaching career. His knowledge of the world was rudimentary at best, but his saving grace was a desire to learn, something any teacher would like."

Early in their relationship, Flye had given Ed a dictionary, saying: "Use this when you hear or see a word you're not familiar with. Learn the word's proper spelling; learn its meaning; learn when to use the word. This book will be your salvation. From now on, carry this dictionary and use it every day." Ed took Father Flye's advice seriously, and over the next six years, he went through four dictionaries.

Father Flye also gave Ed diction lessons. Yokley's poor grammar and colloquialisms were so ingrained, at times success seemed impossible; however, over a span of years, Flye modified Ed's way of talking. "Ain't," "he don't" and "you-uns," as well as other poor choices, were eliminated from his vernacular. Like professor Henry Higgins in *My Fair Lady*, the teacher taught the student well.

During his senior year, Ed's articulation had reached such a level that he was asked to accompany the Prior, Father Francis Parker, on a fund-raising trip to New York City. On December 18, 1936, at the Waldorf Astoria Hotel, Parker and Yokley spoke to several hundred executives. They returned to St. Andrew's School with $106,000. Father Flye could not have been more proud of his protégé.

In May 1937, at the age of 25, Edward Yokley received a high school diploma. A few months later, he enrolled at Lincoln Memorial University, in Harrogate, Tennessee, where he had a football scholarship. He then faced a major hurdle: anonymity. At St. Andrew's he had been a big man on campus, but now he was just another face in the crowd. He lost his scholarship after his left knee was injured. His grades took a nosedive. Facing failure for the first time in his life, rudderless, Ed dropped out of school.

He held a number of jobs, including managing a restaurant in Brooklyn, and as a handyman at a church mission in Lexington, Kentucky. He was working at a Dallas manufacturing plant when the Japanese bombed Pearl Harbor—three days later, he enlisted in the Army. After boot camp, he was assigned to the Army Air Corps, and became a training instructor at Lowry Air Base in Denver.

The Flyes received a letter from Ed in 1942, and Grace Flye wrote: "We just heard from our sweet Eddy. Censors have mutilated his mail with whole lines cut out. Hal and I are so proud of him. My mind still resonates by his drive to better himself."

Ed Yokley had the talent to impress people in a positive way. At Lowry, Ed's public speaking skills and personality impressed General Joseph P. Arnold. Generals and sergeants do not normally become friends, but with the help of General Arnold, Ed was next assigned to the ultra-secret Manhattan Project at Oak Ridge, Tennessee. As part of Ed's security clearance, FBI agents questioned Ed's father, Dallas

Ed Yokley's senior class photo, 1937

Yokley, and the senior Yokley feared his son had committed a serious crime.

Ed arrived at Oak Ridge at a propitious time. The atomic bomb was being developed under a cloak of unprecedented security. The secret complex had a surreal quality, as civilian and military personnel learned about uranium, radio-activity and isotopes. It was a technology that was mysterious and dangerous. Meanwhile, the diction lessons Ed had taken at Father Flye's bungalow earned unexpected dividends. Ed's job at Oak Ridge involved hosting seminars on radiation contamination. From a desert bunker in New Mexico, Ed viewed the world's first atomic explosion. On the island of Tinian, he helped load "Little Boy" aboard the B-29 that dropped the atomic bomb over Hiroshima. He later said that despite the appalling death toll, the cataclysmic event saved many more lives.

Ed married a Memphis secretary, Kathleen Smith, in 1946. As the years passed, Ed was involved with veterans' issues, becoming a spokesman for those who had worn a uniform. He testified in 1990 before a congressional committee that was probing Agent Orange exposure during the Vietnam conflict. Ed had come a long way from the isolated log cabin where he was born. Edward Yokley died in 1996, at the age of 84, at a Veteran's Administration hospital in Daytona Beach, Florida.

Kathleen Yokley said: "If Ed hadn't met the ladies from Mississippi, and if he hadn't gone to St. Andrew's, God only knows what would have happened to him. Ed said he was the luckiest man alive. But this wasn't the whole of it. His success was a mixture of ambition and opportunity.

"I was with him when he visited relatives in Tennessee. It was sometimes awkward, a mixed bag of worms. Ed had taken one road, his family another. We went to Jump Off to see where he had lived, but the house wasn't there any-more. Ed always talked about St. Andrew's. Over the years, we visited the school, and on one visit we talked to Father Flye, which pleased Ed so much. Ed once told me that Father Flye was the living spirit of what St. Andrew's was supposed to be all about."

❏ ❏ ❏

The *Chattanooga Times* printed an article in September 1977, in which Oliver Paris Hodge, a 1924 St. Andrew's graduate, was quoted: "The monks of the Order of the Holy Cross went to extremes to avoid contact with women. To show how narrow their thinking was, St. Andrew's students had to ride the train to Cowan and back so the monks wouldn't be sitting alone with a female. Two of us in 1923 were expelled for taking a couple of local girls for a walk in the woods. Our motives were pure, but the Prior, Father Liston Orum, a fanatic if there ever was one, expelled us, saying catch the 10 o'clock train at Gipson's Switch. My suitcase was packed, and I went to say goodbye to my favorite teacher, Father Flye. I don't know what he said on my behalf, but he swayed Father Orum to let me stay. I was lucky, and the other boy wasn't. It was an episode over an innocent walk in the woods. The Prior was ill-suited for his job."

Flye had taught French to Hodge for three years and the boy showed great promise. As a junior, Hodge spoke and wrote French fluently, and Flye thought that to deny Oliver his senior year bordered on the criminal. The history teacher was then in his fifth year at St. Andrew's, and was already complaining in his private journals about the penalties handed down to students who violated school rules. (There may have been some validity to Hodge's opinion that Orum was ill-suited. Father Flye wrote in his journal in 1927: "Fr. Orum is depressed, nervous, full of fears and dreads." Orum died in 1928 at the age of 36.)

The following is part of a Grace Flye letter dated June 18, 1928: "Oliver Hodge just graduated from the University of Chattanooga, and is going to New York to continue his education next autumn. His stepfather is the Superintendent of the big Civil War park, and lives in the historical Craven House on Lookout Mountain. Oliver drove up from Chattanooga to spend the weekend with us. We are so very fond of him. While I was fixing supper, I heard them talking French so quickly. Oliver is an extraordinary French scholar and says he owes it all to Hal's tutoring. He is as handsome as a stage actor. Whenever he visits us, some of the faculty wives find excuses to knock at my kitchen door. I think he could be another Casanova."

A St. Andrew's classmate, David Lockmiller, described Hodge this way: "Ollie had an urbane look, a cut above the rest of us." Oliver Hodge went on to earn advanced degrees, and had a teaching career, in addition to working overseas with the Office of International Development. He taught French at Philadelphia's

Sunday morning Eucharist at St. Andrew's chapel

Girard Institute. He was a Romance Languages instructor at the University of Chattanooga, where he met a librarian, Mary Hale, who later became his wife. Hodge spent many of his later years in France.

Hodge admitted he first agreed to study French with Father Flye because this let him avoid normal work details. He thought studying French would be easier than shoveling snow. Despite his initial reasoning, he was soon excited about the language. In an interview with Gil Adkins, a St. Andrew's employee who was researching the history of the school, Hodge talked about Father Flye's teaching methods: "From day one, he emphasized the importance of knowing Romance root phrases, and he used history and geography to show how French was favored by the world's diplomats. My mind was like a sponge, and he described exciting places, to get his point across. I hadn't been anywhere and the idea of traveling was a narcotic. I never told Father Flye, but I fantasized about speaking French to impress gals in a smoke-filled bar. I dreamed of palm trees in the tropics and French-speaking hula ladies. My teenage imagination was boundless."[1]

Oliver Hodge continued: "The school was a place with hard rules, run by monks who came from aristocratic northern families. They all had an Ivy League education, and a lot could be learned from them. However, their penny-ante rules were sacred to them. The most ludicrous example was that of Si Turner, who was called on the carpet for missing one class. He had walked to Sewanee to vote on election day. He was in the army in France during World War I, so he knew about his civic duties. Si Turner's dismissal was idiotic.

"The Order had no southern monks at that time. I think some of the Order priests thought of St. Andrew's as a Devil's Island, a place of exile. They were essentially gentle men, very devout. But they were seminarians, not school administrators. They did a decent job, everything considered. Nevertheless, I believe the boys' mountain resiliency had a great deal to do with the school's success."

In a separate interview, Oliver Hodge said: "My sister attended St. Mary's

Clockwise from top right: the Rev. James H. Flye, Arthur H. deCourcy, Samuel Martin, George M. Williams, Allious Reid, Philip H. Mankin, the Rev. Liston J. Orum, O.H.C.; bottom row, left to right: Glenn L. Kimsey, Carrie D. Sloan; Price Womak

School near Sewanee, and I remember the nuns who managed that institution. One could say the idea of the two schools was to marry the two sets off to each other to provide little hillbilly Episcopalians on the Mountain. That notion worked to some degree.

"I remember Reverend Claiborne. He was a wonderful giant of a man, who played football for Sewanee at the turn of the century. He started St. Andrew's, and he'd come around to check up on the place. He and Father Flye were dear friends. They looked like Mutt and Jeff; one big man and one small one. Claiborne had a booming laugh you could hear in the next state, and Flye had a quiet giggle. As a regular at the Flye house, I got to know Mrs. Claiborne and her daughter who often visited there. With the passage of time, I think it is now permissible to say that Claiborne wasn't happy with the way the school was being run. I recall him being so angry about a boy forced to stand during his supper in the dining hall.

"I went back to visit the Flyes at their house several times. I met with Father Flye in New York City, Paris, Philadelphia and Washington. He lived vicariously through my overseas mail. Mrs. Flye once told me how he would study the globe after getting my letters. He was happy when I sent a carton from Casablanca with Bedouin trinkets, coins and a shawl for Mrs. Flye. Our letters back and forth were always written in French. Wherever I was, he wanted to know about the area's culture and language. He had an insatiable appetite for knowledge. He once said: 'Learning is God's work.'"

Oliver Hodge spoke of the last time he saw Father Flye: "It was in Europe in 1964. We sat at an outdoor cafe on the Champs Eysees for hours. I was so impressed when Father Flye spoke Arabic to our waiter, who was from Algeria. Father Flye was nearly 80 and showed some wear and tear, but he had the constitution of a Hercules. Our time together in Paris is a precious memory. I thought of him as a friend, maybe the closest I ever had. He once told me he had always considered me among the race horses he had known at St. Andrew's. It is one of my great pleasures he didn't place me with the draft animals. My life would have been radically different if Father Flye hadn't helped me."

❏ ❏ ❏

The Father Flye mythology was enhanced with the 1999 introduction of *A Final Liaison*, a screenplay by Kenneth and Ninian Williams. The following is the story which prompted them to write their dialogue about torn allegiances.

An ordinary letter from Father Flye saved the life of Edward Hubbell. The priest had been Hubbell's Latin instructor at St. Andrew's, and they exchanged letters after the young man left the Mountain.

Shortly after the Pearl Harbor attack, the Japanese invaded the Philippine Islands and despite the fact he was a civilian, Ed Hubbell became a prisoner of war. He had been working with a road building crew in northern Luzon, and found himself in a confused maelstrom. Refugees clogged the roads, and escape was impossible. When he was captured, Hubbell had a crumpled and soiled letter from Father Flye tucked in a shirt pocket. A Japanese interrogator read the letter and spotted a Latin quotation that grabbed his interest. Ed was then called in for questioning. The English-speaking interrogator, an Army lieutenant named Ito, had studied Latin at Oxford University, and wanted to talk to someone else who also appreciated the ancient language.

In the sweltering hell of a Japanese POW camp in the Philippine Islands, the war was essentially put aside as the Japanese army officer and Ed Hubbell spent time together quietly speaking Latin. The two men shared their opinions about Hannibal, Cicero, Caesar, the grandeur of the Roman Empire. Father Flye's Latin lessons were put to good use in grotesque circumstances.

Their prison camp arrangement had to be surreptitious; appearances were everything. Ito had to pretend he was questioning Hubbell about military matters, so when the camp guards were within earshot his demeanor was one of hostility toward the American, to the point of physical abuse. Some degree of brutality was expected. Ed knew this and accepted slaps to his head, shouting in his face, and being knocked to the ground, as a necessity. It was a question of survival. Hundreds of men were dying monthly in the camp from starvation and disease. Those prisoners still living were essentially walking skeletons. In the midst of this nightmare, Ed was kept alive by Lieutenant Ito who gave him rice, soup, tea and quinine pills.[2]

Hubbell's so-called interrogations ended when Ito was suddenly transferred. At their last meeting, the two men exchanged quiet words of affection. The army officer gave Ed a photograph. After Ito's departure, Ed's health worsened. He was close to death when the camp was liberated by American troops. He had lost nearly all of his teeth, could barely walk, and weighed 84 pounds. Nearly 20 percent of the camp's inmates died during their captivity.

Following Japan's capitulation in late 1945, Japanese atrocities were uncovered to an enraged world. The Bushido code of conduct, used by ancient Samurai warriors, had governed the Japanese military mentality. Surrender to the enemy was dishonorable, so anyone who chose surrender over death in battle was beneath contempt. When Japan began its sweep through the western Pacific in the 1940s, Dutch, British and American POWs became victims of savage brutality. War crime trials were conducted in Japan after the war, but the Nuremberg trials in Germany dominated the world's headlines.

Hubbell never told authorities about Lieutenant Ito, afraid he would be accused of collaborating with the enemy. As a civilian, his POW behavior could not be held to the strict military standard, and he thought his liaison with Lieutenant Ito caused no harm. Nevertheless, he felt shame about his good fortune. He was tormented with "survivor's guilt" syndrome.

Hubbell's daughter, Betty Matthews, recounted her father's post-war years: "After he got back to the states, Daddy tried to contact Ito and was told he had been killed at Okinawa. He once said to me that the young Japanese officer was the bravest man he had ever known, and their meeting was a gift from God. He kept a small photograph of Lieutenant Ito on his bedroom dresser. Daddy never did recover. Malnutrition, malaria, dysentery, and so on, had done too much harm; however, Daddy's outlook remained good, he was grateful he survived. He said Father Flye's letter turned out to be his lucky charm."

"Magna Est Veritas Et Traepraevalet" (the truth is great and it prevails) was the Latin quotation in Father Flye's 1941 letter to Ed Hubbell.

The St. Andrew's Headmaster in 1925, Father Roger Anderson, wrote: "One student bartered potatoes to enter our school." Claude Wright had walked to St. Andrew's from his home near Tracy City, and pleaded with the Headmaster to be allowed to attend classes. The young boy was turned away because he could not pay tuition. He was walking past the Flye bungalow with his head down, sobbing, when he was spotted by Father Flye.

The boy lived on a small farm near Tracy City. His father had worked at a local coal mine, but was unemployed because of lung failure, and was currently bedridden with a recurring fever. In the course of the conversation, the boy mentioned an unharvested potato crop. Father Flye walked to Anderson's office and persuaded the Headmaster to accept potatoes instead of cash. Bartering was common in those days.

Father Flye, Grace Flye, an unknown St. Andrew's maintenance man, and Claude Wright dug up potatoes with their bare hands over the following weekend. They loaded them into burlap sacks and took them to a cold storage area in the basement under the St. Andrew's administration building. The four ended up with blisters and aching backs, and the Flye's big Packard smelled of potatoes for a long time. James Hollingsworth commented: "I heard the potato story many times. It sounded like something Father Flye would do. He would get involved if he saw a boy crying. He had a long tradition of being there for any child who needed help."

Claude attended St. Andrew's for several years. After his father died, he went to live with relatives near Nashville. Archives show he corresponded with the Flyes for 20 years. He became an executive in the railroad business. One of Claude Wright's grandsons said: "No question about it, Father Flye saved grandpa's life."

Dale W. Doss entered St. Andrew's in 1951, and graduated as Class Valedictorian in 1954. He then enrolled at the University of North Carolina at Chapel Hill and earned a Bachelor of Arts degree in history. After graduation, he was commissioned as an officer in the U.S. Navy. He was an electronic navigator with the rank of Lieutenant Commander, stationed aboard the aircraft carrier USS Enterprise, when in March1968, his A-6 Intruder was shot down near Hanoi in Vietnam. He endured five years of torture as a prisoner of war.

The communists at Hoa Lo prison (inmates called it the "Hanoi Hilton") were proficient at what they did. They knew how to effectively torture American captives, yet keep them barely alive. Doss did as he was trained to do, giving only his name, rank, serial number and date of birth. He was beaten into unconsciousness when he refused to volunteer more information. Doss recounted: "My first two years were in isolation. My name appeared in *Time* magazine and 'Hanoi Hannah' mentioned my name on the radio, so the commies thought I was someone important to work on. They tried torture, brainwashing and solitary confinement, to get me to sign false statements that America wanted to take over the world.

"We weren't fed much and we didn't have decent medical treatment. Some of the men had broken arms and legs that were never set. I wasn't treated differently from the other men, not one of us had it easy. It was very difficult. After years of torture and being thrown back into a filthy cell, day after day, it got to the point where I withdrew into myself. The other prisoners did the same. Each of us, on an individual basis, had to hold on to what we were individually.

"The memory of my mother, my grandmother, and St. Andrew's helped me. What I learned at the school came back to me like a bright light. Sitting in pain in that cell in Vietnam, those lessons about truthfulness had a new clarity. One of my survival tools was the mental process of building St. Andrew's from the ground up, brick by brick, board by board. I relived discussions I once had with men such as Father Flye and Father Spencer. This kind of mental exercise kept my mind occupied.

"I had to figure out whether it was worthwhile to live. Things got to a point where I questioned my struggle. Is it worthwhile? Is there a God? Did Christ really live? Why am I here? There was a Vietnamese interrogator we called The Bug. He was an expert at inflicting pain, and one day he said to me: 'Your God has put you here for me to torture.' I answered: 'You know, life is predestined.' Him saying what he did and my response, was a turning point. From then on, I knew things would work out okay.

"The Bug tempted me once when he asked me to do something that appeared small. He wanted me to write a personal letter to the camp commander, saying how good my treatment was, and if I did this I would get a package from home. On the surface, it appeared innocent. I was down to 90 pounds. Why not improve my situation by writing an innocuous letter to the camp commander? Who would know? Who would care? The insurmountable barrier was that I would know, I would care.

"And I knew that one lie leads to another lie. Instincts told me to avoid that slippery slope. I concluded that if I died, it was because the Vietnamese had killed me, not because I pulled a blanket over my head and took the easy way out, and died from a kind of moral decay. My stubbornness in my beliefs was the armor they could never pierce. Dale Doss was going to stay alive on his own terms.

"I thought back to my childhood and I realized how important St. Andrew's was to me. What made Dale Doss what he is today? My answer was that all of it came from St. Andrew's and men like Father Flye. I learned about leadership at St. Andrew's, and that early training served me well. In the prison camp some men were saved by moral leadership. We found ourselves in a position of putting our lives up for each other and this commitment gave us a moral compass. In my case, it all began at St. Andrew's. Effective leadership is character, and that's what the school was all about. You could not be there and not have some of it rub off on you.

"We were young boys who had, at one time, been out of sync with society, but the teachers and priests turned us around. They made a real difference. Those morning prayers, the Sunday services, gave me ammunition I would need later on.

"How did I get to St. Andrew's in the first place? My mother worked hard to keep us afloat. A single parent, especially a woman, never had it soft in those days in a city like Birmingham. We didn't own a car, she had to take a bus to work and back. My grandmother came to live with us. I was a rambunctious kid who got into trouble. I was expelled several times. Mother had heard about St. Andrew's, where troubled boys like myself got a second chance. I was homesick at first, but I adjusted and came to love the place. It was a Christian school for boys, not a school for Christian boys.

"My initial job at the school was in the kitchen. I cleaned the cook's pots and pans. The experience taught me something about myself. The hard work, something new to me, became a personal challenge. I finally took pride in something I did. When I got a compliment about how clean those pots and pans were, I felt like a million dollars. Before St. Andrew's, I had way too much idle time, but at the school I was kept busy. I hit the rack at night exhausted. I gained weight and felt great. I got up fresh-eyed and bushy-tailed. I blossomed at St. Andrew's. One good thing was that we received attention when we needed academic help. My mother's friends in Birmingham were astonished when they heard I graduated at the top of my class.

"Father Bonnell Spencer taught Christian Ethics, a stimulating course I found to be valuable. He produced the school's plays and I was involved in all the plays while I was there, most notably our production of *Macbeth*. Bonny was a sensitive man who meant well and took a lot of teasing. Looking back, I wish I had been nicer to him. Self-centered teenagers can be obnoxious. It is a shame we have to go through life experiences before we realize how we were helped by others. If I could turn the clock back, I'd tell Bonnie how much I appreciate him.

"The man I'm most indebted to was my history teacher, Father Flye. He influenced me greatly. He was truly a top-rate teacher. Before I went to St. Andrew's, I had read plenty of books, but they weren't ones with lasting power. Father Flye put me on a regimen of reading two books a month, many of them from his own library. They were histories and biographies. I remember a book about Robert La Follette, a Wisconsin Senator who ran for president in 1924. Father Flye respected his courage.

"Father Flye had an internal fire, a mystical aura that told you he was different from anyone else. When he was upset he would shake his hands and whisper 'Piffle, Piffle,' a characteristic that gave him his nickname. [3] He had an expression that always made me chuckle: 'May jackals eat on the bones of your father's father.' He would first say it in Arabic, and then in English. He knew many languages.

"Today's society tries to give our children a good education, but unfortunately we don't teach manners or morals these days. I wish every child in the country could have the St. Andrew's training I had."

Doss continued: "My naval career included four commands, including being the Deputy Inspector General. The IG's office investigates wrongdoing, and I saw cases where an officer started out with just a minor infraction, but this led to something serious. It was painful to have to read a senior officer his rights and see him stripped of command. In those cases I looked into, it came down to moral behavior. I recall a case where a senior officer had a young secretary, and it had begun with them having a cup of coffee after hours. The slippery decline, the moral slide, can be subtle. He ended up cheating on his wife, and misappropriating funds. It was sad to see him behind bars, his career, essentially his life, now over. I stayed in the Navy and retired with the rank of Captain."

Sustained American military action forced the Vietnamese communists to release the 592 prisoners of war held at Hoa Lo prison. The world watched on television as the men arrived at Clark Air Force Base, in the Philippines, in March 1973. Their physical appearance was clear evidence how they had been treated. They were welcomed back with flowing tears. The media was in a frenzy to get the prison camp survivors in front of a microphone. This led to a St. Andrew's biology teacher, Walter Chambers, playing a role in the emotional reunion of Dale Doss and Father Flye.

A St. Andrew's alumnus, a professor at Vanderbilt University, was scheduled to be the commencement speaker for the school's graduating class of 1973. But, as fate would have it, Chambers was listening to a Nashville radio station when he heard St. Andrew's mentioned by Dale Doss during an interview. He suggested to the Headmaster that the naval officer be asked to give the commencement address.

Meanwhile, the 1973 seniors had dedicated their yearbook to Father Flye, and he had agreed to come from New York City to be present at their graduation.

Walter Chambers recalled: "Commander Doss stayed at my apartment that weekend, and it was there that he and Father Flye were reunited. Dale Doss, my wife, Margaret, and I were sitting in our living room when Father Flye knocked on our door. I let him in, and the atmosphere was immediately charged; it was like some energy had activated the air in the room.

Lt. Commander. Dale Doss and Father Flye at St. Andrew's Commencement, 1973

"The two men looked at each other, taking in the physical changes the years had brought, with a loving recognition and concern. They stared at each other for a long time, neither saying a word. I saw tears in both their eyes. Finally, Father Flye simply said: 'My son,' and they embraced in the center of the room.

"We sat and listened to Dale's account of his many years of imprisonment: solitary confinement, secret codes used by prisoners to communicate, physical and electrical tortures, hellish living conditions, the frequent moving from cell to cell, the marital problems—infidelity by wives—faced by the men. Dale said his St. Andrew's Christian education gave him the courage and strength to survive. Most amazing to me was his attitude. His outlook had an absence of negatives: no bitterness. I listened to Dale Doss with complete astonishment. I was tremendously impressed. He knew about the anti-war demonstrations, and Jane Fonda's visit to North Vietnam. He knew about these things. The man had endured so much, but his time in that dark hell, his own horrific trip to Damascus, had not crushed his spirit. Keep in mind that when we saw him, he wasn't long-removed from Vietnam. He had only been back home for a few months. He was still painfully thin.

"Father Flye responded to Dale Doss' account with his whole body. The old man's posture, eyes, mouth, arms and hands were animated. He literally leaned into Doss' words. While he listened, his facial expressions showed surprise, compassion, grief, shock and concern. His lips were drawn into a small O, emitting a series of oh, oh, oh, oh, indicating a painful empathy. Father Flye's hands were usually on his knees, but at times he raised both hands and covered his mouth. More than once, he took out his handkerchief and wiped his eyes."

Margaret Chambers recalled: "There will only be few moments in your life that are so sensitive, they are made less if put into words. Such a feeling occurred for me when Dale Doss and Father Flye met in my living room. To this day I can feel the moment, the experience, of watching the two men who so cared for each other.

"In the changing of the guard ceremony at the Tomb of the Unknown Soldier in Arlington, Virginia, the retiring guard is asked: 'Do you feel sufficiently honored?' I felt sufficiently honored when I saw those two men together. I was a close spectator to a scene of extraordinary honor and respect. The rarified richness of that occasion still stays with me."

This article appeared in the *St. Andrew's Messenger*: "Commander Doss' address was a moving experience. He did not dwell on his tortures, or his imprisonment, but rather upon the truths which resulted. He turned to face graduating seniors and addressed his remarks to them directly; however, all could benefit from listening to the truths that he had so tortuously learned. He prayed the seniors would never be put to the test but hoped they too had found here what he had found here and in Father Flye that enabled him to endure. How wonderful it was that these two men were together at this time."

[1] Gil Adkins' history of education on the Mountain was never published. He died in 1989 at the age of 60.

[2] The June 1999 issue of *Reader's Digest* included a story about a Japanese guard's kindness toward an American POW in the Philippines during World War II. Like Ed Hubbell's story, the Arthur Bressi story was not revealed for many years.

[3] By the time he arrived at St. Andrew's in 1918, Father Flye had developed the peculiar habit of shaking his hand and muttering "Piffle, Piffle, Piffle" when he was irritated. This is why St. Andrew's students secretly referred to him as Piffle. The nickname was one of endearment.

CHAPTER 4

The Bungalow—Views on the World—Reminiscences —A Microcosm

The palest ink is better than the best memory.
—CHINESE PROVERB

UPON THEIR ARRIVAL AT ST. ANDREW'S in 1918, the Flyes were assigned living quarters in a house across the street from the school's chapel. The bungalow was ideally situated. It was far enough removed from the rest of the campus so that Grace had plenty of privacy for her painting studio.

With 1,700 square feet, the bungalow was big enough for their needs. There were seven rooms: a dining room, parlor, the den—also used as her portrait studio—two bedrooms, kitchen, bathroom. A hallway led through the center of the bungalow. A wide porch spanned the eastern side of the house, and a large half-floored attic and basement provided ample storage space.

Father Flye was a inveterate collector. His residence was a repository for everything imaginable. He subscribed to many magazines: *Colliers, National Geographic, Time, Life, Fortune, New Republic, Atlantic Monthly, Saturday Evening Post.* He also kept copies of the *Congressional Record, Holy Cross Magazine, St. Andrew's Messenger.* He kept articles from the *New York Times, Washington Post, Nashville Tennessean, Atlanta Constitution, Chattanooga Times, Chattanooga Free Press.* Notes, letters, clippings and books eventually filled 14 ceiling-high bookcases. As the years passed, space became more cramped and visitors were forced to negotiate a literal maze. One maintenance man at St. Andrew's remarked: "Don't worry about a fire breaking out in the Flye house. Things are packed so tight, there

Oil portrait of Father Flye by Grace Flye, 1924

wouldn't be any oxygen to feed it."

Few people knew Grace Flye built the bungalow's 14 bookcases, as well as the stairs leading up to the attic. Her outside sawing activities were slow and clumsy, but she always declined assistance. She once said to a concerned friend: "Hal's teaching is what he's good at, not carpentry."

Francis Parker, the Headmaster, while visiting the Flye bungalow in 1938, remarked that the aisles of voluminous books reminded him of the Library of Congress. Grace replied: "Yes, it does look like it, and I'm the curator."

Grace Flye wrote in a 1940s letter to her niece, Mary: "I was terrified about the front room, boxes staggered up the stairs and a solid litter stacked all over. I wouldn't have minded for myself, nor would I have minded if the literary friend Hal was looking for had arrived, but it was for Hal. Not being objective-minded, he does not notice much until it gets awful. We both are prodigious collectors, he even more than I."

In another letter that same year: "What with mile-high mountains of books and piles of newspapers for future archives, I live like the mortals in the fairy tales, Cinderella sitting in the ashes of a dust-disordered kitchen, trying to sort a roomful of feathers which the wicked fairy imposed on the princess. For ten years Hal has used the study in the autumn and spring, and the west bedroom in winter. He spreads papers on the wide bed and writes on a lap-board. He has a one-dimensional sense of order and ought to be a millionaire with an acre to spread his paper on. He doesn't like to put anything on top of another. My aim is to stack all the stuff, the way it is in a lumber yard. I should be shoving things, but there is no place to shove anything to. I cleared the kitchen table and fixed a place for books. He has been writing for weeks and likes the warm air from the kitchen coal range. He has his typewriter and the couch for his siestas. It will be thrilling when I hoist more boxes out and fix a tall bookcase."

Stanley Hole, a 1949 St. Andrew's graduate, said: "The Flye house was chaos, real chaos. Boxes all over the place. Charming. Extraordinarily warm and friendly. You went there and felt right at home in many ways. I must admit that seeing those tall stacks of boxes in their house was an intimidating experience at first."

Throughout the Flye bungalow there were large and small boxes containing: pieces of string, burnt wooden matches, postcards, letters, empty cans and bottles, containers of glass shards, rusty nails, rubber bands, rusty screws, pencil stubs, short pieces of wire, human hair, pine cones, tennis balls, bent paper clips, empty ink bottles, empty oil cans, nails and bolts. Something was jammed into every crevice, ranging from a child's coat to rolled-up oil portraits. The house had unique odors: a combination of tea, coffee, painting oils, wax, solvents, tobacco from his snuff box, glue, cobwebs.

Father Flye used the broken glass to scrape away lacquer from his classroom's desks. He did this every two years or so, because students invariably carved their initials on the desk tops. For about five years in the 1930s, Father Flye collected used coats and shoes from St. Paul's Episcopal Church in Chattanooga. Needy St. Andrew's students with holes in their shoes, or wearing a threadbare coat, found replacements at the Flyes' house. A pair of shoes or a coat in the assortment may not have been an exact fit, but the idea was to be warm and dry, not fashionable.

Unbeknown to most people, there were good reasons behind the eclectic collection inside the Flye bungalow. Every spring, for example, Mrs. Flye would scatter the tiny pieces of string and used wooden matches for birds that were building nests. Human hair was used for pet beds for abandoned new-born wild animals brought to the bungalow by students. Grace Flye kept the animals under her bed. When the school quit using old-fashioned ink bottles, Grace used them as candle holders for gift giving.

Ethel Simmonds, St. Andrew's faculty wife, said: "Once, when I was about to leave Mrs. Flye's house, she pulled out a small box to show me. It was about the size of a child's foot, and inside was a cocoon-looking hollow place. There was a downy-like softness throughout the little box. She explained she had shredded cloth tea bags to make a little mice's nest, and that she kept it under the couch. It was a work of art. Her mice slept more comfortably than humans did. Their place was a menagerie, with all kinds of animals scooting underfoot or tucked behind boxes: baby squirrels, rabbits, mice and raccoons. I could only imagine what the nights must have been like, when those furry creatures were active. How did anyone get any sleep?"

Faculty wife, Mildred Watts, recalled: "I called my husband one afternoon, saying: 'Come quick, Father Flye and Mrs. Flye are chasing each other in their yard.' Well, it turned out they had spotted a snake in a robin's nest, and they were using a rake to scare it away. That couple loved every critter on the Mountain. Father Flye had a poem by William Cowper, 'Epitaph for a Hare' that he had memorized and he said the whole piece with a great deal of emotion. One night a boy stopped by the Flye house and pulled a tiny rabbit out of his pocket, and asked Mrs. Flye if she wanted to keep it. Needless to say, the rabbit was tamed and stayed there. I was over there a year later, and the animal was hopping around casual as could be."

After Grace Flye's parents died, she acquired boxes of antique clothing dating back to the mid-1800s. There was enough variety that the bungalow's attic had a wardrobe for all of the school's theatrical productions.

A wooden plaque was nailed over the kitchen door in the bungalow. It read:

> May those who love us, love us
> And those that don't love us
> May God turn their hearts;
> And if He doesn't turn their hearts
> May He turn their ankles
> So we'll know them by their limping

Particularly during the early years, the bungalow was a popular gathering place for scores of teachers and clergymen at St. Andrew's. William Claiborne, the school's founder, and his wife, Alice, were regular visitors. Erskine and Laura Wright, James Agee's stepfather and mother, were frequent guests. Grace's letters show that from the 1920s through the mid-1930s, the Flyes hosted many overnight visitors from out of town. With Grace's rabbits, raccoons, and other pets scurrying about after dark, staying overnight in the Flye house must have been a unique experience.

Owing to its location, the Flye bungalow was the first occupied building people saw as they entered the St. Andrew's campus. This led to unusual encounters. Grace Flye wrote on July 26, 1928: "This morning as I sat on the porch, a tall mountaineer came up. He asked about the sale of clothes which the school has once a month, and I told him that was only during school terms. He spotted Hal through a window and asked if he was one of the priests. He said he wanted to meet him. Hal came out and the two shook hands with great enthusiasm, the mountaineer saying: 'Well, I certainly want to get to know you.'

"I could see that Hal was fascinated by the dignified air this man had; very confident, very composed. He had a commanding voice with a strange accent that seemed partly high-brow English. He informed us he was from Valley Cove, and had been a Baptist preacher for 35 years. He said he was born in 1845, but he did not look over fifty. An extraordinary man, over six feet tall, straight as any tree, brown hair, firm skin and a pleasing voice. One could see he was a spiritual chieftain to the isolated cove people. We rarely meet authentic mountain people. His conduct made me think of Grandfather Houghton. Hal and I were lucky to have had a glimpse of a forgotten page in history."

Later on, the bungalow became a haven for a number of retired Episcopal clergymen. Grace wrote in 1949: "Our dear friend Fr. Woodward is 70, frail with cardiac asthma and mild angina. For years he's made annual visits to see us, and with us he magically recuperates. Fr. and Mrs. Baasert from Denver will be here soon. He just retired. Yes, it will be cramped, but I'm looking forward to their company. My Noah's Ark serves all of us as a peaceful refuge in this tumultuous world. Why would I want to travel to far-flung places, when I have every happiness here among the tall trees."

Poet Will Percy wrote: "The place where Father Flye and Mrs. Flye call home is where friendships matter most, and life is celebrated, not scheduled. Their crowded house is enchanting, totally free of false values."

Clyde Medford (St. A '43): "As far back as anyone could remember, the Flyes were a soft touch for a cookie or a dollar. One of the first things you learned when you got to St. Andrew's was that Father Flye and Mrs. Flye were responsive to any sad story. For the boys who had a hard time adjusting to St. Andrew's, dropping by their place made life bearable. It was a refuge for the smaller kids. We older boys, if the truth be known, usually visited to borrow some money." In all probability, rumbling stomachs were not what compelled the younger boys to visit; it was a need for adult affection. The younger the boy, the greater the kindness from the Flyes. Cookies were an added bonus.

Lawrence Meyer, a 1951 St. Andrew's graduate, said: "I used to go down to Father Flye's house occasionally. If I needed an extra buck, I borrowed a dollar. I believe every boy at the school did that at one time or another. When I look back and think about Piffle, I think he was trying to tell us to stay positive. I remember him saying: 'Life is a gift.'"

❏ ❏ ❏

Grace Flye was injured in a 1928 auto accident. Windshield 'safety glass' had not been invented, and her face was lacerated when her car was broadsided by a delivery truck. It was foggy day, and she had not seen the truck as she was leaving the school property. The injuries left scars, but did not affect her socially. Throughout the 1930s, she continued to go to faculty tea parties and hosted friends and relatives at the bungalow. She was also involved in another auto wreck in 1939, in which she suffered a broken clavicle.

Sewanee bank official Herman Green reported: "Mrs. Flye was a tiny woman, barely able to see over the steering column, so she always had trouble parking. I can't think of a single time she didn't end up with one tire left up on the curb when she came to the bank."

David McDowell, a 1936 St. Andrew's graduate, said Mrs. Flye had her own "rules of the road." He put it this way: "She had a tendency to hog the middle of the highway and this scared me witless. We were driving back from Sewanee and both of our left tires had to be at least a foot over the center line, and a car was coming straight at us. But instead of turning the steering wheel, she kept her grip and scooted her body over next to me on the passenger side of the front seat. I was terrified. Luck was with us that day; the other driver took evasive action."

Neither of the Flyes was a careful driver. On one occasion Father Flye was driving his huge Packard on the highway to Tracy City, with Grace sitting next to him. Flye was oblivious to everything, singing at the top of his voice when the car leaned into a sharp turn. He glanced to his right and saw that his wife was no longer sitting there. The passenger door was open and Grace was hunched on the running board, clinging on for dear life. He immediately braked, shut the engine off, and asked: "Grace, what are you doing? Why didn't you yell?" She answered: "I was afraid that if I did, you would have an accident."

Like millions of other Americans, the Flyes were captivated by the new device called radio. Grace Flye wrote on June 29, 1928: "The wonder of radio comes through our window, voices booming from the convention at Houston are amplified in the horn at the school hall and are quite plain this far off, though I can't make out the words. I went up with Hal the other evening to listen, but there is so much rumbling, static they call it, that I found it tiresome. But the marvel of it charms my mind.

"A voice booming out across our air from a thousand miles away, and even the wild applause of the people and the marching of the delegates is heard. What soothes me more is drifting music wafted in my south windows as I sit by my sewing machine. Opera singers and violins from thousands of miles away. Down where the Lukes live is a radio. What is still more wonderful is to go over to the Chapman's and listen to music being played in London and to hear the big Parliament clock strike. The voice of the man in London, clear and plain as if he were in the next room. I just read that a radio message went around the world and came back in a few seconds!"

Several days later, on July 2, 1928, she wrote: "All the magic of conveniences in this beautiful heart of nature. Roads like smooth boulevards, cars swifter than antelopes and electric lights and plumbing. To say nothing of radio when one listens to music from the other side of the world. Mr. George Chapman, a radio genius here at the school, says he can easily hear Canada almost every night."

One of Grace Flye's nieces, Mary Boorman, recalled that Father Flye used radio to keep up with world affairs: "I wanted someone to go with me to play tennis, but everyone was crowded around the radio listening to news reports about Mussolini's invasion of Ethiopia [1935]. Uncle Hal was angry about this, he was really upset. He claimed the Italian Fascists were a bunch of strutting buffoons who would lose their pants if they were up against a modern army."

Eleanor Talbert, another one of Grace's nieces, had a similar experience: "We were visiting their house and Uncle Hal and my dad [Charles Houghton] were listening to the radio so intently about Hitler's soldiers going into Czechoslovakia [1938]. I was a high school junior and didn't care a whit about it, but I knew by their seriousness that something important was going on."

Herman Green recalled: "I was at their house to talk with the Flyes about their property off Sherwood Road. We never got around to it, because Father Flye waved me off to listen to Prime Minister Neville Chamberlain announce: 'There is peace in our time' [the 1938 Munich Pact]. I didn't follow European politics as closely as I should have, so the news didn't mean much to me at the time."

Father Flye was emotionally shaken in 1940 when he heard Winston Churchill offer Britain nothing but blood, toil, sweat and tears. He mentioned the Prime Minister's radio address at a faculty meeting, and was disappointed in the reaction. He wrote: "Everybody looked at me with an uncomprehending bovine stare." Flye was addicted to Edward R. Murrow's radio reports during the Blitz of 1940, when London was bombed for 57 consecutive evenings. Entire blocks of the city were razed by the Luftwaffe. From September to November, raids over London killed 14,000 people. The England he first visited back in 1908 was being defiled. At Andrew Lytle's Monteagle home, Flye said one evening: "I heard on the radio that the Waterloo train station was bombed." Lytle reported: "His pain was acute. He was a devoted Anglophile."

Whereas her husband was a slave to newscasts, Grace Flye treasured their huge radio console—it was nearly four feet tall—for its entertainment value. Her eyes brightened nightly as she listened to the popular radio personalities of that era: Eddie Cantor, Jack Benny, George Burns and Gracie Allen, Abbott and Costello, Fred Allen.

From China to Iceland, from India to Bolivia, the world was breathlessly fascinated with the 1927 Charles Lindbergh solo flight across the Atlantic Ocean. However, Lindbergh's name never appeared in Flye's journals. His journal entries were usually restricted to more humdrum matters. His correspondence, on the other hand, frequently mentioned current events. In a letter written in July 1925, he instructed Grace: "Save the *Chattanooga Times*. I want to read all about the monkey trial." John Scopes, a science teacher in Dayton, Tennessee, had broken state law by teaching evolution, and his trial was one of the most publicized in history. Reporters from around the world traveled to Dayton to hear William Jennings Bryan clash with Clarence Darrow over a literal interpretation of the Bible versus Darwinism. The trial basically centered on freedom of speech in Tennessee public schools. Scopes was found guilty and sentenced to pay a minor fine. The law was eventually revoked by the Tennessee legislature.

Father Flye's interest in the trial was intensified by his long-time readership of H. L. Mencken, an anti-establishment columnist based in Baltimore, Maryland. On the first day of the Scopes trial, Mencken had angered church conservatives when he wrote: "This circus in Dayton is being held in a part of the Coca-Cola belt where Episcopal and atheist mean the same thing."

Father Flye's letters in the 1930s reflected his concerns about the turmoil in

Europe and Asia. He wrote that when a nation's currency loses its value, its citizens look for quick solutions and are receptive to fire-breathing demagogues: "People may resent authority, but they think they can't live without it in unsettling times. Then it will be inevitable that poverty, politics and propaganda will be the troika that propels the barbaric sled of jingoism."

He also had strong ideas about domestic politics. He was critical of American artistic and intellectual activists who were drawn to communism, claiming they were simply misguided. He loathed hate-mongers such as the "Radio Priest," Charles Coughlin, who said big business was to blame for the country's financial woes. Father Flye noted that this theme went as far back as the founding fathers. He dismissed Ezra Pound as "irritating riffraff."

Flye voted for Calvin Coolidge and Herbert Hoover, and frowned on Franklin D. Roosevelt's New Deal, saying it put "addicts at the federal trough." Flye disliked socialism, and he absolutely detested communism. He wrote in 1934: "Hitler and Mussolini and their fascist lackeys are seen as threats to peace, but why is it the newspapers don't write about communism? How any person in this country can be attracted to the brutal Russian government escapes me."

The history teacher remained optimistic about the United States: "The people of this country don't have a tradition of total acquiescence to absolute authority which is necessary for fascism or communism to take a hold." Nevertheless, the 1930s were marked by hard times and fear. One quarter of the nation's households did not have a steady income. President Franklin D. Roosevelt said: "I see a nation ill-housed, ill-clad, ill-nourished." Conditions were worse elsewhere. There was mass starvation in Asia. As early as 1921-22, a wheelbarrow of deutschemarks in Germany only bought a loaf of bread. Such wretched conditions allowed Adolf Hitler, Benito Mussolini, Hideki Tojo and Joseph Stalin to solidify their power. Their rise did not go unnoticed by Father Flye.

Flye went to California in June of 1936 to see Dunning Sumers, a former St. Andrew's protégé, who was then enrolled in the Army's Officer Training Corps at the Presidio Military Complex in San Francisco. Flye's journals contain few mentions of Sumers, but Mrs. Flye often wrote about him in her letters. Sumers had learned French from Father Flye at St. Andrew's, and apparently had been an excellent student. Dunning was now wearing a military uniform, and with war looming on the horizon, the priest was worried about his former student's future.[1]

On July 17, 1937, Father Flye wrote Charles A. Mark, a high school English teacher in Knoxville: "Every politician in the world should have to take an extensive history course. Otherwise history will repeat itself and the results will be horrible. The world is heading toward a disaster."

On August 25, 1939, Father Flye wrote James Agee: "Another European crisis is at hand, due to Hitler's demands, and complicated by the signing of a pact between Germany and Russia. This has produced, I take it, considerable indignation among our left-wing friends. I have thought for about a year that it was possible for the two countries to get together." Exactly one week later World War II officially began when Germany invaded Poland.[2]

In a 1940 letter to Jack Hauper, a New York City acquaintance, Flye wrote: "A man like Hitler doesn't have any spiritual dimension. His story is the ultimate cautionary tale. Dictators always use patriotism to disguise their lust for power. Hitler will never be remorseful, he doesn't have a conscience to begin with."

❏ ❏ ❏

In an article published in 1932, Father Flye wrote: "Childhood is not just preparation for life. It is life at that stage. As well say that the age of forty five is a preparation for being fifty or sixty. The age of ten or twelve is totally justifiable in itself. Why not say that perhaps the intrinsically worthwhile age is childhood?"

This excerpt is from Father Flye's private journal in 1936: "I am a person to whom companionship and cooperation mean a great deal. I like the idea of mutual aid. I dislike competition. To win over someone is not a pleasure to me."

Father Flye wrote in October 1937: "The King James Bible and the words of such a writer as Shakespeare give the English language a precious currency. The United States is the beneficiary of a splendid legacy and should not sanction multi-tongues. To do so, our nation would run the risk of having a fractured culture with demands for official documents to be written in foreign languages. Babel wasn't successful and we should be mindful of that."

This journal notation in 1937 indicated Father Flye had talked to a student and was troubled by what he heard: "The discussion with Charles was depressing. I know why he acts as he does. The results are usually catastrophic when parents don't invest in time and love. Ten minutes of encouragement does wonders for a child's esteem. Charles will be here several years, and I will try to direct him in a positive way."

From Father Flye's "American Neutrality," published in the *Sewanee Review* in 1938 and reprinted in the 1979 St. Andrew's *Calendar:* "Provided it is not at the expense of sympathy, we would in a world like this surely wish for mirth."

In his dealings with students, Flye was sometimes severely tested. Grace Flye wrote in March 1937: "Hal is so perturbed by little Tommy's questions. He is a slight boy with much intensity. How can anyone adequately explain to an orphan why he was abandoned at birth?"

Flye wrote in October 1938: "Crime stems from a lack of self-discipline and respect for others. It represents a collapse of inner values. The idea that poverty and crime are inextricably linked is dangerous, and is an insult to millions of poor people who lead lives of dignity, order and nonviolence. I have met individuals who moved to this country with nothing more than dreams for a better future. Poverty for them was the reason to pull together and work harder, never the excuse to commit crimes."

An undated entry: "Those ceremonies we respect are founded in tradition. If you take away rituals on special occasions, you take away any sense of responsibility. Marriage vows given before a justice of the peace in the middle of the night borders on the obscene. Of course, not all marriages work, but those which begin under the auspices of the church, with time-honored ceremonies administered by an ordained clergyman, are more likely to succeed. The record speaks for itself."

From Father Flye's journal in 1938: "Young men are usually good-natured, but self-centered and aggressive, immersed in their world of athletics and newly-discovered masculinity. Left without any guidance, they tend to be crude, devoid of manners. Young women of the same age seem to be more aware of those around them, more cognizant of other people's feelings, more caring. In this sense, young women could have a civilizing influence. One would think having boys and girls together would make for a more agreeable atmosphere. Perhaps this is so, but what is the purpose of a school? Human intellect is like a muscle in that it needs discipline in order to grow. My fear is that a co-educational environment would be one of great distraction. A co-educational environment may produce better-adjusted people at social functions, but what about the training of a mind?"

Father Flye had strong feelings about gender mixing in the classroom. He was born at a time when sex, race, and finances determined the level of education a person achieved. He came from a generation that proclaimed: "Women have their place." He was born into a culture that considered a woman who "painted her lips" nothing more than a harlot, unless she was an actress.

Father Flye in 1949: "Our national conduct is a continual challenge in this country, where the question is clouded with political rhetoric. Legislatures and courts struggle with these issues. Change is inevitable, and how the country adapts to these changes is important. The adage about being careful you don't throw the baby out with the bath water is one to remember. Because of the uprooting of families now happening, I fear there will be a loosening of acceptable behavior."

❑ ❑ ❑

William Peyton, a 1925 graduate of St. Andrew's, recounted: "One evening in late September1921, I got off the train at St. Andrew's; a 16 year old boy who hadn't been 50 miles away from home before. I found boys there from nine years old to 19. Some were as rough as pine knots; their actions and coarse language left much to be desired. Our school work schedule would change every 30 days, so that each boy worked on every job by the end of the school year. In those days, rich people from out of state shipped boxes of clothing to the school. We did extra chores for credit slips; these in turn were used to buy the clothes. You can't imagine how this helped us.

"The curriculum was below current standards, but it should be remembered we had boys two or three years older than they should have been for their grade level. Their situation was caused by cash problems, illness, family troubles; no two cases were the same. These boys were under tremendous pressure, with little time, to obtain a basic high school education. Generally speaking, St. Andrew's did a good job of filling our gray matter with some useful information.

"We had four major subjects through my high school years: Math, English, History, Science. Some boys studied Latin and French with Father Flye. We also had trade school subjects such as carpentry and cabinet-making. Most of the faculty were secular clergy. Mrs. Barbour and Mrs. Sloan taught bookkeeping.

"It didn't take long for a boy to learn about the peculiarity of a teacher. Dr. Naylor had a goatee and taught English. We called him 'Billy Goat,' and he would cry at the slightest provocation. The science teacher, Sam Martin, was a veteran of World War I. Any mention of the war set him off; the day's lesson was ignored and he talked about his war experiences until the bell rang. One day he threw sodium into a beaker of water and it exploded. The test tubes on the shelves were in a shambles.

"We loved Father Campbell, a man with a spring to his step; Father Orum dispelled our homesickness with his stories; Father Whitall was tough as nails; Father Lorey gave advice about our problems; Father Baldwin was known as Mr. Serious. I don't think there was an intellect or genius among the five men, but they accomplished miracles against great obstacles."

George D. Wilson was also a St. Andrew's student in the 1920s. He recalled: "For a mountain boy whose family did not have much money, St. Andrew's was the place to get an educational foundation. My parents paid the school a monthly tuition of $15. We had teachers who lowered the boom if you didn't follow the rules. Boys being boys, four of us couldn't resist the chance to see lions and elephants, so we sneaked off to see Haig's Traveling Circus in Tracy City. We were caught, and our penalty was shucking corn every weekend at the school farm for a month. One thing about the school was that you learned discipline the old fashioned way, no hand-wringing, and no apologies. St. Andrew's was a no-nonsense place when I was there. You were given a good educational base to work with, and you walked a straight line."

Floyd Garner, a 1937 graduate of St. Andrew's: "The student body when I was at St. Andrew's was around 120; boys from Memphis and Chattanooga as well as boys from local valleys and the Mountain. We also had a few from Texas and Alabama. I came from Sherwood, and I went home for Thanksgiving and Christmas. That is, if the winding road down to Sherwood wasn't impassable due to ice and mudslides.

"I was there from '34 to '37. I worked there during the summer on the farm as part of my tuition. We worked out in the fields growing vegetables and corn. We worked five days a week during the summer. We also had a dairy. In the wintertime at school we didn't just go to class. We had assignments such as working in the school laundry, cleaning tables, washing dishes, cleaning the dormitory, it varied. My allowance was one dollar a week. My sister attended St. Mary's School, and twice a year, St. Mary's girls came over for dances. The Order priests were insistent that we dress properly for those shindigs. We had to clean up, and be on our best behavior.

"I have fond recollections of St. Andrew's, warm and friendly memories, because we were in a real family setting. My dad said St. Andrew's would make a man of me, and he was right. The school tried hard to get me ready for college. I went on to Georgia Tech and the University of Tennessee, and graduated with an engineering degree. The regimen at St. Andrew's was beneficial. It put me on the right course.

"Boys would walk or hitchhike to Sewanee on Saturdays to see a movie. For my part, I enjoyed visiting the university's book store. I couldn't afford to buy any books, but the lady who ran the store let me browse through the damaged books that were kept in a back room. There was a place in Midway where you could get a sandwich, and it was there I got to know some of the old-fashioned mountaineers, down-to-earth folks with no axe to grind. One of the old men in Midway was an expert at whittling, and he gave me a tiny horse. It was a work of art. The mountain men appreciated what the St. Andrew's monks were trying to accomplish, but they didn't understand why a man would voluntarily stay unmarried.

"I was a dormitory prefect my senior year. The Headmaster and Prior laid down the rules and the prefects enforced them. We handled the discipline. In most instances, it was a matter of a boy having to do some extra work, or he was grounded from going into town for several weeks. The school had one young man who was an incorrigible trouble-maker. He was a runaway, but this rarely happened.

"Riding on the train down to Cowan was an experience. It was an old-time train with wooden seats that snaked up the mountainside, whistling at every curve, with no air conditioning or heat. It had an old coal-burning engine and you would be covered by ashes by the time you arrived at the top near Sewanee. It was a small train, normally pulling two passenger cars. The 'Mountain Goat' went once a day to the coal mines located near Tracy City.

"I remember Father Webb and, of course, Brother Dominic, a jolly old man. He was the one man at St. Andrew's whom everybody liked. It is strange what you recall. The contrast between Father Flye and Father Parker, for instance. Father Parker conducted Mass quickly, but Father Flye took his time and seemed sincere, speaking each word clearly. Father Flye took his early morning chapel duties seriously."

World War II profoundly affected St. Andrew's. Everyone had a relative, or knew someone, who wore a military uniform. Rationing was a way of life; trains and buses were invariably crowded with servicemen; women went to work in defense plants. Dunkirk, Tarawa, Tobruk, Stalingrad, became well-known to the armchair warriors studying the combat from afar.

Small to begin with, the school's population shrank even more after the war erupted. Bishop Robert Campbell wrote in his post-holiday "Friends of St. Andrew's" letter in February 1943: "Just a thank you for your Christmas offerings. It helped pay bills at the end of the year. We are grateful. With the reopening of school in January, the war came closer to all of us and took our Headmaster, and two other members of the faculty. We are glad to report that after strenuous readjustments and the fortunate finding of new helpers, we think we can pull through successfully till the close of the school year.

"Over a dozen boys did not return; because they were so close to 18, it did not seem worthwhile. Our reduced enrollment has the prospect of staying here till summer as the local Draft Board has deferred till then all who are, or will be, 18 by next Spring. We are not building our bridges very far ahead. God bless us all!

"As for our boys, there is a certain unceasing restlessness. The stark realism of war which awaits them makes the daily, common task of school seem unimportant and trifling. It is harder to concentrate in class, and to conform to pettifogging rules and regulations. But, don't think of us as 'down.' We have a grand basketball team, with splendid spirit, and we have yelled ourselves hoarse over many a victory. Before Lent, we plan for the performance of Gilbert and Sullivan's *Pinafore*. Some of our boys, and a group of girls from St. Mary's, will form the cast. It is a beautiful indication that the young people are eagerly working to produce this rollicking classic."

Bishop Campbell's letter concluded: "Every day now at St. Andrew's we can hear the thunder and jar of the great guns at Camp Forrest below us in the valley, practicing day and night on the testing ground. How calmly we take it. 'Just the guns,' people say, as they feel the houses quake and the windows rattle. Yes. Just the guns!"

Rod Colson, a 1945 St. Andrew's graduate: "Let me mention a few things I can never forget: Winters of snow and fog, Piney Point, nights spent fighting forest fires, a pretty campus with the old chapel, the barn in the distance and the beautiful monastery, that cow trellis at the entrance, white-haired Brother Dominic playing the organ, Dr. Hannah's slow way of saying 'yes,' and his old Pearce-Arrow car, Mr. Matthews who made boys in trouble walk around a tree for several hours.

"Hawk-Eye Ricketts, the night security guard, carrying his time clock slung over his shoulder, trying to keep us on campus, my first chew of tobacco and then vomiting, listening to the news about Pearl Harbor on the radio, the laundry with the number 69 printed on my clothes, students denied going to the movies, because they were being punished and had to rake leaves, Father Flye's warm house and him shaking his enormous hands when he was agitated and saying: 'Piffle, Piffle.' And Mrs. Flye who was so nice amidst her paintings that were stacked just everywhere. Her house had a pleasant oily odor that permeated the place.

"Church everyday and twice on Sunday became so much a part of our lives. I will never forget those lovely religious services. My problem during my senior year was being Head Prefect, having to sit in judgment and dole out punishment for fighting, skipping class, mouthing-off to a teacher, slipping-off to town. The war cut into the student body; my graduating class was only six. As I reflect back to those years, I can appreciate the hardships with rationing, yet these problems were not conveyed to us. The spiritual guidance at St. Andrew's will always be a high point in my life."

R. E. Goodwin, a 1945 graduate: "My five years there were during the war years. Classes were small, especially in the upper grades. There were five seniors in my graduating class. It was the popular thing in those days to quit and join the military. Mr. Koski was Headmaster when I entered St. Andrew's. He joined the service in 1942 and was replaced by Father Turkington. I have fond memories of him and the other faculty members. They had the patience of iron to work with boys in our age bracket."

Harry Knight, a 1947 graduate: "My four years on the Mountain are etched with memories of homesickness, first dates, first dances with St. Mary's girls, new girlfriends, fights, comradeship, educational development, athletic successes and failures. Nicknames were the order of the day: Hamo, Argo, Apeman, Plop, Abie, Tot, Wild Bill, Pusso, R.D., and even our girl friends were awarded such titles as Goose Neck, Slim Lips and KiKi. Verbal imitations of Father Turk, Piffle Flye, Smokey Tate, Miss Brown, Doc Hannah, Mrs. Willis were heard every time we boys got together. [2]

"The school went through many phases in its history, and it underwent a big change during World War II. New policies, students from a wider geographical area, new faculty and many new ideas were instituted when I was there. Both track and boxing were major sports in the 1940s. Once in a while, I spotted alumni in their military uniforms, but I didn't talk to them. I was more concerned about going to Sewanee and having a date than I was in thinking about the war."

In a 1945 letter, Father Flye reminisced about one of his former students: "He was in the class of '42, of happy disposition, who without cowardice was depressed about going to war. I tried to cheer him, telling him of the uncertainty of life, but also of the strong odds of one's coming through. He was killed in the Philippines."

Grace Flye's letters indicate that in 1945 Father Flye was notified that one of his favored students, a boy who wrote poetry, died when his naval vessel was rammed by a Japanese Kamikaze pilot. During World War II, St. Andrew's teachers dreaded looking at the casualty list pinned to the school's bulletin board.

In 1945 the *Holy Cross Magazine* included "Reminiscences and Reflections" by Father Flye. The following are excerpts from his article: "A former student with whom I have exchanged letters is now in the armed service. He had ability far above the average, a thoughtful and wide reader, and a youngster for whom the very best in teaching would be none too good. In a letter to him three years ago, I suggested his keeping a journal of observations. Recently commenting on this, he wrote to me: 'Like you, I am aware of the microcosmic value of a place such as St. Andrew's.' A microcosm; yes.

"A St. Andrew's boy now in the Military Police and back at the school recently for a visit was telling me of his training. He said he was trained to deal with angry people with the least trouble and to avoid fights. I remember thinking when I heard this that here is the whole problem of government anywhere. A microcosm; yes.

"What should be the conception of government, and what attitude toward it would one want to foster? Obedience and conformity within proper limits are good. Because without them there would be disorder and lawlessness. But carry them too far and a good example of what one gets can be found in Germany or Japan. What I have seen, whether in school or in the world generally, has made me conclude that one of the most searching tests of a person is how he uses power or authority. I think of one boy at St. Andrew's many years ago of common sense, intelligent with a nice disposition. He is now a fine man. A microcosm; yes.

"I think of an illiterate oaf of low mentality but much brawn who somehow managed to be shoved along to the eleventh grade when he dropped out of school. He has now been decorated for distinguished service in this war. A microcosm; yes.

"I remember an exceptional boy of thirteen among whose many cultural interests was poetry. There was very little to offer such a boy in companionship at the school. Few boys and faculty staff were of his world, and he was lonely and uncomfortable. I was sad when he left the school in the middle of the year. We still write to each other. He is now a high-ranking officer in the Naval Intelligence Service. A microcosm; yes.

"I was teaching ancient history, and I gave this question on the final examination: 'Briefly write the career of Julius Caesar.' This particular boy closed with these words: 'The Ides of March killed him because they thought he was going to be King.' But despite his lack of knowledge about Julius Caesar, he graduated with my concurrence. He is now a prominent property owner. Nobody will ever again ask him about Julius Caesar. A microcosm; yes.

"What are St. Andrew's boys like? What are Americans like? What kind of men are soldiers? Or sailors? Or airmen? I remember a boy who was in my American History class. After we went through the War of American Independence it was not clear to him whether the French and perhaps indeed the British were on our side in that war. Some would say that a person so ignorant of our history is incompetent as a citizen. This young man is now teaching Instrument Flying in the Army Air Corps. In civilian life he will be a satisfactory member of his community. Not all boys respond in the classroom environment, and this has little to do with their intelligence. Some people develop at a separate pace, in different ways. A microcosm; yes.

"A school for boys in the Tennessee mountains: that sounds picturesque, and perhaps one expects to find a school 'up thar in them hills' with boys climbing high mountain trails carrying a rifle and a jug of moonshine whiskey. I have frequently been amused at the surprise shown by persons who came to the school expecting to find that sort of place. I remember three boys who graduated from St. Andrew's in the 1920s. They enrolled at Columbia University and did very well. The three were of local mountain stock. A microcosm; yes.

"What have we gained, and lost? Stephen Vincent Benet wrote:
> But when the last moonshiner buys his radio,
> And the last, lost, wild-rabbit of a girl
> Is civilized with a mail-order dress,
> Something will pass that was American,
> And all the movies will not bring it back."

[1] Father Flye shared this anecdote from his 1936 trip to California: his bus had stopped in the desert town of Elko, Nevada. Flye had traveled aboard ocean steamers, so he had seen celestial displays; however, on this night, he was so awed by the stars he failed to notice when his bus left the depot. The priest said he was stranded in Elko until the next day. During his 1936 trip to the west coast, Flye visited Stanton and Mary Chapman in Solvang, California. They were poets who had lived in Sewanee in the 1920s, and who fell on hard times during the Great Depression. Father Flye mailed them money over a period of many years. There were rumors of other trips to the west. One story was that Father Flye went to Los Angeles to visit James Agee, and while there he met Charlie Chaplin and Rita Hayworth. No documentation of such a trip was found.

[2] Father Flye's mind was not totally occupied with world affairs in the 1930s. Like most of the students and faculty at St. Andrew's, he watched movies Saturday nights in the Assembly Room. He wrote in his journal that he liked Clark Gable and Loretta Young. The films were a weekly "free loan" from The Bijou, a Chattanooga movie theater.

[3] Nicknames were a long-established St. Andrew's tradition. The 1926 senior class had these colorful nicknames: Slacker, Flops, Preacher, Crack, Pants, Roots, Pinky, Big Louie.

ST. ANDREW'S SCHOOL CHRONOLOGY

1905	School officially opens
1905	First non-cleric teacher, Samuel Chapman
1906	Telephones installed
1907	First female students, Gertrude Collins and Ethel Medford
1908	Year-round classes begin (abandoned 1914)
1911	High school instruction begins
1912	First campus death, Jackson Rollins, 18, from typhoid
1912	Tom Bierry opens store, St. Andrew's Crossing
1913	School put on graded basis
1914	First chapel service
1915	First wedding of St. Andrew's-St. Mary's pupils, Art Garner and Dolly Gipson
1915	First graduate, Allious Reid (became Headmaster 1932-38)
1916	Sam Lackey opens St. Andrew's Crossing post office
1916	Electricity installed
1918	James Harold Flye, first married teacher, arrives with his wife, Grace
1919	Prefect System initiated
1921	First female graduate, Helen Goodwin (married Winthrope Puffer)
1921	First issue of *The Mountain Lion*
1924	Colmore House, oldest campus building, destroyed by fire
1927	First orphan student arrives
1930	Administration Building destroyed by fire
1932	School receives academic accreditation
1935	First Student Council
1937	Grades One through Six abolished
1938	Entrance roadway pillars built
1942	Football abolished (resumed 1949)
1945	Grade Seven abolished (resumed 1972)
1947	School dairy and farm discontinued
1953	Typhoid outbreak, 50 boys ill
1961	Hughson Hall dedicated
1962	Gunn Lake constructed
1965	Alligood gymnasium dedicated
1965	First black student, William McCadden (graduated 1968)
1966	Grade 8 abolished (resumed 1972)
1968	Three St. Mary's girls enrolled: Nina Barry, Mary Chapman, Laura Chapman
1970	Order of the Holy Cross announces divestment
1981	Merger with Sewanee Academy, St. Andrew's becomes St. Andrew's-Sewanee School

PRIORS AT ST. ANDREW'S SCHOOL

Fr. Sturges Allen	1905-1906
Fr. Shirley Hughson	1907-1914
Fr. McVeigh Harrison	1914-1918
Fr. Robert Campbell	1918-1922
Fr. Edwin Whitall	1922
Fr. Liston Orum	1922-1925
Fr. John Baldwin	1925
Fr. Robert Campbell*	1925
Fr. Roger Anderson	1926-1931
Fr. McVeigh Harrison	1931-1932
Fr. Francis Parker	1932-1938
Fr. Robert Campbell	1938-1947
Fr. Bonnell Spencer	1947-1955
Fr. Julien Gunn	1955-1965
Fr. Murray Belway	1965-1968
Fr. Lee Stevens	1968-1970
Fr. Sydney Atkinson	1970-1972

*In 1925, Fr. Campbell was Prior for three months before being consecrated as Bishop of Liberia.

HEADMASTERS AT ST. ANDREW'S SCHOOL**

Mr. Robert Hazzard	1905-1906
Fr. Louis Lorey	1906-1911
Fr. Robert Campbell	1911-1921
Fr. Edwin Whitall	1921-1922
Fr. Liston Orum	1922-1924
Fr. John Baldwin	1924-1925
Fr. Roger Anderson	1925-1932
Mr. Allious Reid	1932-1938
Fr. Francis Parker	1938-1939
Mr. Augustus Koski	Sept. 1939
Mr. Herman Matthews	through
Dr. Francis Thompson	Nov. 1942
Fr. Hiraim Wolfe	
Fr. William Turkington	1942-1953
Fr. Bonnell Spencer	1953-1955
Fr. Warren Steele	1955-1957
Fr. Joseph Kelly	1957
Fr. Julien Gunn	1958-1960
Fr. Franklin Martin	1960-1980

**At times Frs. Campbell, Whitall, Orum, Anderson, Gunn, Baldwin and Spencer were Headmaster and Prior simultaneously.

LOCAL MISSIONS

Starting in 1909, the Order priests at St. Andrew's became involved in local mission work, which had been established by William Claiborne, the Rector at Otey Parish in Sewanee. He supervised the work of university theological students at nine nearby missions, and, at his request, the Order of the Holy Cross performed mission duties at Battle Creek and Sherwood. Just getting to Battle Creek was a test of endurance. Father Hughson wrote these instructions: "Wear rough clothes for branches. Go southeast by way of Monteagle. Use path at the edge. Mission building is about two miles after you reach the valley floor." The descent off the Mountain was a steep 1,100 feet, and both hands were needed for balance on the foot path. The mission was 10 air miles from the school, but the return trip to St. Andrew's at that time took hours. The Battle Creek mission was successful despite the hardships. Thirty-seven children were attending Sunday school there by 1912. The path down the side of the Mountain to the Battle Creek mission began in the now-ritzy area of Monteagle called Clifftops. Harold Kennedy wrote about the mission in Sherwood: "The Order met with constant opposition from other religious sects and the Klan. These groups were suspicious of the Order's rituals, and the clothes the monks wore were discussed on a frequent basis. Father Mayo was the first to go to Sherwood and he was threatened with violence. In 1924, while Father Orum was holding the Three Hour Service, someone was ringing a bell in the nearby school house to annoy the worshipers. One member of the congregation left; he came back with a black eye, but the bell ringing had stopped." The monks had to cope with local suspicion and fear when they started their mission work at Battle Creek and Sherwood. This kind of resistance was not unique. People who live in isolation are normally wary of strangers. This has been true in Maine and Oregon, as well as Tennessee. A problem for the Order priests was their differentness. Their vestments looked like women's dresses. Their northern accents were considered strange, almost foreign. In the beginning of the 20th Century, Episcopal clergymen of heroic dedication made every effort to bring enlightenment to the secluded parts of the Cumberland Plateau and the surrounding valleys. One church historian wrote: "Getting their hands dirty, as the mission priests had to do on a constant basis, carried on a tradition that began in Biblical times."

CHAPTER 5

The Teacher—The Man

Even while they teach, men learn.
—SENECA (4 BC - 65 AD)

GRACE FLYE FELL IN LOVE with St. Andrew's. The beauty and isolation of the school were a tonic to her spirits. In May of 1919 she wrote in a letter to her step-mother: "It is lovely here. Such a sweet spring jumping out of its shoes for sheer joy. One can see the flowers unfold and wave their hands. I rush out of bed to see how much farther along the leaflets are each morning."

Her husband was more restrained. Father Flye wrote in 1920: "The students here are trusting and friendly. They come from poor but loving families. They look to be thin soil in which to plant knowledge, but I hope some of them will bloom. The saddest observation one can make is that they come from homes where low expectations are ingrained, generation after generation. They have boxed-in lives. When I notice a boy who can escape such expectations, I encourage him."

Everyone agreed that Father Flye was an exceptional teacher. He was eccentric with peculiar ideas, but he was remarkable in the classroom. He could reduce everything, no matter how complex, to the simplest terms. Arthur Ben Chitty wrote: "Father Flye was a man who spoke with great authority on an astounding range of subjects."

From 1918 to 1954, boys at St. Andrew's were beneficiaries of his teaching skills. He taught Latin, French, American Government and English, but he was better known for being a history instructor. One telling aspect of his tenure was that many of his former students majored in history in college, and a number of them became history teachers themselves at high schools and universities. An educator could not ask for a higher tribute.

David Lockmiller reported: "Father Flye's class was the most memorable thing I recall about St. Andrew's. He talked about all aspects of history, not just names and dates. His chief characteristic was his genuine interest in us. He was not just drawing his pay; he was doing a job he loved. Even today I can close my eyes and see him, right at the top of my list. Father Flye was in a category all by himself." Dr. Lockmiller's remembrance carries weight when you consider he was a history professor himself at North Carolina State University, before he became President of the University of Chattanooga.

Teaching is a demanding job; however, the quality teacher overcomes demands by having a genuine excitement about his profession. The motivation of successful teachers come from passion, not a paycheck. What is needed to be a better teacher? Father Flye may have answered it best in 1927 when he wrote: "Children cannot be taught by someone who doesn't love them."

Flye did not insist that a particular date be memorized by his students. That was not his style. Instinctively knowing what would keep the boys' interest high, he taught history as a series of biographies. He had the ability to make an individual from the past emerge in his classroom.

During the 1920s and 1930s, the history books at St. Andrew's were frayed hand-me-downs from other schools, and Flye seldom used a textbook to teach history. Not having audio or visual aids available, he used initiative to make his courses lively. He read aloud from material he had personally saved: a newspaper, a book of poetry, a biography, a magazine article, a diary or letter. Some of Flye's classroom props had originally been the property of the Major. As a wedding gift, his father-in-law handed over priceless letters and newspapers from the Civil War period.

Flye usually lectured without notes. His memory was exceptional, and he used it effectively. Once he told his class about a Army lieutenant who faced a court martial in the Seminole Indian War, because he refused to take part in a campaign designed to massacre Indians. Only after relating the story, did he reveal the officer was Jefferson Davis, who later became president of the Confederate States of America.

That same day he also talked about Varina Howell Davis, widow of the Confederate leader. After her husband's death in 1889, in dire financial straits, she went to live in New York City to work as a book reviewer for publisher Joseph Pulitzer. When she died in 1906, her casket was draped by a Confederate flag and a military band played "Dixie" as it accompanied the hearse to a train bound for Richmond. A unit from Governors Island escorted the cortege to the New York train station. Varina Davis was the first woman accorded such an honor by federal troops.

Little-known facts were part of his repertory. Frank Caldwell, a 1930s St. Andrew's student: "I was fascinated when Father Flye explained the Civil War spawned 50 years of feuding in the border states. Kentucky and Missouri had mixed allegiances, brother against brother, creating voting patterns that lasted into this century. Father Flye told us that the Confederacy never had complete control

south of the Mason-Dixon line. Around Knoxville there were up to 30,000 Union sympathizers during the Civil War. The average history book does not tell you this."

The St. Andrew's history teacher said the Confederacy was plagued with rivalries. One day in class he passed around some letters that were encased in glass. They were old with age, yellowed and brown. One letter was written by a general in Mississippi, who complained his request for cannons had been ignored. The second letter came from a Confederate general in Louisiana, who replied that his field pieces were taken in blood and would stay where they were. Written in 1863, both letters began with extremely courteous salutations.

Floyd Garner, a 1937 graduate, said: "Father Flye was noted for caring about how well you were doing. If you had a problem, he would stay after class and go over it with you, back and forth. He found out what you needed to know, and made sure you solved your problem. His time was yours; he would take any amount of time you needed. He had a lot of respect as a teacher. He was the only teacher at St. Andrew's who didn't have a paddle board to keep discipline."

Hartwell Hooper, a 1948 graduate, recollected: "The unique thing about Father Flye was that if you raised your hand and asked a question while he was lecturing, he didn't seem to mind. Other teachers took your head off if you did this, but not him. This give-and-take made his classes more interesting. He always put us on an honor code, something we didn't have with other teachers. During exams he would nonchalantly walk out of the room. His trust was never violated, we respected him too much.

"One thing really sticks out in my mind. He was teaching European history and had been explaining the French revolution. For about a week he had been reading out of this book, an account of the brutal conditions during the revolution. This one time he was reading out loud and suddenly he stopped. He was having trouble expressing himself. He put the book down on his desk and it was then we realized the book he had been reading from all week was written in French. Piffle had been translating into English the whole time. It was awesome."[1]

Flye was not angry if a boy fell asleep in class; however, what looked like leniency was really consideration. He wrote in his journal on March 14, 1922: "I heard Henry Slater was given a red mark for sleeping in English class. The day students shouldn't be treated this way. He is a splendid child who gets up before sunrise and walks three miles to get to the morning chapel services on time. No wonder he needs his sleep." There is the famed tale of Father Flye along with the other students tip-toeing out of the classroom, so that a sleeping boy could continue his nap.

Dale Doss: "He had a photographic memory. It was really phenomenal. If someone in class asked Father Flye a question he couldn't answer, he would get this kind of puzzled look on his face, put his hand to his chin and walk a few steps in one direction, and then the other. His mind was very far away. He would suddenly reach up like he was pulling a book out of the air, from an imaginary library

St. Andrew's history class, spring 1939

shelf, and give the answer. The first time I walked into his house, I knew where he was pulling his imaginary books from. His place had thousands of books.

"He used inspirational stories to keep our interest. I remember the case of Heinrich Schliemann, the amateur archeologist, who battled great odds before he found the treasures of Troy. The way he described the excavations, we were there, up to our hips in mud, finding plates of gold. His lectures were hypnotic; I rarely wanted his class to end. His teaching was why I majored in history in college."

Flye was a magpie who never discarded anything. It was a habit which he put to good use. For example, he would stop lecturing and announce: "I'll be right back" and dash out of the classroom, run the 35 yards to his bungalow and charge through the back door shouting something like: "Grace, find me the 1916 file on Woodrow Wilson's neutrality." Despite the incredible clutter in the bungalow, Mrs. Flye knew where to look. The history teacher would return to his classroom in minutes, a little breathless, with the item he needed.

Ethel Louise Simmonds, faculty wife and close friend of the Flyes, remarked: "Father Flye was the only teacher in the country who could leave his class, run home, find a piece of paper, and be back in class in just minutes. He couldn't have done it without Mrs. Flye's help." The history and civics instructor was usually well-prepared, so his rushing to the bungalow did not happen often. However, doing it once or twice was enough to embellish the Flye mythology.

During a visit to the Flye bungalow in the 1940s, faculty wife Mildred Watts learned about their filing system: "I was impressed with their cataloguing everything. All over their house, books and magazines were put vertically on tables or stools by their size and kind. Each stack looked as if a ruler helped line it up. Mrs. Flye told me when her husband wanted something, she knew the size of the book, its title, and when it was printed. This told her where the correct stack was located, and how far down the stack to look. They had their filing system down to a fine science."

Stanley Hole remembered: "Father Flye's dedication was extraordinary. We had been studying the 1415 Battle of Agincourt, one of the most momentous battles in world history. He took the class out to the big athletic field south of the classroom. He had gotten up at dawn and staked out red and blue wooden markers over a quarter of the big field. He walked around and said: 'The French were here, and the English were here.' He then recited from memory the unforgettable Henry V speech written by Shakespeare:

> From this day to the ending of the world,
> But we in it shall be remembered;
> We few, we happy few, we band of brothers;
> For he today that sheds his blood with me
> Shall be my brother; be he ne'er so vile
> This day shall gentle his condition:
> And gentlemen in England, now a-bed
> Shall think themselves accursed they were not here,
> And hold their manhoods cheap whiles any speaks
> That fought with us upon Saint Crispin's day.

"Father Flye's presentation that day was extraordinary. In all his history classes, you were there when it occurred. I recall the time he read from a letter General James Longstreet had written to his wife on the morning of the battle of Manassas. The general had gotten up at 5:30 a.m., had breakfast with his aides, and he was worried about his supply lines. It was educational to learn about the responsibilities of a high-ranking military officer."

❑ ❑ ❑

Father Flye believed the Civil War was the central event in American history. He was not alone. More than 50,000 books have been written about the Civil War, and the world still remains interested in the bloody conflict. Every year, there are Civil War battle reenactments and this is puzzling to foreign observers. One English professor exclaimed: "Hell will freeze over before the French get with us to honor Waterloo." It was Father Flye who told his students about current military bases named to honor *Confederate* generals: Bragg, Hood, Pendleton. He said this was a certification of the marrow of the United States.

He emphasized the positive facts that the Civil War preserved the Union and ended slavery. He added, however, that contrary to simplified versions of events, the typical southerner fought to defend his home territory—not necessarily to preserve slavery. The teacher read in class from a *London Times* article about the siege of Richmond. A British reporter asked a Virginian why he was there. The answer was: "Because the damn Yankees are here."

Flye's interest in the Civil War came early. His father's general store in Haines City had customers who were veterans of that conflict, both northern and southern, who sometimes discussed their war experiences. One man in particular, Sam Hodgeman, left a mark on young Hal Flye. Hodgeman served in a Michigan regiment that fought at Chickamauga. Inside a field hospital in northern Georgia, Hodgeman's leg was amputated.

Thomas Church, a 1950 graduate, had this to say: "Father Flye hated Margaret Mitchell. He said her *Gone With The Wind* had a romanticized representation of the Old South that was absurd. He told us that the average prewar southern farmer lived hand-to-mouth and didn't own a single slave, and, as a matter of fact, was indignant that the large plantation owners had the economic edge over everybody else."

The St. Andrew's history teacher made a valid point. According to the 1860 census, southern states had seven million whites and 6.6 million of them did not own a slave. Another interesting statistic was that there were southern "free blacks" and Indians who were slave owners.

The author of this book remembers: "We were shocked when Father Flye said Negroes had fought for the south. He noticed our reaction and he showed us some old newspaper clippings kept between panels of glass. The *New York Herald* had printed a story about Negro troops defending Richmond. Father Flye explained they were probably slaves who had been pressed into service by their owners."

Flye's students learned about the strong feelings of state sovereignty which existed in the 1860s. A man went to war as a Georgian or a New Yorker. Military units carried state banners into battle, equally important as the Union's Stars and Stripes or the Confederate battle flag. It was almost unheard of for a Civil War soldier to fight with a unit other than one from his native state.

Oliver Hodge remarked: "Even at the college level, I never met a teacher like him. His knowledge was incredible. I recall him telling us about Winchester, Virginia, that changed hands no less than 72 times in the Civil War! Another tidbit I remember is that Abe Lincoln's three brothers-in-law fought for the south. Father Flye taught history through a prism of the present; we heard the whine of the bullets at Antietam. He read to us parts of *Red Badge of Courage* by Stephen Crane, and also *Andersonville Diary* by John Ransom. Most history books are as dry as a west Texas riverbed, but his classes were engrossing."

Flye never portrayed war through the filter of romanticized nostalgia. During his childhood he met crippled Civil War veterans. In Milledgeville, where he served as a novice priest, he saw the aftermath of General Sherman's scorched-earth policy. His father-in-law, A.C. Houghton, had been seriously wounded in the Civil War. The priest-teacher knew combat's high tariff. He hated violence; it was not possible for him to glorify warfare. He felt obligated to teach history, as he once said:

St. Andrew's students, 1938

"With all the bark off the tree."

Astute St. Andrew's pupils noticed his regard for the "gentleman's code of honor' practiced by southern aristocracy in the 1860s, but also that he was happy the Union remained intact. His students were mostly attuned to the southern culture, so Father Flye had to use a delicate finesse when he praised a northern leader. To his credit, he made every effort to paint an honest picture of the Civil War.

Father Flye said the tragedy for the south was not losing the Civil War, it was the travesty of the Reconstruction era. He characterized John Wilkes Booth as a fanatic who poisoned the post-war well. He told his history classes that Abraham Lincoln had a conciliatory attitude about the Confederacy, but his assassination created an atmosphere of revenge. In turn, the south had to endure carpetbaggers, unfair trading dictates, federal garrisons, and ludicrous political alignments.[2]

James Hollingsworth recalled visiting Missionary Ridge with Flye in 1947: "It was a windy day and we parked near some cannons. We got out of the car and I started to read some of the metal plaques, while he walked over to the edge of the parking lot. I couldn't handle the cold wind so I returned to the car, but he stood there looking out over the city of Chattanooga. He stayed there for a long time, unmoving, as if in a trance. When he finally returned to the car I asked him what took him so long. He replied: 'I saw those brave men climbing up through the boulders.' As we drove away to see my sister who lived in Red Bank, he proceeded to tell me about the battle of Missionary Ridge. And the way he told it, with such detail, for a brief moment (and I know this sounds crazy) I thought to myself: 'My God, he was actually there!"

Andrew Lytle, noted Sewanee author, observed: "Father Flye believed Robert E. Lee and Abraham Lincoln were exceptional men, but tragic victims of their time. He said the Gettysburg Address was poetry of the highest order. We frequently talked about that time in history. Come to think of it, if he had lived before the Civil War started, he would have been an Abolitionist. Nothing like a John Brown, nothing so violent, but he would definitely have been against slavery."

Father Flye held Robert E. Lee in the highest esteem. This is not surprising when one considers Lee's excellence at everything he did from his West Point

St. Andrew's student Harold Dering, October 1939

days to the end of his life. Following Lee's death in 1870, even northern newspapers eulogized him. During his twilight years, Flye was chauffeured by Marnette Trotter on a trip from Tennessee to New York City. They passed through Virginia and visited Washington and Lee University. Marnette said: "We went to the university chapel, and the young tour guide explained: 'This is the chair where General Lee sat for his daily prayers.' She asked Father Flye: 'Would you like to sit there?' He answered: 'Oh, my, no, no, I wouldn't presume.' We went outside and saw a big statue of the general. Father Flye took his hat off and held it over his heart. It was clear to me that General Lee was one of his heroes."

Flye said history was not just words in a book; it was emotions, smells, sounds. He brought hardtack, a hard biscuit, into his St. Andrew's class for inspection. He then strummed a banjo and sang Civil War tunes. One of his favorites was the northern marching song—"Battle Cry Of Freedom":

> Yes, we'll rally around the flag boys
> We'll rally once again
> Shouting the battle cry of freedom
>
> The Union forever, hurrah boys, hurrah
> The Union forever, hurrah boys, hurrah
> The Union forever, hurrah boys, hurrah

He then sang the southern ballad — "The Bonnie Blue Flag":

> First, gallant South Carolina nobly made the stand
> Then came Alabama, who took her by the hand
> Next, quickly Mississippi, Georgia and Florida

All raised the Bonnie Blue Flag that bears a single star

We are a band of brothers, and native to the soil
Fighting for our liberty, with treasure, blood and toil
When our rights were threatened, the cry rose near and far
Hurrah for the Bonnie Blue Flag that bears a single star

Thomas Church, a 1950 graduate: "His side-bar stories stayed with you. He told us the custom of laying flowers on a grave started with the death of General 'Stonewall' Jackson. Unable to go to the funeral, Confederate soldiers had asked that a bouquet be placed on the General's grave. The whole world now puts flowers at cemeteries. Father Flye was a walking almanac. He shared information with us that you wouldn't find elsewhere."

Flye told his classes about what happened to the Mayflower. Following its historic trip to North America, the ship returned to England where it was dismantled, and its huge timbers were used to build a horse barn. He explained why any dead tree at the White House is quickly replaced. The tree's role is basically symbolic, maintaining permanence, vital to the nation's feeling of stability.

There was a scattering of Seminole Indians in the Haines City area when Flye was a child. Billy Bowlegs, Timmy Tiger and Alligator Chipco were customers at his father's store. Through this early exposure, he acquired an empathy for native Americans. He became emotional when he talked of The Trail Of Tears, the relocation of the Cherokees to the Oklahoma Territory in 1838-1839, that cost 4,000 lives.

Father Flye did not restrict his comments to distant events; in the 1930s, he told his pupils about President Franklin D. Roosevelt being paralyzed from polio in 1921, and this was why newspaper editors never published a photograph showing FDR in his wheelchair. In those days, newspapers felt it was their civic duty to shield the White House from embarrassment. Former students recalled being surprised when Father Flye told them about newspapers intentionally never reporting Woodrow Wilson's incapacity in the last days of his presidency. Mrs. Wilson and presidential doctor Cary Grayson, a Sewanee graduate, made the major executive decisions.

The St. Andrew's history teacher warned students to be dubious regarding "breaking news."[3] He told about the hysteria after Lincoln's assassination when innocent people were jailed and executed. Phillip Cook (St. A '50) recalled: "Father Flye explained how the Hearst newspaper chain created the toxic atmosphere that led to the Spanish-American War. It was 'yellow journalism' with no attempt to be accurate. He said truth is often the first casualty of war."

Flye's passion for history was displayed in a letter he wrote to Charles Riggins in July, 1937: "Studying history means getting to know great individuals, great events, great thoughts and great writing. The study of history is learning about the insight of Plato; the zeal of Christopher Columbus; the uncommon intelligence of Benjamin Franklin. It is being in Congress and hearing Henry Clay desperately trying to get a compromise. It is realizing the reasons behind the writing of Luther's Ninety Five Theses; the Magna Carta; the Constitution. It is visualizing Egyptians building the Pyramids; wondering about the intellect of Octavian; having a dialogue with Aquinas. It is seeing extraordinary courage at Missionary Ridge; being in the laboratory when Marie Curie isolated radium; sharing the moment when a European explorer stepped ashore for the first time at the mouth of the Congo River.

"Learning about history forces you to study geography, meteorology, psychology and all the other fields of science. It forces you to study the world's different cultures and major religions, and realize that all men have had similar needs, goals and patterns of behavior. History is all the glory and disaster, deeds and misdeeds, which have taken place since man first appeared. No fictionalized book, stage play or motion picture, can come close to, much less equal, the excitement of history.

"No matter what technical marvels materialize in the future, what political doctrine is dominant, what national borders change, what languages are spoken, man will still be a product of what went before him. So in order to understand man today, you must first know about his past."

It was 1950 and World War II was still fresh in everybody's memory. Father Flye had been talking to his class about the enormous scale of the Normandy invasion on June 6, 1944. He stopped talking, was silent for a moment, and then related what had also taken place on June 6, 1944, off the island of Crete. German soldiers had forced nearly 1,000 Greek, Italian and Jewish captives onto a freighter that was taken out to sea and scuttled. All of those aboard drowned. The teacher said: "This atrocity shows why the Nazis were held accountable in world opinion." His knowledge went far beyond what he had read in a musty textbook.

He always said history was a chain of events, and his students should know how the past has shaped the present. He frequently quoted philosopher George Santayana's observation: "Those who cannot remember the past are condemned to repeat it."

Father Flye's civics classes were as brisk as his history courses. True to form, he often used history to buttress his interpretations of how state legislators and congressmen reviewed, debated, and then passed laws. He excelled at telling stories of the famous debates in the halls of Congress. His methods were consistent; he read aloud from biographies, letters and newspaper stories to illustrate the difficulties faced by the people involved at the time.

The St. Andrew's teacher was intense in his regard for the U.S. Constitution and the Bill of Rights, saying they were the most significant documents in modern times, not just for the United States, but for the world. Benjamin Franklin, George Washington, John Quincy Adams, Thomas Jefferson, as well as all the other founding fathers, were portrayed as men who used their knowledge for honorable purposes.

Flye stressed the point that they had customarily studied ancient and contemporary history, and this gave them an understanding of what would work, and what would not work, in the formation of a viable government. He said the men who wrote the Declaration of Independence knew a great deal about human nature.

He told his students that they should appreciate the sacrifices made by the men who signed that document. Most of them lost their personal wealth. Father Flye made it clear that he admired the English culture, particularly the Common Law precedents that were brought to North America, but the colonists had no choice but to fight for their independence. He asserted taxation without representation was evil.

On the wall in his classroom, under glass and framed, was this commentary published in a North Dakota newspaper. It left a lasting impression.

•Have you ever wondered what happened to the fifty men who bravely signed the Declaration of Independence? Five of the signers were captured by the British as traitors, and tortured before they died. Twelve had their homes ransacked and then burned. Two lost their sons serving in the Revolutionary Army, another had two sons captured. Nine of the men died from wounds or hardships in the Revolutionary War. They had pledged their lives, their fortunes, and their sacred honor.

•What kind of men were they? Twenty four were attorneys and jurists. Eleven were merchants, nine were farmers and large plantation owners; men of means, well-educated. But they signed the Declaration of Independence knowing full well that the penalty would be death if they were captured. Carter Braxton of Virginia, planter and trader, saw his ships swept from the seas by the British Navy. He sold his home and properties to pay his debts, and died in rags. Thomas McKeam was so hounded by the British that he was forced to move his family almost constantly. He served in Congress without pay, and his family was kept in hiding. His possessions were taken from him, and abject poverty was his reward. Vandals looted the properties of Hall, Dillery, Clymer, Walton, Gwinnett, Heyward, Rutledge, and Middleton.

•At the battle of Yorktown, Thomas Nelson, Jr., saw that the British General Charles Cornwallis had taken over the Nelson home for his headquarters. He urged General George Washington to open fire. The home was destroyed, and Nelson died bankrupt.

•Francis Lewis had his home and properties destroyed. The enemy jailed his wife, and she died within a few months. John Hart was driven from his wife's bedside as she was dying; their 13 children fled for their lives. His fields and his gristmill were laid to waste. For more than a year he lived in forests and caves, returning home to find his wife dead and his children vanished. A few weeks later he also died from exhaustion and a broken heart. Norris and Livingston suffered similar fates.

•Such were the stories and sacrifices of the American Revolution. These were not wild eyed, rabble-rousing ruffians. They were soft-spoken men of means with an education. They had security, but they valued liberty more. Standing tall and with an unwavering spirit, they personally pledged: "For the support of this declaration, with a reliance on the protection of the divine providence, we mutually pledge to each other, our lives, our fortunes, and our most sacred honor."

•They gave us a free and independent America. The history books never told you a lot of what happened in the Revolutionary War. We did not just fight against the British. We were British subjects at that time in history and we fought our own government. Some of us today take these liberties for granted ... and we shouldn't.

❑ ❑ ❑

Ethel Simmonds, a St. Andrew's faculty wife, recalled Father Flye's enthusiasm: "He had very big hands, expressive hands. I remember his hands when once we had him over for supper. He had brought some coins with him, and he handed them to our son, Andy, who was 17 at the time. He said: 'These were in use at the same time our Savior walked on earth.' He also had some seeds which he said were from Biblical days. I remember how exhilarated he was when he talked about how he would show the coins and seeds to his classes. His excitement was marvelous."

Father Flye's classes were not only informative, but entertaining as well. When he saw boredom taking over, he energized the atmosphere with an unexpected burst of dry humor. The older St. Andrew's students suspected some witty poetry was coming when he would suddenly stop talking, and start to grin from ear to ear.[4] This was one of his favored Prohibition era lyrics:

> Four and twenty Yankees
> Feeling very dry
> Went across to Canada
> To get a keg of rye.
> When the keg was opened,
> They all began to sing
> Who the hell is Hoover
> God save the King!

He liked to recite this ditty from the 1936 Alf Landon campaign:

> The alphabet we'll always have
> But one thing sure is true
> With Landon, the New Deal's
> Out and that means PDQ

> Alf Landon learned a thing or two,
> He knows the right solution,
> And in the White House he will

Stay with the Constitution
Oh, Alf Landon!
He's the man for me
Cause he came from prairie Kansas
His country for to free

Students recalled his witty reference to Gertrude Stein:

I don't like the family Stein
There's Gert, there's Ep and there's Ein
Gert's poems are bunk, Ep's statues are junk
And nobody understands Ein

Another Flye favorite was Dorothy Parker's: "Joe says: 'Calvin Coolidge has died.' George says: 'How can they tell?'"

St. Andrew's Prior, Father Bonnell Spencer, wrote: "I watched Father Flye put on his magical performance for years. There is no question his eccentricity was a component of his teaching bag-of-tricks. He had a fun classroom according to the boys I talked to. The boys never knew what to expect from one day to the next."

Phillip Cook, a 1950 graduate: "In many ways, Father Flye was as much a showman as he was an educator. His classes could be very entertaining. Better orators, those with a passion, intuitively have ways to keep your attention. He was otherwise shy and soft-spoken, but his mannerism changed when he walked into the classroom. Every boy at St. Andrew's saw this transformation happen."

Russell Wheeler, a 1952 graduate, talked about Flye's teaching style: "Piffle had the class spellbound when he told how one of Napoleon's soldiers noticed the Rosetta Stone stuck in the mud near the mouth of the Nile (1799), and how it enabled scholars to decipher Egyptian hieroglyphics. The Rosetta Stone had duplicate stories in several languages (Demotic, Greek and ancient Egyptian) and it really caused excitement in the world of archeology. They went crazy over that slab of rock.

"Father Flye's description of the Pyramids was incredible. Constructed as tombs for ancient Egyptian royalty, with stone cubes weighing many tons each, they were one of the Seven Wonders of the Ancient World. Imagine a half million slaves taking 20 years to build one without any modern machinery! But, as mind-boggling as that is, what Father Flye zeroed-in on were the inner chambers. He told us about the secret passages inside the Pyramids that were storage areas and royal tombs. I came from a generation that used to sit outside at night to listen to scary ghost stories. I'd have goose bumps.

"Well, Father Flye told stories with the same kind of whispery suspense. I recall him asking the class: 'Do you know what they found in the Queen's Tomb deep down inside the Pyramid?' Of course, nobody knew the answer, so he then dramatically, ever so slowly, opened his hand to show us a small dog-faced figurine, a replica that was probably purchased at a museum shop, that was passed around the classroom. Piffle was so good at storytelling, that we all had the eerie sensation of stepping back into antiquity. It was weird."

Joseph Crankshaw attended St. Andrew's during the 1947-48 school year: "I recall the night Father Flye showed me a naval sextant. We were on his front porch and we couldn't get a fix on the horizon so we climbed to the top of the fire tower. He told me how early mariners needed an accurate clock and a sextant to know where they were located. At the top of the tower, I used the sextant to get a fix on a star and calculated that St. Andrew's was 200 miles east of Delaware! He chuckled and said I'd get the hang of it later on."

Crankshaw continued: "Father Flye was a champion teacher, who thought faster than he talked. He was one of the two most significant educators in my life. I vividly recall his history class when we studied the Viking raids in northern Britain. The class had a huge mural that showed the Vikings' weapons, boats, tools and clothing.

"Because of his influence, I became a journalist. I remember Father Flye saying that when you read history never accept the words without finding out who wrote them, because history is usually written by the winners, and they aren't always honest. It was this understanding that shaped my career as a newspaper journalist."

Parker R. Lowry, a 1953 graduate, spoke the sentiments of countless people when he said about Father Flye: "I was impressed with his knowledge of world events, both ancient and contemporary, especially as to how history repeats itself. I remember Father Flye saying Mass, when he said: 'It is more blessed to give, than it is to receive.' I have never heard it said since, that I did not think of Father Flye. I can't say enough good things about this man. Piffle had a saintly quality about him."

❏ ❏ ❏

Archival records do not show an instance where a St. Andrew's administrator found fault with anything Flye said or did in class. But letters and interviews do hint that his maverick methods caused some heartburn.

On a Saturday morning in 1924, he drove several students to the Bethel Methodist Church in Victoria, Tennessee, near the town of Whitwell. The church's belfry was a gift from England's Queen Victoria in 1887. Being a dedicated educator, he wanted the boys to see this nearby part of history. However, the Prior, Liston Orum, became furious when he heard that St. Andrew's students had been taken to see a church of another denomination. Flye was already at odds with Father Orum, and this event only added to his chagrin. The Oliver Hodge walk-in-the-woods expulsion had taken place one year earlier, and this was another example of the history teacher and Father Orum locking horns. It is not known if

Flye ever revisited the church in Victoria. If he did, he probably went alone.

James Hollingsworth recalled that Father Flye referred to the "Scottsboro Boys Trial" in his classroom: "I told him, in the most diplomatic way I could, that it was stupid to even mention the trial. He agreed it was a delicate subject. His students had been raised in a segregated environment, and they naturally had firm feelings about racial matters. The local mountain boys probably had never even seen a Negro, but St. Andrew's boys from the cities certainly had.

"I knew what was bothering him. We often talked about the awful way Negroes were treated, and I recall how mad he was in Chattanooga one day when we walked past a 'Colored Only' drinking fountain. Nevertheless, it was dumb for him to bring up the trial in class. The Order of the Holy Cross gave Father Flye a lot of latitude."

In 1931, nine black teenagers were arrested near Scottsboro, Alabama, and charged with raping two white women. The case was a civil rights *cause celebre* that involved the American Communist Party, the NAACP, liberal writers, the Alabama National Guard, and the U.S. Supreme Court. From the start, it was clear the state had a very weak case, but the controversy was not resolved until Governor George Wallace granted full pardons more than 30 years after it all began.

Two mentions of the Scottsboro case were found among Grace Flye's letters. In one of them, she wrote: "Hal and I wonder how men of Christian faith can allow such an injustice." Hollingsworth's concerns were valid. Jim Crow had a firm grip on southern society in those days, racial attitudes were on a short fuse.

Father Flye's outlook on racism was exhibited in a letter of August 1, 1939, when he wrote of an episode in New York City: "I talked today with a boot-black who did my shoes, a colored boy of about 13. He lives in Harlem and comes by subway down to 34th Street, where he works between 7th and 8th Avenues. He is in the 6th grade, friendly and responsive to questions. I said in parting: 'Thanks and good luck.' And he replied: 'The same to you.' Three minutes and only a few scattered words between us. I could have taken him in my arms. God bless him."

Flye's vacation relief job during the summer of 1934 was on Eleuthera Island in the Bahamas. While there, he wrote to Grace: "The Bahamians are very engaging. They are a fine people." That same summer, he wrote Ralph Warren: "Race relations here are not so bad as to make one feel restricted. What a contrast to my childhood when northern Negroes were loved as a race and despised as individuals, while southern Negroes were admired as individuals and hated as a race."

Ex-St. Andrew's Headmaster, Father Franklin Martin, said Father Flye telephoned him and offered congratulations when the school was racially integrated in 1965. It was Father Martin's understanding that St. Andrew's was the first private high school in Tennessee to break the racial barrier. St. Andrew's is prominently mentioned in *They Took Their Stand*, a book on the integration of southern private schools.

Andrew Lytle remembered Flye's criticism of the nation's educational system:

"He said our ignorance of history can be traced to lousy books and lousy teachers who pawn off their monographs as textbooks. He was right when he claimed most history books are notoriously dull. I remember one textbook that was required reading in a history course at Columbia. It was tedious, esoteric nonsense. Such a book has the impact of sour milk. The challenge is to make history exciting and relevant. Father Flye did this, and St. Andrew's was lucky to have had him.

"I thought of him when I watched that excellent Civil War documentary on public television. Utilizing only narration and photographs, Ken Burns brought the Civil War into millions of homes in a fashion Father Flye would have liked."

Sewanee professor, Robert S. "Red" Lancaster, reflected: "There is no doubt Father Flye had one of the best minds this part of the country ever had. I never understood why he wasn't on the faculty in Sewanee. [4] His insight was something to behold. His poetry kept me in stitches, of course, but beyond that he was a scholar and an astute philosopher. I remember him saying that a nation with a low literacy was destined to be one of low morals. I've wondered if he was forecasting our future."

❑ ❑ ❑

Mr. Lancaster's question brings up an interesting point. The history teacher complained about conditions at St. Andrew's, yet there was the university located just two miles away. He had a Master's degree from the University of Virginia, and advanced theological training, so what stopped him from relocating to Sewanee? Arthur Ben Chitty observed: "Especially during his early years at St. Andrew's, the university beckoned. He was the kind of teacher Sewanee wanted. However, there were high hurdles to overcome. Dr. George M. Baker became Dean after World War I, and he used the Ph.D. as a guide in hiring faculty members, and Father Flye didn't have a doctorate. The faculty from the 1920s were still on duty up until World War II; there was very little turnover. In those subjects where Father Flye was proficient, the vacancy rate was an absolute zero. Sedley Ware taught history until retirement, as well as Tudor Long in English." Even if the Ph.D. requirement had been waived, there were other factors to consider. Flye's maverick behavior was tolerated by St. Andrew's administrators, but Sewanee department heads would not have been as generous. But Flye had autonomy at St. Andrew's, with an aloofness toward many of his fellow teachers. He was not known as a "team player." There was also the issue of Grace Flye. Sewanee faculty wives were duty-bound to a variety of obligations, including entertaining students at "Sunday Night Visitations." Grace's habits were idiosyncratic, and university careers have been ruined by spouses who did not fulfill social expectations. There were no similar burdens for Grace at St. Andrew's School. Regarding the notion of Father Flye teaching at Sewanee's seminary, his Anglo-Catholic opinions and his free-wheeling teaching methods, as well as his lack of a Ph.D. degree, put this possibility beyond his reach. Over the years, when he contemplated his options, teaching at the nearby university was never considered. His niche was established at St. Andrew's, but at the University of the South he would have been on the lowest rung of the hierarchy. Given his personality and independent nature, he would have found this intolerable.

❑ ❑ ❑

This "wish list" was written by Father Flye in 1931: "I fancy indeed that hardly any kind of writing would interest me more than the frank expressions, real feelings and attitudes, toward life from people of other lands and other times.

"How interesting it would be to know how life seems to a Japanese farmer or teacher, a Chinese scholar or carpenter, an Arab of the vast deserts, or a person picked purely at random out of a village in Tibet, a Greek or Spanish peasant, a fisherman or sailor of Brittany, a village school teacher in Ireland, a scribe in Tehran, a silversmith in Damascus.

"How glad I would be to have a journal of the life and thoughts of my grandparents. I want to know of their difficulties and triumphs, their most quiet meditations on life as they saw it. And jottings by those who lived long ago and far away. Their value to me would be inestimable, even though they were not the work of literary geniuses. Having such knowledge is my greatest desire."

❑ ❑ ❑

[1] In addition to his proficiency in Latin and French, Father Flye routinely read Italian, Spanish and Greek newspapers. He admitted his Arabic "needed work." Robert Costa, his New York City friend, reported: "His German was excellent, with no accent whatsoever. He could recite the original *Silent Night* in German." Even more remarkable was that in the evening of his life, at age 90, Father Flye was studying Mandarin Chinese.

[2] The St. Andrew's history teacher was convinced it was the harshness of Reconstruction that led to the fractious racial feelings that plagued the South. He wrote: "History shows us that human conflict has been nothing but cause and effect. Southern legislatures packed with exslaves, federal governors and scalawags brought on the white man's polarization. This led to the Ku Klux Klan, poll taxes and segregation. The irony is that the former slaves and their descendants were the ultimate victims of those deplorable post-war events."

[3] Flye's cynicism was verified after the assassination of President John F. Kennedy, November 22, 1963. Radio listeners were told that Dallas school children cheered when they heard the president was killed. The facts were that elementary school pupils yelled with delight when a principal went on the public address system and announced that classes had been canceled.

Another case of the media's rush-to-judgment was that of Richard Jewell in connection with the bomb explosion during the 1996 Olympics in Atlanta. The security guard was the center ring of a "news circus" for 88 days, as the media butchered his reputation. Jewell was eventually cleared of all suspicion.

⁴"Ten Little Motorists" was one of Father Flye's favored witticisms:
Ten little motorists, driving in a line;
One tried to pass the rest —
Then there were nine

Nine little motorists, sadly I relate;
One passed a traffic stop —
Then there were eight

Little motorists, young and very deft;
One tried to show his skill —
Seven were then left

Little motorists, touring in the sticks;
One failed to dim his lights —
Then there were six

Little motorists, very much alive;
One did not see the train —
Then there were five

Little motorists, driving in the rain;
One skidded on a curve —
Four now remain

Little motorists, coming from a tea;
One faced about to chat —
Then there were three

Little motorists, sad but true;
One slumbered from fatigue —
Then there were two

Little motorists, racing just for fun;
One passed upon a crest —
Then there was one

One little motorist, though it's seldom done;
Lit a match to gauge his tank —
Now there are none

CHAPTER 6

DuBose—EQB Club—
Close Friends—High Jinks

We can evade reality, but we cannot evade the consequences of
evading reality.
—AYN RAND (1905-1982)

*F*ATHER FLYE NEVER HAD AN EMPTY DAY. Besides grading
papers, browsing through his private library, reading newspapers,
and hosting visitors, he also tried to keep up with his massive correspondence. Samuel Lackey, manager of the St. Andrew's Crossing post
office, once exclaimed: "Father Flye gets more mail than the governor."

For much of its history, St. Andrew's did not make a strong effort to keep track
of its graduates. The school periodically mailed *The Messenger*, a fund-raising cir-
cular, but because they were mailed by third class postage, the circulars were not
forwarded or returned if they were sent to an invalid address. Alumni visiting St.
Andrew's discovered the school could not supply the current address for a former
classmate, so Father Flye was asked to help. It was well-known that his address
book contained at least 500 names.

A study of the letters to Father Flye show a wide range of subject matter.
Some are only humdrum and gossipy, whereas others are more interesting. One
example is this letter from Andrew Chenson, dated November 18, 1947: "Your
words about Europe were welcome. Of late, I've given considerable thought of
going to France. David Potter, professor of history at Yale, whom I read for my
Master's Degree, is the Harmsworth Professor of American History at Oxford
this year. I want you two to meet, provided I could be a minuscule fly on the wall
listening to your exchange. Ah, that would be a delicious treat.

"To answer your inquiry, I'm presently an instructor of American history and

English at Schofield Junior College, located on the Army base here in Hawaii. The students are varied: men and women, Army, Navy, Marines, and civilians. What a mixture I have in class: Americans, Hawaiians, Filipinos, Japanese, Chinese, Koreans, enlisted men as well as officers. Here at Iolani I'm regarded as an eccentric character, but a fairly effective teacher.

"If I haven't told you already, I'm an admirer of the Oriental, with friends who are Chinese, Japanese and Korean. The Japanese are the friendliest of the three groups; they are sensitive to a fault. The Koreans are seen as being argumentative, the Irish of the Orient, but I've had no difficulty along those lines. When my students ask me when I'm going to get married, I answer: 'Whenever I find a tall Chinese lady whose father has a million dollars!' That always gets a chuckle.

"One of my colleagues at the school is Major William Bruce Sharp, who remembers you from his seminary days in Sewanee. He is currently the post chaplain, and he has some funny stories about you 'scholars' drinking port with Will Percy on your front porch, and singing bawdy college songs. I can see it now. Thanks for filling me in on the status of David McDowell. I remember meeting him at your St. Andrew's house. Has he mellowed, or is he as much of an egotist as before?"

Chenson concluded his letter: "I've begun the research on the episcopate of Dr. Thomas N. Staley, Lord Bishop of Honolulu, 1861-1870. And, yes indeed, your ideas on how to proceed have turned out to be the best approach. I wish that your travels would bring you in this direction. I would relish a long conversation. Additionally, I would like for you to see these tropical sunsets. Please pass along my fond regards to Mrs. Flye. From what I've seen, no local artist would dare compare against her work."

❑ ❑ ❑

The St. Andrew's history teacher had a busy social life in Sewanee and Monteagle.

In 1919, Flye met William Haskell DuBose, a mission priest and teacher of Old Testament studies at the theology school in Sewanee. Flye and DuBose entertained each other, and bystanders, by challenging each other's memory of scripture. Their friendship was linked to an extraordinary school in Monteagle, and the person who made the school possible. Before the DuBose Memorial Church Training School was founded there was no official Episcopal agency to lend a hand to rural ministries. The Episcopal movement in the United States was historically centered in cities and larger towns. A visionary cleric, William Sterling Claiborne, set out to change this.

Claiborne's idea was to create a school to train men of humble beginnings to be rural pastors, giving them a practical, rather than intellectual, preparation. He argued that his school would not be in competition with any existing seminaries,

DuBose Training School

but theologians would always call the DuBose school "a backdoor to the ministry," because it did not require a college degree for admission.

After serving as an Army chaplain in World War I, Claiborne was determined to obtain backing for his idea. Coincidentally, the 1919 Episcopal General Convention loosened the educational requirements for ordination—Latin, Greek and Hebrew were no longer part of the clerical examination for local ministries.

A few years later, a board of nine trustees, including four southern bishops, agreed to purchase 58 acres in Monteagle from William Haskell DuBose. The school's name was picked to honor William's father, William Porcher DuBose, who had taught at the theological school in Sewanee from 1871 to 1908. The training institute, known officially as the DuBose Memorial Church Training School, opened in Monteagle on September 21, 1921.

Three St. Andrew's priests taught at DuBose between 1921 and 1924, but Flye never did, even part-time. On August 9, 1928, Grace wrote her father about the ray of hope the training school represented: "Hal's spirit will be broken if he can't get away from here. I hope he goes to DuBose. They all love him there. He can't teach history, because Prof. Cole has that permanently." In Flye's mind, the training school in Monteagle was his ace in the hole if he needed another job on the Mountain. His theory about this was never tested. Nevertheless, the DuBose school fed his dreams and he found companionship there.

On and off, William S. Claiborne taught at DuBose until he died January 7, 1933. His exit marked the end of an era. His contribution to the neglected people of his time and place is beyond estimation. He salvaged St. Mary's School. He founded St. Andrew's School. He was the driving force behind the rural missions near Sewanee. He built the Otey Parish Rectory in 1907. He made the DuBose school possible. He was responsible for the first hospital in Sewanee.

Father Flye said of him: "There are countless recipients of William Claiborne's noble works in this part of the world." Grace Flye wrote in a letter dated January 10, 1933: "We are devastated over Father Claiborne's passing." Grace Flye and Alice Claiborne, and their husbands, were the closest of friends.

Over 23 years, before it closed in 1944, DuBose had 273 students from 75 dioceses. 171 of them became ordained priests, and six of them became bishops. The DuBose Training School had a large impact on the nation's Episcopal rural ministry.

□ □ □

Ecce Quam Bonum ("Behold How Good") is taken from the 133rd Psalm. The EQB Club in Sewanee was a treasured outlet for Father Flye. Founded in 1870 for faculty members of the University of the South and other "gentlemen of the Mountain," the EQB Club kept Flye's intellectual juices flowing. He became a member of the EQB Club on November 26, 1930. One time in 1936, when his Packard would not start, Flye walked through a rainstorm to an EQB meeting 2 miles away in Sewanee.

The club met every two weeks and featured a presentation (called a "lead") by a club member (the leader) on a subject not related to his profession. An English professor talked about history, a physics teacher discussed poetry, and so on. After the lead, in a question-and-answer period, the leader defended his thesis.

Elizabeth Nickinson Chitty, wife of historiographer Arthur Ben Chitty, said the EQB Club meetings were lively: "The Q-and-A's were tough to handle. The meetings were more academic in Father Flye's time, and some of the club members were vicious in their questioning. Father Flye prepared for months before he gave a lead. He wasn't loud, but he held his own. He loved the EQB."

Flye served as Secretary of the EQB Club from 1933 through 1935. His minutes of the November 9, 1933, meeting read: "Met at General Jervey's grand place. Present were Kirkland, Bruton, Long, Knickerbocker, Myers, R. B. Davis, MacKellar, Woodward, DuBose, Baker, Lindsey, Thompson, McConnell, Finney, Gen. Jervey, Col. Smith, Bearden, Hodgson, Gass, Atkins, Ware, Kayden, Scott, Guerry, and Flye. Minutes of the previous meeting were read and approved. Dr. Knickerbocker was announced as the leader at the next meeting, his subject will be Adolf Hitler."

His notations about the club's meeting on February 6, 1935, had a poetic tone: "The landscape is that of a traditional northern Christmas scene, snow falling lightly, earth and roofs white under soft diffused moonlight from behind the clouds, club members assembled for this meeting. Eighteen men were present. The lead of the evening was by Prof. Gass, who dealt with Sappho, the lyric singer of ancient Lesbos whose fame has come to us through twenty five centuries. Some consideration was given to the setting, the Aeolian culture of the Eastern Aegean where there was to be found by the 7th Century B.C. a civilization filled with the interest and joyousness of living where poetry and art were cultivated with enthusiasm." Father Flye then went on to write several pages of lyrical descriptions of Sappho's poetry.

He concluded with: "The Prof. Gass paper was praised for its interesting charm of style. It set one musing; the writer of these notes can bear witness that during the past several days he has found his thoughts turning often to an island in the blue Aegean where in the morning of Greek history, under sunny skies, a woman gifted with rare genius, where her songs placed our Sappho among the immortals."

Sappho held a special place in Father Flye's heart. If he had an appreciative audience, he loved to recite her poetry. According to those who witnessed him reciting her words, his eyes always had a tearful misting.[1]

Father Flye's EQB Club presentations were:

February 1931   Movements in Modern Education
March 1933   Propaganda
January 1935   Lawlessness
April 1937   American Neutrality
May 1940   Government Considered
April 1943   Some Thoughts on History
January 1945   Freedom of Thought

Two were published in the *Sewanee Review:* "Movements in Modern Education" (January 1932), and "American Neutrality" (April 1938). [2]

Father Flye presented "Freedom of Thought" at the EQB Club on January 25, 1945. His talk was given at a time when Germany's military collapse was obvious, and there were questions about the Soviet Union's post-war aims. He essentially forecast the Cold War, and this angered many in the audience. After all, the Soviets had been our brother-in-arms against Germany. The only explanation was that the priest was an uninformed hysteric. Flye may not have changed any minds that day, but he knew his appraisal was accurate.[3]

Robert S. "Red" Lancaster, a University of the South professor, recalled an outdoor discussion on literature after an EQB meeting: "Father Flye said he feared we, as a people, were becoming addicted to forgettable slap-stick entertainment, and were ignoring good literature. A Sewanee professor loudmouth in the crowd declared this was due to the fact that the country didn't have any great writers. Father Flye replied that there were still great writers, what was missing were great readers."

□ □ □

William Percy at his "Mountain Cabin" in Sewanee, circa 1939

Father Flye had three special friends who kept his intellectual plate filled: Will Percy, Andrew Lytle, and James Hollingsworth.

Their love of Sappho was the common denominator in Father Flye's friendship with Will Percy, a noted author, poet and attorney. Quoting the ancient lyricist became part of their *entente cordiale*. The history teacher especially liked Sappho's poem about the evening star Hesperus: "Bringing back everything that shining dawn scattered, you bring the goat, you bring the sheep, you bring the child to its mother." When he was asked why classical poetry was important to him, Flye replied: "We need heroic examples. There can never be too much heroism or love in literature."

William Alexander Percy was born into a prestigious Greenville, Mississippi family. He wrote three noted volumes of poetry: *Sappho in Levkas and Other Poems* (1915), *In April Once* (1920), and *Enzio's Kingdom* (1930), as well as a volume of *Selected Poems* (1930). His autobiography *Lanterns on the Levee* (1941) won critical acclaim.

Will Percy was a man of moral and physical courage. Serving with the American 37th Division in France during World War I, he achieved the rank of Captain and was awarded the Croix de Guerre. He led a successful campaign against the Ku Klux Klan in Greenville in 1922. He inherited his *noblesse oblige* from his father, LeRoy Percy, a 1879 Sewanee graduate, who was a U.S. Senator from Mississippi, and a wealthy land owner. Following his father's footsteps, Will Percy graduated from the University of the South in 1904.

To escape the summer heat and humidity in the Mississippi Delta, the Percy family had a summer cottage near Sewanee. Will had a deep attachment to the Mountain. He wrote in *Lanterns on the Levee*: "The Mountain is so beautiful that folks who have once been there always, one way or another, come back."

Will Percy made it a point to see Father Flye when he came to stay at his mountain cabin. Their get-togethers were sometimes boisterous. Grace wrote on September 18, 1942: "Hal has me worried. He stayed up nearly all night on the porch giggling and laughing with Will Percy, reciting poetry until the dawning hours. Hal enjoys Will being here, but he goes to extremes and doesn't get enough sleep. He sometimes pays a heavy price. Of course, I enjoy Will Percy as much as Hal does. Mr. Percy is such a refined gentleman."

In a thank-you note to Grace Flye, Will Percy once wrote: "Due to your husband's keen insight into things past and present, I think his mind is better company to him than most people are. This is why I feel so honored when he welcomes me into your warm home." *Through The Eyes Of A Teacher*, a booklet of Father Flye's photographs taken around 1930, includes a photograph of Will Percy.

The Percy literary lineage was continued by Will's adopted son, Walker Percy, the author of many outstanding works including: *Lost in the Cosmos, Message in the Bottle, Second Coming,* and *The Moviegoer.*

❑❑❑

Flye first met Andrew Nelson Lytle at a EQB session. A prolific man of letters, Lytle gained prominence as one of 12 writers known as The Agrarians. They believed that literature should have a regional flavor in order to survive, and that industrialization would destroy the South's unique homogeny. Their hypothesis did not have universal acceptance. For instance, a *New York Times* editorial described them as a dozen men trying to hold back the sea of change.

Begun at Vanderbilt University, the movement spawned celebrated essays during the 1920s and 1930s: *I'll Take My Stand: The South and the Agrarian Tradition* and *Who Owns America? A New Declaration of Independence.* The group included Andrew Lytle, John Crowe Ransom, Donald Davidson, Allen Tate, Robert Penn Warren, Frank Lawrence Owsley, John Gould Fletcher, Lyle H. Lanier, Herman C. Nixon, Henry Blue Kline, John D. Wade, Stark Young. Some later became literary icons.

Andrew Lytle wrote several noted novels, as well as short stories and essays. David Madden, Director of the Civil War Research Center at Louisiana State University, judged Lytle's *The Long Night* (1936) one of the best novels ever written about the Civil War. Lytle's *Bedford Forrest and his Critter Company* (1931) was considered an historical *tour de force.* Many critics believe his most enduring novel is *The Velvet Horn* (1957).

Andrew Lytle was a 1920 graduate of the Sewanee Military Academy. He attended the Yale University School of Drama, and later appeared in Broadway plays.

He was Managing Editor of *The Sewanee Review* from 1942 through 1944, and Editor from 1961 until 1973. He taught English at Sewanee from 1961 through 1973.

Lytle said Father Flye had a way with children: "He helped people without drawing attention to himself. When I visited him, it was great to sit back and watch his effect on boys who came to his house. He was courteous to children. You know how rare this is? When he was with youngsters, he always chose his words carefully. He knew how easily their feelings were hurt. He knew children did not have the veneer adults have through years of experience.

"In his house, there was an absence of stiff formality. If a boy entered and found an adult visitor, Father Flye would introduce the boy to the grown-up, whether it was a college dean or a business tycoon. He had an innate kindness toward everyone, no matter their age or station. Contrary to those formal courtesies so often demanded by men of the cloth, Father Flye had a breezy unpretentiousness."

Andrew Lytle added: "Here was a man who was humble, never taking credit for what he did. He always sang the praises of others, never of himself. God only knows how many times he helped someone by giving them money or doing a good deed. He did this quietly, without fanfare. The Orange Bowl in Miami couldn't hold all the people he helped. He was never too busy to do a good turn for a student, or even a stranger. I admired his intellect, his generosity, his charity of spirit. It was no mystery to me why he was so popular."

Flye's friendship with Lytle gave the priest entre to literary circles he would not have had otherwise. He liked his visits to Lytle's huge log cabin home in Monteagle where writers and poets congregated. He met and liked Caroline Gordon (married twice to Allen Tate), author of nine novels and several short stories. Flye said she had a "first-rate mind." Loving all things poetic, he was happy to meet The Fugitives," writers who had published a poetry magazine while students at Vanderbilt University.

Grace wrote on June 5, 1944: "Yesterday Hal performed the marriage of two young people who had met only several weeks ago (a wartime romance one sees these days) at the Lytle house. Following the wedding, he got into a hot discussion with Andrew Lytle and Allen Tate. The pair of them claimed the Confederacy would have won the Civil War if Nathan Forrest had commanded the southern army. Allen Tate believes Robert E. Lee was stricken with a 'Virginia only' mentality and never had a strategic viewpoint. Hal naturally took exception. He and father always agreed the south could never have won that awful war. Despite the occasional clashes of opinions, being at the Lytle place gives Hal a feeling of time well-spent. He returns energized and can't wait to tell me about who said what to whom."

Whereas the love of poetry bonded Will Percy to Father Flye, the love of history cemented the Lytle-Flye friendship. One observer, Buck Jackson, wrote: "When they got together they seemed to lapse into being two men from the

19th Century. It was like they were using lines from a play, using language that had a grace you don't hear anymore."

James Hollingsworth in Coast Guard uniform, 1918

Another of Flye's friends was James Butler Hollingsworth, a retired geologist and widower who lived in a two-story house a few miles east of Tracy City. The walls of his house were covered with memorabilia from his years working for petroleum firms in Asia and the Middle East. He dabbled at being a "gentleman farmer," raising goats and chickens. He was a history buff and loved stimulating dialogue, so it was natural that he liked the St. Andrew's teacher. In many ways, they were like two peas from the same pod.

One conversation at Hollingsworth's house, in the late 1930s, was interrupted by the sound of gunfire. It was hunting season and rifle shots were expected. The geologist remembered: "Father Flye quietly put on his large overcoat and walked out to the front yard. The shooting was off to our left; he turned and shouted at the top of his voice: 'Stop that.' He then came back inside, took off his coat and sat down. The look on his face was one of pure hatred. His hands were shaking. For the longest time, we didn't say a word to each other. Beyond his being a vegetarian, Father Flye hated the notion that someone would kill a harmless animal."

Hollingsworth and Flye had a long-standing chess game that may have set a record for longevity. Only one move per player was allowed when they socialized. If it was the priest's turn to make the next move on the chess board, Father Flye entered Hollingsworth's living room and said: "I move this rook to here." The chessboard was then ignored until the next visit. Nobody knows if one of their chess games was ever finished.

Father Flye's demeanor was Victorian, quaint, even chauvinistic, depending upon one's point of view. If he was sitting down he stood up whenever a woman entered the room. He removed his hat when introduced to a woman. He adhered to a rigid code of civility, rooted in his turn-of-the-century idealism. By contemporary standards, he was a moss-backed traditionalist; on the other hand, his old-world courtesy made him incredibly charming.

He almost never uttered a word of profanity. James Hollingsworth did recall one time he used a four-letter-word: "Goat's milk was as popular as cow's milk is today, and I used to sell a few buckets to my neighbors. My male goat had died and I wanted to go down to Cowan to see a man about buying one. I invited Father Flye to go along. Keep in mind that he always wore a black suit with a starched white clerical collar.

"When we got there, the old farmer was sitting in his front yard under a shade tree, not too far from his front porch. There was a large table and a few lawn chairs. The goat, which was a big brute, was chewing grass ten yards away. After introductions, we sat down with the old timer and we started off with inane talk about the weather and such. In those days you didn't rush into serious business talk; you had to proceed with a modicum of sociability. Well, as we began to talk, this goat walked over and began to sniff us, like a dog would.

"For some reason, the goat took a dislike to Father Flye. The animal began to lower his head and gently push against him. Father Flye took it in good cheer, moving his chair and saying 'nice goat,' or something to that effect, as he patted the horns.

"This happened several times, with Father Flye getting up and moving his chair and trying to calm the animal saying 'nice goat.' The old man and I were fascinated by all this and we soon both began to chuckle. We could see that Father Flye was becoming increasingly agitated. Finally, the goat rammed him hard enough to knock him over. By now, the old man and I couldn't contain ourselves and we were laughing out loud.

"Father Flye was trying to get to the front porch on his hands and knees, while the goat butted his behind. He crawled up on the front porch where the goat couldn't get to him. Father Flye was angry. His face was crimson red and his hair was a mess.

"He yelled to the farmer: 'What is wrong with this goat?' The old man, who was now laughing his head off, replied: 'I don't know for sure, but my guess is he doesn't like Catholic priests.' Father Flye shouted back: 'Would you please tell this damn brute that I'm Episcopalian?'"

The following was one of Father Flye's favored jokes: "The loud temperance preacher said from the pulpit: 'If I owned all the beer in the world, I'd throw all of it in the river.' With even more enthusiasm, the preacher said: 'If I had all the wine in the world, I'd throw all of it in the river.' Then working himself up to a fever pitch, the evangelist yelled: 'If I owned all the whiskey in the world, I'd throw all of it into the river.' Then he sat down. The church's song leader then stood up and announced with a smile: 'For our closing hymn, let's sing 'Shall We

Gather At The River?'"

He recited this one frequently:

> At an ecumenical meeting, a secretary shouted: "The building is on fire."
> The Methodists gathered in the corner and prayed.
> The Baptists cried: 'Where is the water?'
> The Quakers praised God for the blessings that fire brings.
> The Lutherans posted a notice that fire was evil.
> The Roman Catholics passed the plate to cover the damages.
> The Jews posted symbols hoping the fire would pass.
> The Congregationalists shouted: 'Every man for himself.'
> The Fundamentalists proclaimed: "It is God's vengeance.'
> The Christian Scientists concluded there was no fire.
> The Presbyterians appointed a committee to study the fire.
> The Episcopalians formed a procession and left the building.
> The secretary grabbed a fire extinguisher and put out the fire.

❑ ❑ ❑

For decades some of the St. Andrew's students and local taxi drivers had a cooperative arrangement. If a boy left money at the highway entrance to the school with a handkerchief stuck on a stick, approximately an hour later a case of beer was left in nearby bushes. Carling's Red was the beer of choice in the 1930s and 1940s. Student drinking, especially at the college level, was part of the Mountain's culture. Shake Rag Point was the place where young men would go to shake a bush with a rag attached, leave cash, and come back later to find a jar of "white lightning." Father Flye knew of this, and casually took it all in stride. His friend who lived near Viola, Tennessee, Ralph Warren, said: "Father Flye took a nip without any apologies. I recall him saying Jesus drank spirits, and, as a matter of fact, his first miracle was converting water into wine at a marriage in Cana."

On November 15, 1938, Father Flye wrote: "I was talking to Charles [a student] about drinking and I said: There's no harm in taking a drink if you know when to stop; but you realize that if you get in a state where you take risks which you would not ordinarily, that is bad. I have never seen a drunken man I envied." He had a casual attitude about drinking, but he deplored drunkenness.

Father Flye sometimes demonstrated a rebelliousness that bordered on the bizarre. He had a history of defying authority, and clearly his activities at Clara's tavern in Monteagle went over the line of propriety. They never acted on it, but St. Andrew's administrators knew he violated some fundamental tenets of good conduct.

After the repeal of Prohibition in the mid-1930s, Clara's became a popular "watering hole" with local residents. In his Packard, Flye gave a lift to boys he

"Clara's Place" in Monteagle

saw walking at night toward Monteagle. They were driven straight to Clara's, no questions asked. Hartwell Hooper, a 1948 graduate, said: "We boys would be out on the highway hitch-hiking and Father Flye would come along in that enormous car of his and he would give us a ride. He didn't want to be seen letting us out right at the entrance to Clara's, so he would let us out nearby."

At times Father Flye went to Clara's with a St. Andrew's student. The teenager was clearly "underage," a fact the owner and the priest ignored. William Jackson, a 1951 graduate, said: "He would turn his clerical collar around, put on a tie, and wear his black suit. I felt privileged to be at Clara's with him. I recall there was always an absence of small talk in our discussions. Father Flye would recite from an esoteric poem that, strangely enough, fit in with what we were talking about. I remember him saying: 'Make ye no truce with the bear who walks like a man' from one of Rudyard Kipling's poems about Russia. I know folks from the school spotted us at Clara's, but nobody said a word to me about it. Looking back, I suppose St. Andrew's didn't want a scandal. In my opinion, we didn't do anything wrong."[4]

Arthur Ben Chitty: "My roommate in Sewanee in 1932 was 'Whiskey John Brown,' who once brought a five-gallon jug of it up to our room. It was a dance weekend and the two of us were very popular that weekend. Whiskey John practically paid his way through college this way. He would sell you a pint bottle for a dollar. He made great profits doing this kind of thing. He bought five gallons for five dollars and would sell forty pints.

"Father Flye socialized with a philosophy professor at the University of the South, Hugh Caldwell, and the two of them went to Clara's. The place was

St. Andrew's dining hall

always loud. It wasn't a large bar, about 30 to 40 feet long, and it had exposed ceiling rafters. When you got sufficiently drunk, you'd show how sober you were by hanging by your knees from the rafters. To prove you could get home by yourself. Typical drunken logic."

Father Julian Gunn, who served at St. Andrew's in the 1950s and 1960s, had this to say about Flye's behavior: "How he took St. Andrew's boys to Clara's was a flagrant violation. It is no wonder Bishop Campbell and Father Spencer dwelt on his acts of disloyalty. Discussing the issue with me once, Bishop Campbell answered my inquiry as to why the Order put up with Father Flye: 'We couldn't put him out in the cold. Where would he have gone?' St. Andrew's was the only place he could have done that. No other institution would have given him such leeway. During his last years at the school he sat in the dining hall and flipped peas off the end of a knife at the head table. This amused the boys sitting at his table, but it was a juvenile defiance. The Headmasters gritted their teeth when it came to Father Flye."

Father Bonnell Spencer wrote about Flye's behavior at the 1950 commencement: "I was expressing gratitude for all that Father Flye had done for the school, and I looked at him sitting beside me. He was making derogatory faces at the audience, and I was shocked he felt that way. I never understood the man."

❑ ❑ ❑

From time to time, St. Andrew's boys were also mischievous. One Saturday night a cow was left inside the Assembly Room, also called the Honors Room or Study Hall. The cow remained calm until it was discovered by one of the cooks the next morning. The woman screamed and ran for help, waking up everyone

Brother Dominic and pupil at the St. Andrew's chapel organ

she could find. Her reaction was a mistake. With all the yelling and confusion, the frightened animal started urinating and defecating as its feet became entangled with overturned desks. Windows, desks and one door frame were destroyed as the cow tried to find an exit. It was finally subdued and taken back to the school farm. The barnyard odor in the Assembly Room made it unusable for days.

A few rebellious boys led some of the farm's cows into an onion patch one night. The next morning onion-flavored and onion-smelling milk was served for the students' cereal.

Nobody has yet explained how an automobile owned by a St. Andrew's chemistry teacher was parked on the roof of one of the dormitories. Ann Tate, a school employee, said: "Believe it or not, this actually happened."

Two students sneaked into the chapel in the middle of the night and played rock-and-roll music on the chapel's organ. The rotund organist, Brother Dominic, was a good-humored man, but when he was informed "Fats Domino" was rattling the rafters, he made a beeline to the chapel, wearing only his sandals and long johns. This was the only time known in school history when the Infirmarian had to give Brother Dominic a sedative. Later, one the boys said: "I didn't know he knew such language." The two rock-and-rollers survived Brother Dominic's wrath. After leaving St. Andrew's, Lawrence Meyer became a student at Auburn University, and Paul Lowdenslager went to Annapolis.

A St. Andrew's boy had parked his father's automobile south of the football field, and was spooning with his sweetheart. Somehow her foot became jammed under the car's dashboard. A maintenance man at the school and a Sewanee policeman were stymied, so they telephoned a local doctor for help—after all, he had plenty of experience in evacuating people from mangled car wrecks. The physician used a "surgical saw" to free the girl's foot. Then the car was taken to the school's maintenance shop and the damage under the dashboard was repaired. The embarrassed young lady from Cowan sustained nothing more serious than a bruised ankle. The policeman didn't file a report, and the doctor didn't send a bill. The episode was kept secret by all concerned. The couple married each other some years later, and both the policeman and the doctor attended their wedding.

Administration Building at St. Andrew's School

At dusk one October, following an evening meal, a mathematics teacher was walking across the St. Andrew's quadrangle when he heard a strange sound over his head. He looked up and saw a footlocker suspended about 10 feet over his head, hanging by rope from a tree limb. He slowly lowered the trunk to the ground. When he looked inside, he discovered a terrified freshman. The boy had been inside the footlocker for about 15 minutes. The perpetrators, three sophomores, polished brass, swept floors, and received no weekend passes for the next three months.

Research for this book uncovered many such stories. One student showing his "fast draw" to several roommates accidentally shot himself in the foot. A dormitory pillow fight turned serious when one boy put a rock inside a pillow case, and another boy's skull was fractured. A skunk was left inside the school's library, forcing an evacuation of the Administration Building. Snakes, spiders, dead birds, raw eggs were secretly placed in dormitory beds.

Then there is the story of the missing school bus. The St. Andrew's football squad had played a Friday night game in Chattanooga against Notre Dame, and was getting dressed in the locker room when the substitute bus driver, a Sewanee student, entered and announced meekly: "I can't find the bus."

This is what happened. After the team had unloaded before the game, the driver had parked the bus two blocks away from the football field. He had earlier arranged for his sweetheart to meet him in Chattanooga, and they wanted privacy in a secluded area of town. Leaving the bus behind, they walked back to watch the game during halftime. Unfortunately, the bus was in a restricted parking zone, and was towed away to the police compound. The school bus could not be retrieved until the next morning. Emergency arrangements were made, and the coaches and the football team stayed overnight at the ritzy Read House hotel in downtown Chattanooga. This turn of events had a happy ending as far as St. Andrew's was concerned. The parents of the embarrassed substitute bus driver paid the expenses.

□ □ □

[1]The fame of most early Greek poets was eclipsed by Sappho of Lesbos c. 630 B.C. - c. 570 B.C. Plato called her the Tenth Muse. It is believed she wrote close to 500 poems; most of them about her affection for female friends. Sappho's poetry had two themes: love and the eternal value of words. Despite her approval in antiquity, some Greek comedies mocked her works, which led to negative tales about her morality. Lesbian originally meant women of Lesbos.

[2] Dating back to 1892, *The Sewanee Review* is the country's oldest literary quarterly. The magazine's longevity and prestige is remarkable when one considers it has been produced at a small liberal arts university in Tennessee. As editors in the 1940s, Andrew Lytle and Allen Tate established *The Sewanee Review* as a quarterly with both national and international connections. T. S. Eliot, respected man of letters and *Review* contributor, wrote in the 1950s: "*The Sewanee Review* has reached the status of an institution ... its loss would be something more than merely the loss of one good periodical: it would be the symptom of an alarming decline in the periodical world at its highest level." Contributors to the *Review* have included an impressive number of noted authors and poets, including William Faulkner, Shelby Foote, Thomas Merton, Saul Bellow, Ezra Pound, Dylan Thomas, W.H. Auden, Katherine Anne Porter, Caroline Gordon, Jacques Maritain, Joyce Carol Oates, Flannery O'Connor, Robert Penn Warren, Conrad Aiken, Andre Dubus, Albert Camus, Peter Taylor, Kenneth Burke, Malcolm Cowley, Carlos Baker. And the not-so-famous have had their words published in the magazine. After Father Flye's "American Neutrality" appeared in *The Sewanee Review* in 1938, in a letter to her relatives in Florida, Grace Flye wrote: "Hal was surprised editor William S. Knickerbocker took such an interest in his thoughts on the subject of war. I am so proud of Hal. He doesn't say much, but I think his chest is full. His article is kicking up dust here at St. Andrew's. At yesterday's tea, I detected envy among the faculty wives."

[3]The Cold War dominated American foreign policy for the next 44 years.

[4] Clara's was also a popular restaurant. The owner, Clara Shoemate, prospered. Following the death of her husband, Tom, she remarried and moved to California.

CHAPTER 7

The Bishop's Anger— Dark Journals— The King's Beard

The truth doesn't hurt unless it ought to.
—BERTIE C. FORBES (1880-1954)

*M*ONASTICISM HAS NEVER BEEN ASSOCIATED with the mainstream of the Episcopal church. To churchgoers, especially in the South, the image of monks and monasteries has had the repugnant odor of Roman Catholicism, and the elaborate chapel services at St. Andrew's reinforced this idea—the use of incense, bell ringing, holy water, Biblical statues, icons on the wall, a crucifix instead of a vacant cross. The Benediction on Sunday evenings at St. Andrew's included rituals that dated back to the Middle Ages. Acolytes secretly called the services "smells and bells."

James Ward Lee, a 1948 graduate, said: "The monks of the Order of the Holy Cross were so 'High Church' they made the Pope look like a Methodist. Both the Order priests and the secular fathers said confession was good for the soul. We all tried to line up at Father Wright's booth, where a couple of Hail Marys would do penance for our boyish sins. With the Holy Cross priests, individual salvation was day-by-day and week-by-week; confession, communion and chapel every single day, then at least twice on Sunday."

Father Flye never faulted the religious ceremonies at St. Andrew's; on the contrary, he liked the ancient pageantry. To him, the more dramatic the church services, the better. Regarding the issue of Roman influence, he liked the words of the English prelate, Parry Liddon (1829-1890), who had promoted

Incense, a symbol of the "High Church" services at St. Andrew's

Roman Catholic practices.

Father Flye never understood why some Episcopalians were agitated about Roman Catholic influence, real or imagined. His opinion was expressed in an article he authored for the May-June 1919 issue of *American Church Monthly.* He wrote: "There are three branches of the Catholic Church, the Eastern, the Roman, and the Anglican, each keeping the succession of bishops and sacraments. The differences between the three branches are few and mostly concern matters of usage rather than doctrine. The Roman branch requires priests to be unmarried, the Eastern branch requires them to be married, and the English branch leaves it optional. The Roman branch prefers Latin services, the Eastern and Anglican use national languages. The big difference is Roman Catholics believe the Papacy to be the head of the whole church, a principle which has never received universal Catholic consent."

As Flye saw it, there was little to get excited about. The three branches of the Holy Catholic Church were of the same ecclesiastical family, with no major differences between them. He said he was an Anglo-Catholic clergyman. Father Flye endorsed the premise that the history of the church was also the story of Western civilization. He had read about the establishment of monasticism during the 4th century in Europe. He accepted at face value the *opus Dei* inherent in monastic life. He did not believe a celibate life was unnatural, as such, but he knew becoming a monk was not for him. He could never be that subservient to authority.

The monks at St. Andrew's were quietly dedicated. Flye admired their devotion, but thought they were not as well-read as they should be. He hated intellectual laziness and said a university degree was never an end in itself. He judged adults by what they read outside of their chosen profession. He particularly was at odds with the Order priests, because they had little interest in current affairs. This baffled him. He could not imagine a day without reading newspapers and, after the late 1920s, listening to radio newscasts.

Though they were not as informed as he was, the monks had their share of secular contacts. Running St. Andrew's was an exercise in reality. Haggling with a contractor about building a water tank or concerns over a leaky roof were not ethereal exercises. The monastery hosted weekend retreats for alcoholics, mostly from Chattanooga, and the Order priests spent hours counseling these troubled men. This duty was just as tiring as any physical labor. The monks spent hours on their knees every day praying for the salvation of other people. This was the calling God demanded of them, it was their spiritual foundation. Staying abreast of today's headlines was not a priority for the monks.

Bonnell Spencer, the Prior at St. Michael's Monastery from 1947 until 1955, wrote: "Father Flye never did fit in. He regularly skipped faculty meetings. He had an aloofness toward the Order Fathers. He was a remarkable teacher, and a blessing to

Crucifix at the entrance to St. Michael's monastery at St. Andrew's School

those boys in whom he took a personal interest, but he always had contempt for the Order of the Holy Cross. He was an intellectual snob. He never gave credit where it was due." Spencer's assessment was accurate. Flye's attitude was obvious when he wrote in his journal: "Faculty meetings are dominated by trivia easily forgotten."

Shortly after moving to St. Andrew's in 1918, Father Flye and his wife fell into a daily routine. From all appearances, their lives had settled into a contented pattern. But a sequence of events in 1921 permanently stained their serenity.

It is one thing for an established monastic Order to go against the ecclesiastical grain, but it is quite another thing for an individual clergyman to do so. James Harold Flye normally avoided confrontation; however, in 1921 he inexplicably challenged a high Episcopal official on a personal level. At the time, he had been at St. Andrew's for three years, and he was a nobody in the educational and priesthood fraternities. Without knowing it, he made a decision that became a defining moment in his life.

On September 25, 1921, Father Flye wrote to Bishop Coadjutor of Tennessee, the Right Reverend Troy Beatty: "I was away last summer at the Cathedral parish

The Rev. Bonnell Spencer, St. Andrew's Prior 1947-1955

in Chicago. A few days after my return here, I was looking over the Diocesan Journal, and was amazed to read that you noted during your two trips to St. Andrew's School last year, the Sunday worship service was in no sense in accordance with the Prayer Book. This is a grave charge. Our ceremonial is, I grant you, different from that of the Episcopal churches in this region, but I challenge your statement. My type of Churchmanship is what many would call extreme, like that of the Holy Cross Fathers, but I keep close to the Prayer Book. I have not consulted with the OHC Fathers about this, and am writing purely on my own initiative."

Bishop Beatty's reply was laced with sarcasm. In a four-page letter dated October 7, 1921, the Bishop made it clear he thought Father Flye had violated church protocol and was wrong about the Prayer Book. In essence, he said: "You feel a responsibility for what goes on at St. Andrew's, even though you are not a member of the Order. Now that you have challenged my statement, I remind you that we, as clergymen, have sworn to uphold the law of the Protestant Episcopal Church; the only Service Book recognized by the Church, in addition to the Bible, is the Book of Common Prayer. You wrote that you intend to keep pretty close to the Prayer Book; however, your oath requires you to stick to it absolutely. We are solely commissioned to obey the law as it is now, not as we think it was 500 years ago."

Father Flye did not let the matter rest. He wrote back on October 20, and gave the Bishop a lecture on church history. His six-page letter covered a variety of subjects: salt added to the Baptismal water, vestment colors, ancient Canons. What started as a disagreement about the Book of Common Prayer was now a dialogue on every ceremony practiced in the Episcopal church.

The Bishop Coadjutor responded in a letter dated November 10: "We are so apart that if we were discussing this subject face to face, I question if we could accomplish anything! You continue to write Mass, a Roman Catholic designation, which I find strange. Must I remind you that we serve in a Protestant church?" Bishop Beatty then informed Father Flye that the word Protestant originally meant those people who protested against Roman Catholicism, and bloodshed accompanied the historic cleansing of Roman beliefs from the Church of England.[1]

Father Flye wrote back on November 18, with yet another discourse on church history. Bishop Beatty did not respond. Their correspondence was at an end. However, the opinions expressed in the letters were now a matter of record. Like Caesar crossing the Rubicon, Flye's disagreement with Bishop Beatty was pivotal to his future. As the years went by, he sometimes daydreamed about once again being a parish priest, but his rashness in 1921 had doomed his chances.

Those angry letters permanently soured his relationship with the Order of the Holy Cross. After notification of the acrimonious correspondence in 1921, St. Andrew's Headmasters and Priors knew they had an iconoclast on the faculty roster. Father Julien Gunn, who worked at St. Andrew's for 10 years, remarked: "Starting with the outrageous letters to Bishop Beatty, the Order knew Father Flye was a loose cannon. He had been hired to be a teacher, and to conduct sunrise chapel services. He had not been hired to be a defender for the Order of the Holy Cross. His recklessness was embarrassing."

The Beatty letters caused a furor in the Flye bungalow. Mary Boorman recalled: "My family was very upset with him. He had no right to go off half-cocked. St. Andrew's officials were irritated about his unauthorized campaign about some esoteric church rituals. For a time, my family was convinced he was going to be fired. There was a lot of hand-wringing, especially by Aunt Grace. He once got into a screaming match with the Major over the business. It was awful. I know nearly everyone thought of Father Flye as a mild-mannered, ultra-polite priest. But, believe me, in those days, he had a terrible temper and was as stubborn as a mule."

James Hollingsworth said: "Father Flye was not realistic in a couple of areas. Vicars aren't hired sight unseen. He didn't have the temperament for a parochial ministry. He was too set in his ways, too opinionated. He was extremely informed on most subjects, but he was blind about some things. It was puzzling. He never saw that his time in Milledgeville had been a disaster.

"His confrontation with the Bishop was also a monumental blunder. There is no doubt he burned his bridges behind him in 1921. The Episcopal church made him persona non grata. To be the Rector of a church requires a Bishop's approval, but it is not needed for temporary summer work.

"He once told me he was known as 'The Cardinal,' due to his vast knowledge of church history when he was a seminary student in New York. Adding two and two together, his knowledge of history is what caused his run-in with the Bishop. Father Flye may have been too smart for his own good. Privates don't lecture generals."

Flye's disenchantment at St. Andrew's started with the Bishop Beatty controversy. He had defended the Order, yet he ended up feeling betrayed. He believed his well-meaning efforts were not appreciated, and he would never forgive the Order for what he saw as a betrayal. His harsh journal comments about the school's day-to-day operations first appeared in 1922. His viewpoint had permanently soured.

St. Andrew's acolytes , 1932

From then on, his outlook never varied. He had other complaints, but the issue of punishment for St. Andrew's students was a recurring theme. His attitude about the various Headmasters was in stark contrast to his non-judgmental views about almost everyone else.

Robert Campbell was the Headmaster when the Flyes arrived in 1918. They liked him. But in late 1921, Campbell was replaced by Edwin Whitall, who was strict about rules and punishment. Whitall became a regular entry in Flye's journal. The history teacher thought the Headmaster was arbitrary and cruel, and that he passed his attitudes to the prefects. He wrote in 1922: "The prefects shouldn't have this much power over younger boys. Who watches over the prefects?" However, Father Flye never wrote that any prefect abused his position.

The Prior and Headmaster selected the dormitory prefects and the head prefect, a process the two men took seriously. The boys chosen for the positions of trust had been observed for a period of time. Their personal behavior, judgement, character and maturity were closely examined before they were selected.

Father William Turkington, St. Andrew's Headmaster from 1942-1953, recalled: "The finest head prefect I ever had was a chap named James Seidule [a 1950 graduate]. He was a born leader, excellent athlete, and a boy who believed in honesty and fairness. Just before dinner one day a seventh grader was in the library and couldn't get the librarian's attention, and so he wet his pants. He made a dash for the dining hall when the bell rang. Everybody knew about the little fellow's accident, and I saw that the story was being passed around. Boys being boys, the seventh grader was in for some hazing when the meal ended. I rang the bell and said the final prayer of thanksgiving. Seidule got up from his chair, walked over and put an arm around the boy, and escorted him out of the dining hall, thus sparing him any more embarrassment. This is what you look for when picking a leader."

What would Flye have proposed as an alternative to the prefect system? The school's boarding students were there 24 hours a day, seven days a week. Usually no more than several monks lived in the monastery at any given time. Two of them, the Prior and the Headmaster, were fatigued by the demands of managing the school. The monks had sunup to sundown obligations. Every day they spent four hours praying. Their first obligatory prayer began at 5 a.m. The Order priests were soft-spoken by temperament. They had worked hard to rid themselves of any coarseness. It was uncommon for one of them to raise his voice. However, someone had to keep order in the dormitories. The prefect system was the logical way to maintain discipline, but Father Flye never agreed.

Beginning in 1922, his journal notations had a recurrent theme—he was critical of the way administrators punished rule breakers. He wrote on September 3, 1926: "James Roberson (15), Louis Rosen (12) and Sanford Perry (15) wanted to go out west. A policeman in Nashville picked them up. An escapade like this is from the standpoint of mature judgement, unwise, but I see nothing intrinsically bad in it. A sense of adventure is a fine quality. These youngsters will be severely punished."

The Rev. William R.D. Turkington, St. Andrew's Headmaster 1942-53

Flye wrote on September 10, 1926: "Paul Green wanted to light a candle in the chapel to hold a sweet vigil in memory of his mother. The Headmaster [Fr. Roger Anderson] wouldn't hear of it so the candle was taken away. This child's effort to make this offering, in piety and affection, was roughly trampled out by the head of the school, a priest. Deplorable. His knowledge of what makes a boy act as he does is identical to his knowledge of the ocean, he only sees the waves. He doesn't know what hopes and fears are swimming beneath the surface."

October 14, 1926: "The new boys haven't yet been assigned a seat in the dining hall. Often they can't find a place to sit down and don't eat at all. It is a crime that a boy has to miss a meal. How can the Head Table be so uncaring?" That same month he faulted the rule that the dining hall door be locked at a precise time. Flye wrote: "Nothing can justify this. Growing boys need their meals."

In November 1926, Father Flye wrote a petition criticizing the dining hall rules, but no other faculty member would sign it. Disappointed and frustrated, he handed the petition to the Headmaster with his sole signature on it. His bitterness regarding the Order of the Holy Cross intensified.

Meals were brought to dining hall tables in bowls or platters that were given to the person in charge of the table: a prefect or faculty member. After serving himself he then handed over the bowl to be passed down the table. The bowl occasionally had little food left in it when it reached the younger boys at the far end of the table. Father Flye was always popular in the dining hall, because at his table the youngest boys received extra attention.

St. David's dormitory at St. Andrew's School

Larry Meyer, a 1951 St. Andrew's graduate: "One of the things I recall as a young boy at St. Andrew's was that Father Flye made sure the ones at the far end of the table, the smaller guys, got enough to eat. Upperclassmen usually got the left-overs. I thought I would starve my first year there, so being at Father Flye's table was always a privilege."

Parker "Peanuts" Lowry, a 1953 graduate: "I relished being assigned to Father Flye's dining hall table when I was a young student at St. Andrew's, for it meant I would get a fair share of the food. We sat higher forms to lower forms, and at most tables the bowl was empty when it reached the bottom. Father Flye didn't allow it at his table."

Boys were locked out of the dining hall if they were late for meals, as a lesson in punctuality. During the school's early years, many mountain boys had a casual attitude about arriving on time. They came from homes without clocks. Locking the dining hall door sent a forceful message; headmasters knew the impact of a missed meal.

Flye wrote in his journal about two boys fighting over a slice of bread in the dining hall. In truth, the boys disliked each other anyway, and had fought frequently; their fisticuffs were not about hunger. He also wrote about a boy who crawled through a utility tunnel to reach a food storage area in the kitchen. The facts had nothing to do with hunger pangs; the boy was trying to make money, pilfering grape juice and sugar to make "dormitory wine."

At one period in the school's history athletes ate at separate tables in the dining hall; there was a ambivalent validity to Flye's charge that this was preferen-

A page from the St. Andrew's yearbook, 1926

tial treatment. The idea at the time was that separateness created *esprit de corps* for athletes. This practice did not prevail, and only lasted two years.

In the fall of 1930, Father Flye wrote the following in his journals:

September 11: "This morning at roll call Fr. Anderson said: 'Where is Sam Carter?' 'Ans. 'Right here.' Fr. A. 'Oh, right here? Well, I want to say to you, Sam Carter, that if I catch you blowing that bugle any more after bedtime at 8:30, you won't have any bugle, and you won't be able to sit down. The idea of you making that racket after bed time. It was outrageous.' Sam Carter is a little boy from Atlanta, only 12 years old and a bit small for his age, but in the eighth grade and remarkably bright and well-informed, well-behaved. To address him in this way was counter to fundamental principles. It shouldn't have been made a public matter, shouldn't have been said in the presence of the school. It was not courteous, and one who does not consider that a child is entitled to courtesy ought not, of course, to have to deal with children. One would not treat an adult that way. A child has feelings. That was no way to speak to Sam in public. To some this would seem only a small matter, but I don't regard any incident in dealing with a child as of no importance."

September 12: "This morning Fr. Anderson came to breakfast in a riding costume, white sport shirt with white knickerbockers, golf stockings. He went horseback riding after breakfast and was at roll call in the same costume. Three boys were late coming to breakfast. Fr. Anderson noticed one, Clyde Baumgartner, and called down from the head table 'Fatty (a horrible nickname) why are you late? What time is breakfast served?' Ans. 'a quarter to seven.' ' Yes, a quarter to seven. And what time is it now?' 'Ans. ten minutes to seven.' 'Yes, ten minutes to seven, and you know breakfast is at a quarter to seven. Oh, Fatty.'"

September 13: "There are 86 boarding boys on the roll. The meals are much as for some time past. Besides breakfast there is a light meal and one something like a full meal. During the football season the light meal is in the middle of the day, lunch, with the larger meal at night. I don't get enough to eat on this fare, I am sorry to say. I should think the boys need more than this light lunch.

"At supper Fr. Anderson said the same thing in detail about reading books or writing letters in Study Hall, reminding boys that they would get demerits for reading, and lose the privilege of using the school library. This procedure seems idiotic; incredibly bad practice."

September 25: "At roll-call this morning Fr. Anderson referred to Frank Long having taken books that were read in study hall and listed the names of offenders, and declared the Headmaster would back up Frank Long in his maintenance in the Study Hall. Such a situation cannot be handled by a penalty system. It is time to see someone beat this wooden system. For lunch today there was for each person two sandwiches, one with potted meat, one with jam, (thin bread) and a cup of cocoa. Think of this as a meal for hungry boys."

November 18: "As I write this afternoon, there is another hateful thing to chronicle in the running of this school and makes one rage against the heartless-ness and stupidity of the administration. Having the late mass I didn't go to breakfast and was not up about the school till dinner. At dinner I heard two boys had been expelled, Shirley Tate and H.D. Harris. Shirley Tate is from Battle Creek, seven miles from here at the foot of the mountain, where the Tate family has lived for generations. The boys were under the influence, so Fr. Anderson expelled them.

"They were not disorderly but in their rooms, having had a little too much. These are good boys and need a helping hand instead of a kick. Warr and Lauzenheiser tried to put in a word for them. The faculty was not consulted. Many boys feel so indignant about the way H. D. Harris and Shirley Tate have been dealt with."

Following are excerpts from Father Flye's journals during the 1931-1932 school year:

"Fr. Harrison raised some money. One check for $2,000 came in. Another one from the DuPonts for $4,000. During Fr. Harrison's absence there was nobody living at the monastery and some boys got drunk from drinking sacramental wine kept in the sacristy. They're gone from the school forever. Fr. Taylor was to be in charge, but he couldn't keep up the monastic house, and he too got drunk on wine, but he won't be expelled like those unfortunate boys were. This situa-tion could have been handled in a more civilized and fair manner. It is amazing that an institution run by priests can be so pig-headed and cruel."

"The tone of the school is not good, much worse than in past years. Little interest in reading and studies, boys slack and lazy. Honesty here at a low ebb and a good deal of drinking. Many boys seem to me to be trash, not particularly worthy of trying to educate. Few boys have qualities of leadership, ambition, character, ideals, and those who do would have these fostered better in other surroundings. The attitude of the Order is criminally inefficient. This is a place of wasted opportunities, inconsistent policies, mismanagement, bungling."[2]

In September 1939, the St. Andrew's Headmaster, Mr. Augustus A. Koski, issued this proclamation to the teachers, whom he called Masters:

"So many complaints have reached me from boys who have gone on to col-lege, that it seems necessary to establish the following rules:

1. Masters will use the class period to discuss main subjects, nothing else. If assignment is completed before the end of the period, the remaining time is to be used for review or drill. Reading stories is strictly forbidden.
2. No Master may dismiss his class before the signal for dismissal is given. Dur-ing exams, Masters must keep boys in the classrooms for the full period.
3. All written work will be corrected and returned, as soon as possible, to the pupil. Monthly and term examinations, and notebooks, are to be returned to the pupil and mistakes explained. They will be collected and turned over to

the Headmaster.

4. Study Hall Masters will observe the following regulations to the letter: The roll is to be called at the beginning of the Study Hall period. Not more than five minutes is allowed to sharpen pencils, get paper, books. Each student is to occupy a seat by himself. Studying together is forbidden. Silence will be strictly observed in the Study Hall. There will be no letter writing or reading of books not on the posted list. Only the Headmaster and the Infirmarian give permission to be absent from Study Hall. Permission must be in writing; no excuses will be accepted.

5. Except for illness, no Master may be absent or dismiss his class.

6. Unless excused by the Headmaster, all Masters will attend morning Roll Call.

7. On leaving classrooms, Masters will see that windows are closed, and everything is in good order. Classes will pick up paper before dismissal. Sharpening of pencils on the floor, or on desks, will not be allowed.

8. Masters will refrain from discussing school policy. All criticisms will be brought to the attention of the Headmaster."

In September 1939, Father Flye wrote: "I was talking to Mr. Koski, and he told me he had lost his temper. I said: 'Good, I hope you never find it.'"

Throughout the 1930s, Flye's journals were filled with criticisms of the way the Order managed St. Andrew's.

However, his iconoclastic outlook was not shared by everyone. Former faculty and former students generally gave the Order high marks for a job well done.

Father Flye did not go home each day and kick the cat, beat his wife, or get drunk. Instead, he vented his feelings in his journals, which were never meant to be read by anyone else. This activity let him carry on. His private writings were genuine, but they were unbalanced, unfair. For example, his 1930s complaints about meals never mentioned the Great Depression. In his journals, he did not mention the responsibilities carried by school administrators. His journals had plenty of criticisms, but never any solutions.

The Order monks led lives governed by exacting rules, so it was natural that they set down rigorous expectations for students; however, one would be hard-pressed to agree with Father Flye that the Order of the Holy Cross was "criminally inefficient" at St. Andrew's, as he wrote in his private journal.

One of the amazing characteristics of the history teacher was his ability to hide his true feelings. Students attending St. Andrew's did not know of his discontent. This is remarkable when you consider he worked at St. Andrew's for 36 years. Only through his journals and Grace's letters do we know of his torment.

Father Flye was remembered fondly for his friendliness toward St. Andrew's students, but the record shows he did not waste time with dimwits. He took a special interest in boys who showed intelligence, curiosity or creativity. Father

St. Andrew's chapel

Bonnell Spencer said the history teacher had a misplaced measure of superiority, especially toward the Order priests; however, Flye's "snobbery" was never obvious to most people.

An instructor at the University of the South, Robert S. Lancaster, reflected on Father Flye's quirky temperament: "When I looked at all the practical aspects of running St. Andrew's, and his complaints about mismanagement, I concluded the school wasn't about efficiency or even common sense. The place was about faith and love, and no person can argue that St. Andrew's School wasn't a big success."

❏ ❏ ❏

The March 16, 1924, edition of the *New York Times* carried a story with a provocative headline: "Ancient Rites Add To Episcopal Rift." The sub-headline read: "Liberals assail rites in which hair from the beard of Charles I is blessed at mountain school."

The article began: "The forthcoming issue of the *Churchman*, an organ of the liberal branch of the Episcopal Church, reveals that monks of the Order of the Holy Cross celebrated 'St. Charles's Day' at St. Andrew's School in Tennessee, by blessing and carrying in solemn procession a venerable relic, a single hair, from the whiskers of the martyred King Charles I of England. The ancient rites have created a controversy in the worldwide ranks of Episcopal church leaders."

The article explained: "St. Andrew's is located near the University of the South in Sewanee, where Bishop William Manning received his ecclesiastical training, and the controversial blessing of the King's beard had the Bishop's prior approval. The Order of the Holy Cross has its headquarters in West Park, N.Y., and a spokesman for the monastic order said the responsibility for the 'St. Charles Day' ritual lies elsewhere."

Subsequent to the *New York Times* article, the *Churchman* carried a blistering attack against Bishop Manning and the Order of the Holy Cross. Describing the order as a propagandist society against Modernists in Episcopal ranks, the article accused the order of "flooding the mails, over past months, with pamphlets attacking forward- thinking Modernists." The *Churchman* article continued: "St. Charles Day is not in the church calendar. This magazine asks, as the church spends money as 'defenders of the faith,' why it permits such celebrations as took place recently at St. Andrew's, constituting, in the opinion of the Modernists, a troubling standard of morality."

The event created a furor in church circles from London to San Francisco— one that placed St. Andrew's on the map. The St. Charles incident generated unprecedented heat. The rituals of January 30 were first reported by the *Nashville Banner*; however, Episcopal leaders did not take notice until the *New York Times* published the story on March 16, 1924, six weeks later.

The initial story in the Nashville newspaper was an account of what the reporter had seen—he had no idea his story would create a firestorm: "Visitors to the mountain school of St. Andrew's found the pages of time turned back to a long gone era. On this special day, monks celebrated the feast of St. Charles the Martyr, known to the world as Charles I of England, a man of purity and a martyr in that he gave up his life rather than forego his church. The pious fathers at this tiny school keep this day in memory of his death at Whitehall Palace. He was beheaded January 30, 1649."

In 1924, the Order of the Holy Cross was already in disfavor for its elaborate church services that smacked of Roman Catholicism; Episcopal liberals believed the blessing of a single hair was nothing less than medieval extremism. However, Father Liston Orum viewed the St. Charles the Martyr celebration as the high point in the school's history. Orum, who was serving as both Prior and Headmaster at the time, scheduled an unprecedented chapel ceremony lasting four hours, with an abundance of pomp that included Order priests wearing colorful, special-made vestments.

Father Flye did not participate in the festivities; however, Father Orum persuaded Grace Flye to get involved. Before the January 30 ceremony, she kept busy for three weeks designing and painting a silk banner honoring King Charles I. It was the only time she took part in any activity held inside the St. Andrew's chapel.

Walter Chambers, a St. Andrew's biology teacher and school historiographer for a number of years, wrote: "Mrs. Flye did a lot of work on the project. She painted a portrait of St. Charles on the purple banner, crowned and robed, holding in his hand an axe, symbol of his passion, and the palm, symbol of his victory. However, she did not attend the elaborate ceremonial, because she did not approve of it."

It is true that at the time of the controversial 1924 St. Charles Day celebration at St. Andrew's, the Order of the Holy Cross priests held church ceremonies with medieval elements. Depending on the service, their rituals had included monks lying prostrate on the chapel floor, the kissing of garments, and so on, but such practices were phased out by the late 1920s.

The hair from the beard of King Charles I was kept at St. Michael's Monastery on the St. Andrew's School campus for many years, but was eventually returned to the Order of the Holy Cross headquarters in West Park, New York.

❏ ❏ ❏

Rod Colson, a 1945 St. Andrew's graduate, said: "We had church every day and twice on Sunday." Chapel attendance was mandatory for students in his time, and had been for most of the school's history. However, beginning slowly in the late 1950s, and accelerated during the 1960s, there was a changing of the guard. The chapel services at St. Andrew's were modified to the extent that the solemn High Church liturgy was eliminated.

The St. Andrew's chapel was basically stripped of its Roman influences. The holy font near the chapel's entrance was removed. The Stations of the Cross were taken down. The Sunday night Benediction was terminated. One former faculty member described the period this way: "Students were no longer required to go to chapel. Those who did go had a nonchalant attitude. It was awful."

Traditional chapel services were replaced with Rejoice Mass, which consisted of "rock" music amplified through an electronic keyboard, with accompanying drums and guitars. Churchgoers heard tunes akin to those from Broadway productions such as: *Jesus Christ Superstar, Hair* and *Godspell.* The Age of Aquarius had arrived at St. Andrew's.[3]

The Episcopal prayer book was changed. Different versions of the prayer book were tried. One was called the *Zebra Book*, another the *Blue Book*, and yet another the *Red Book*. The Lord's Prayer was altered.

Traditionalists believed the Order of the Holy Cross had mislaid a precious spiritual dimension. Father Julien Gunn, who served as Prior at St. Andrew's from 1955 to 1965, and who resigned from the Order, wrote this: "To give you some idea of how poisoned the environment was, an entire class of seminarians was deemed unfit, not qualified. Homosexuals and draft dodgers were making a mockery of monasticism. It was best that the Order stepped away from running St. Andrew's."

Sunday evening Benediction at St. Andrew's chapel, 1940

Juanita Barry, former employee, reported: "My three children were students at St. Andrew's. All things considered, I thought the school did okay. However, when I went to work there in the late 1960s, it was a time of great change. The Order was falling apart up north and out west, and then it finally did leave the Mountain. The things that led up to it quitting the school were there for anyone to see. I was Father Martin's secretary for years, and I saw everything unraveling for the Order."

The sacred Stations of the Cross were removed from the chapel and simply discarded. The chapel's wicker chairs, dating back to 1917, were burned in a mammoth bonfire. Historical and religious artifacts, as well as tradition, were thrown out the window. The tenure of Father Franklin Martin, the Headmaster from 1960 through 1980, was marked by turbulent change. He reported: "From my start at St. Andrew's, I knew the Order was losing interest in the school, and it was more pronounced with every passing year. The basic values of the Order changed. The West Park monks had lost the dedication of the Order's founders back at the beginning of this century."

There was no question the Order was undergoing dramatic changes. The Father Superior of the Order of the Holy Cross, Father Leopold Kroll, resigned from the Order and married a former nun in 1957.[4] Father Flye knew that events taking place at St. Andrew's reflected changes that affected the the Episcopal church everywhere. During this period, he visited St. Andrew's School a number of times. It is not known if he discussed church problems with the Headmaster

Graduation day at St. Andrew's, 1950

or faculty members. In any event, he could only be a spectator to the fluctuations of the times. Change affected cultural values, politics, technology, and ecclesiastic traditions.

Late in his life, his personal pastor was Bishop William Millsaps, who recalled: "My talks with Father Flye were very revealing. Our views were the same on a number of matters. We went over the changes that were happening in the Episcopal church, and he was worried about the future. Long before the 1979 Prayer Book appeared, some were advocating rash liturgical changes, changes of language, even some changes in doctrine. Father Flye was one of those who saw the change of doctrine had to do with de-emphasizing the fallen nature of man, a watering-down of the sense of sin.

"He believed the 1928 Prayer Book with its emphasis upon sin and redemption was balanced, but the 1979 Prayer Book, while it has a reference to sin, also offers words which can be substituted for traditional prayers, and this type of thing chipped away at the holiness of our Christian doctrine. Father Flye said there had been a watering-down of genuine humility.

"I'm sure that if Father Flye were here today, he would claim that the 1979 Prayer Book isn't all bad, but there are weeds in the garden; in other words, the beginning of the end for the more valuable plants found in the church's garden. Father Flye really knew the 1928 Prayer Book, with its beautiful language. I don't know it for a fact, but I suspect, given his age and interests, he might have known a lot about the old 1896 Prayer Book also. He wouldn't have thought of it as just an historic relic. His refusal to use the 1979 Prayer Book was based on doctrine.

"In the 1920s, prior to the Wall Street crash, there were popular songs that every day told our ancestors: 'I'm getting better and the world is a happy place,' but along came the Great Depression followed by World War II to knock that into a cocked hat. This analogy shows the Christian faith can't afford to kid itself. If you don't take sin seriously, then Jesus didn't need to be crucified, and his death meant nothing. I'm talking about basic Christian values. Either Jesus was the Son of God, or he wasn't. Now, if he wasn't and he didn't have a direct link to God, what are we talking about? The revisionists are trying to change things to fit a false 'let us feel good' approach. I agreed with Father Flye, who had the conviction that there should be continuity. What was correct then should be correct now."

During an interview on June 22, 1995, Bishop Millsaps also explained why Father Flye opposed the ordination of women: "He was against it on the grounds that Jesus and the apostles were uniquely inspired, that even though Jesus honored his mother, and other women as well, he did not set them apart as apostles. It would be a crucial mistake to go against thousands of years of Christian heritage. I've tried to accept the Church has new insights, but I can't willy-nilly throw out everything to be politically correct for today's feminists. It would give a false image to the liturgy."

❏ ❏ ❏

[1] To many, Eucharist, Communion and Mass are interchangeable. The same can be said for the words Episcopal, Anglican and Church of England. In the Episcopal church, Communion was the term used for many years, but Eucharist is the favored one in use today. Mass is the term preferred by Roman Catholics.

[2] Father Flye's major complaint about St. Andrew's was that the school's rules were linked to the individual Headmaster. Some Headmasters were martinets; others "ran loose ships." No set pattern of rules and punishment was passed on from one Headmaster to the next. This lack of continuity put the history teacher in a fury. The Order of the Holy Cross provided Father Flye plenty leeway. For instance, several of his articles were published in the *Holy Cross Magazine*, and his writing always was critical of how students were treated. The Order simply ignored his ongoing dislike of the way St. Andrew's was administered.

[3] This description of the church services at St. Andrew's in the 1960s does not portray the present church services at St. Andrew's-Sewanee School. Currently, the 1979 Book of Common Prayer is used, and the chapel services are traditional in nature. The current student body is required to attend chapel services at least three times a week.

[4] The headquarters of the Order of the Holy Cross is still at West Park, New York. During a telephone interview in May 1998, Brother Robert Sevensky reported the size of the Order was 36 "life-professed" and 40 novices. The Order no longer uses the title "Father" for its ordained priests—they are now called "Brother."

CHAPTER 8

James Agee and David McDowell

The greatest pain is when you know the consequences too late.
—RUSSIAN PROVERB

*T*HE FATHER FLYE-JAMES AGEE FRIENDSHIP became famous in 1962 with the publication of *Letters of James Agee to Father Flye*. Out of nearly 1,000 letters from Agee, Flye chose a relative few to submit to the George Braziller Publishing Company. The priest had an enormous editing job, because many of the letters contained matters too personal for public viewing. Flye also had to struggle to decipher Agee's penmanship. He reported: "Jim's scratches are a combination of Swahili and Egyptian hieroglyphics."

In a letter dated August 3, 1962, Father Flye wrote to Arthur Ben Chitty: "In the project of publishing those letters I was not looking for any publicity for myself. The title of the book was the selection of the publisher. This is Jim Agee's book, not mine. After his death I felt they should be shared with others." At the time of the first printing, nobody had any inkling of the impact the letters would have. As it happened, they recharged an interest in James Agee and also put Father Flye under a spotlight.

Despite the impression given by *Letters of James Agee to Father Flye*, the two men did not have an inordinately close relationship. Their contact was generally confined to letters. For long periods of time they did not see each other in person. Agee was never the central figure in the priest's life. However, the Agee-Flye linkage took on legendary proportions.

Flye was ill at ease at the suggestion that he was a substitute parent to Agee. He said: "Some have felt Jim saw in me something of a surrogate father, but this

129

Oil portrait by Grace Flye of James Agee as a St. Andrew's acolyte

was not the case." Their bond was never like father and son, with mixed emotions of competition and commitment. Most fathers would have been critical of Agee's excesses; Flye kept his disapproval to himself. Onlookers thought the priest was overly tolerant of Agee's failings. In fact, Flye was nonjudgmental when it came to all his friends.

Father Flye met James Agee in 1919, when the boy was nine and a St. Andrew's pupil. Jim lived in a dormitory even though his mother, Laura Agee, resided nearby in one of the campus houses. The priest remembered: "Rufus, as he was then called, was an intelligent boy, fond of reading. He was interested in fossils and shells, and knew many by their scientific names. We discussed numerous subjects: foreign countries, rabbits, kangaroos. He was tender-hearted, with a sympathy for suffering. I had an affection for him at that lovely age."[1]

Agee was at St. Andrew's for several years before he left to attend his first year of public high school in Knoxville. He hated Knoxville, and began writing Flye on a regular basis. Their camaraderie was enhanced when they toured parts of England and France by bicycle in 1925. Agee's stepfather, Father Erskine Wright, financed the trip. The following fall Agee entered Phillips Exeter Academy, a highly regarded private high school in New England.[2]

Agee then enrolled at Harvard University. While at Harvard, Agee developed an interest in Hollywood films. He spent his weekends watching movies at all-night theaters. He was so enamored with camera angles, lighting techniques (and actress Helen Hayes) that he saw *Coquette* seven times in one week. His keen attention to details paid dividends later when he became a film critic.

During his college tenure, he wrote poetry that was favorably reviewed by well-known critics such as Edna St. Vincent Millay and Robert Frost. Agee wrote: "Their verdict is that I can do a lot if I don't give up and write advertisements." He published a book of verse titled *Permit Me Voyage*. While at Harvard, he began to drink heavily.

Agee's Tennessee childhood provided the backdrop for his two novels, *The Morning Watch* and *A Death in the Family*. He also wrote *Let Us Now Praise Famous Men*, a nonfiction study of a southern sharecropper family. He wrote features for *Fortune*, *Time* and *The Nation* magazines. He wrote Hollywood screenplays, and is best known for his work on *The African Queen* and *Night of the Hunter*.

As a movie critic, Agee had few peers. He had a remarkable talent for the high-sheen writing then associated with *Time*, but he had a nagging feeling that he should be doing something more artistic and creative. Despite the financial hazards, he left the magazine to strike out on his own as a free-lancer. He was alternately a film critic, poet, screenwriter and novelist. His successes were erratic; to meet expenses he was constantly forced to go back into journalism. He was plagued with self-doubt, depression, and extreme mood swings. He engaged in periods of intense work, but lacked self-discipline. Biographers agree that his literary output was small.

Agee's personal routines were self-destructive. By the time he was voting age, he had formed his work habits—he wrote late into the night in small penciled script, while sipping gin, chain-smoking and listening to jazz. Insomnia and alcohol assaulted his gangly body, guilt and indecision took a toll on his psyche. Adultery and drinking ruined his three marriages. He wallowed in regret, but refused to curtail his excesses. He neglected his teeth and went days without bathing. His life was full of failed dreams.

George Fielding, a Greenwich Village neighbor, said: "Jack London wrote fifty books before he died at 40. If Jim had worked that hard, he would have done outstanding work. God only knows what he could have accomplished. But, no, he was up all night drinking and playing his damn jazz records."

By the 1940s, Agee's reputation as a promising writer had grown, and he mingled with a number of eminent poets, artists and authors, including Truman Capote and Thomas Wolfe. He also rubbed shoulders with pretenders to the throne in the artistic world of Greenwich Village. When Flye began his summer duties in New York City in the early 1940s, he had not seen Agee for some years, and he looked forward to seeing him again. He suspected he would meet interesting conversationalists at Agee's apartment, and he did. For example, one night at Agee's place he met Whittaker Chambers, the ex-communist who had been the key witness in the 1949 perjury trial of Alger Hiss. Flye and the journalist became friends, and Flye visited Chambers several times at his farm near Westminster, Maryland.

On May 16, 1955, James Agee had a fatal heart attack. He was 46. He had not achieved what he sought as a writer, and considered himself a failure. None of his work was in print. He left $450 in a savings account. He did not own a life insurance policy. His widow, Mia, was left destitute. His death went unnoted except by a few friends.

However, less than a decade later, Agee was famous, almost a cult idol. His posthumous fame came after *A Death in the Family* won a Pulitzer Prize in 1958. Then, in 1961, Tad Mosel's stage adaptation of the novel, titled *All The Way Home*, also won a Pulitzer. The prizes drew attention to Agee's work and life, and in literary circles his writings, including his poetry and film reviews, became fashion-

David McDowell, 1935

able and were re-visited. One critic wrote: "When a writer drinks too much, smokes too much, declares he is placing life before art, and dies early, he almost certainly will be the stuff of legend." Twenty years after he died, all of Agee's books had been reissued and were back in print. The legend of James Agee has had the real lasting power. His agonized life captivated critics, perhaps as much as any words he put to paper. Time has been good to his literary reputation.

David McDowell, a 1936 St. Andrew's graduate, was the person who made James Agee famous. David had an aptitude for writing, which came to Father Flye's attention. When Agee visited St. Andrew's in the mid-1930s, the teacher introduced him to David, a senior at the time. McDowell later said: "I was in total awe when I first met Agee. He was an author and I was a schoolboy. I had a bad case of hero worship."

McDowell excelled at St. Andrew's. He was class valedictorian and a star athlete, earning a football scholarship to Vanderbilt University. He later transferred to Kenyon College. While at Kenyon, McDowell married another student, Margene Smith, who later gave birth to a boy named Alan.

McDowell graduated from Kenyon College, served in the U.S. Army in World War II, reached the rank of Lieutenant, and was wounded in the North African campaign. While convalescing at a military hospital in Italy, he met Maria Luisa Taglienti, who came from a well-to-do Italian family with ties to royalty. Her family called her Mara.

Mara was only 17 and smitten with the handsome American officer. She did not speak English then, so she and McDowell conversed in French. Mara's family opposed her seeing him; however, she was hopelessly in love.

McDowell obtained a divorce from Margene, married Mara, and they moved to Paris where he studied at the Sorbonne, supported by the G.I. Bill. At this time, for some unexplained reason, McDowell began to insist that his young wife be called Madeline.[3]

After several years, David and Madeline McDowell moved to New York City. McDowell's writing and editing skills were easily recognizable. He worked at Random House, and then was a senior editor with the *Saturday Evening Post*, and then Crown Publishing. Meanwhile, McDowell began to socialize with Agee.

They stayed up all night drinking, while their wives stayed home alone.

McDowell eventually became editor-in-chief at McDowell-Obolensky, a publishing house that printed esoteric books by unknown authors. They were quality works, but never best-sellers. David's decision to publish the melancholy *A Death in the Family* made publishing history, and his role in creating the Agee legend was pivotal.

McDowell-Obolensky did not have a big budget, so David circumvented traditional marketing methods and instead used his personal contacts to spread the word about the novel. He was no stranger to wealthy patrons of the arts, and he was a frequent guest at manicured estates in Scarsdale, White Plains and the ultra-rich

Maria Taglienti, age 17

Hamptons on Long Island. He wrote in his diary: "I like Gloria Vanderbilt, but I can't stand her shit husband." His position as editor-in-chief of a publishing firm gave him entree to the rarefied world of *belles-lettres* influence.

David McDowell's 1952 Christmas card mailing list was impressive: Bennett Cerf, Truman Capote, Robert Fitzgerald, Dylan Thomas, Gore Vidal, Robert Bly, Marilyn Monroe, Tennessee Williams, John Gielgud, John Stuart, William Carlos Williams, Tallulah Bankhead, Caroline Gordon, Agatha Young, John Carridine, Mario Puzo, Louie Armstrong, Benny Goodman.

McDowell frequented the Century Club, an exclusive Manhattan club for movers and shakers in the literary world. Without being too obvious, he planted the idea that Agee's novel deserved recognition. His efforts had a word-of-mouth ripple effect among the powers-that-be.

Warren Eyster was the Managing Editor at McDowell-Obolensky at that time: "We were a small publisher, only six people on the payroll. My job was a catch-all from the designing of book jackets, deciding what paper to use, to arguing about prices. McDowell ran the operation when *A Death In The Family* appeared. He was the very best at public relations. He knew everybody who was somebody in town. Salesmen don't know books and editors don't appreciate sales departments. David knew both from all angles, and this gave him an edge.

"Questions of worthiness and politics aside, the Pulitzer is a much-desired honor, and being an opportunist, David ran with the ball as far as he could. He knew the Agee book had a good chance of securing the Pulitzer, so he cajoled the sappy owner we worked for, Ivan Obolensky, to spring for some money.

David bought advertising in trade magazines and newspapers. He took advantage of the fact that Agee had the reputation as a New York movie critic. David cleverly took the approach: 'Look here, one of our own makes good.' He knew New York writers were clannish to a fault."

Warren Eyster added: "McDowell was respected. If he said it was important, then reviewers and people awarding prizes listened. Half of his job was to get reviewers to pay attention. He was the one with the clout where it counted. Jim Agee would only be an obscure footnote if it had not been for David's efforts."

David Madden, prolific southern writer, reported: "I first met David McDowell when he was at Crown Publishing. He published two of my volumes: *Cassandra Singing* and *Bijou*. My sense about the Pulitzer is uneven. People in Hollywood will tell you the movie getting the Oscar isn't necessarily the best one, but it is an honor. A friend of mine, Robert O. Butler, got a Pulitzer, and I saw what it can do. It can change your life. Regarding Agee's sad novel, David McDowell was powerful enough to make a difference. He knew the right people."

McDowell fraternized in the high social strata, and took Father Flye to upper-crust parties, where they mixed with such luminaries as Cerf, Elsa Lanchester, Jascha Heifetz, and Celeste Holm. The priest liked being at the wine-and-cheese gatherings, but he was never awed. McDowell recalled: "Father Flye was more interested in meeting the better-read person than he was a show biz headliner."

Father Flye was pleased when his association with Agee drew wide interest; by proxy, the soft-spoken priest was suddenly famous also. His Manhattan apartment became a magnet for feature writers. In the late 1950s and the 1960s he was interviewed numerous times by publications such as the *New Yorker,* the *Village Voice,* and the *New York Times,* but the resulting articles never reported the priest's contributions to Agee's literary prestige.

The facts are irrefutable: David McDowell put Jim Agee's name on the literary map, and it was Flye who brought the two together. When Agee died, *A Death in the Family* was a collection of scraps and pieces; no finished manuscript existed. Mia Agee, Flye and McDowell put the parts together that became the finished novel. McDowell did the final editing at a secluded house near Millboro Springs, Virginia.

Father Flye spent more than two years sorting through the correspondence that became *Letters of James Agee to Father Flye.* A *New York Times* review claimed the book was similar to F. Scott Fitzgerald's *The Crackup,* as a self-portrait on the American scene. *Nashville Tennessean* reviewer Louise Davis wrote: "Once under the Agee spell, the hunger for more is sharp. The tragedy in the revealing letters is that he was beginning to harness his gifts when suddenly it was all over." Bowen Ingram, Tennessee novelist and short story author, wrote: "These letters bring James Agee to life again. I'm glad he is back. What a wonderful thing it is that Father Flye kept the letters. That he allowed them to be published is best of all."

After *Letters of James Agee to Father Flye* was published, at McDowell's urging,

St. Andrew's Messenger

James Rufus Agee
1909-1955

Spring 1973

Above: 1972 "Agee Week" panelists Dwight MacDonald, Robert Fitzgerald, David McDowell, and Father Flye

Right: Author Bowen Ingram, Father Flye and Dr. Charles Carr at Agee Week festivities, 1972

Agee Week panelists, left to right: Dr. Andrew Lytle, Mr. Brainerd Cheney, Mr. Warren Eyster, Mr. Frederick Manfred, Mr. David Madden, Mr. David McDowell, the Rev. James H. Flye, Dr. William Stott, 1972

Father Flye visited various universities, including Vanderbilt, Rollins, and Syracuse, to speak about James Agee. This amplified the writer's mythology.

Arthur Ben Chitty observed: "There were tons of articles about Father Flye and his kinship with James Agee. But there was a lot more to the man that was never put in a magazine. Father Flye's main characteristic was humility, a total absence of pride. He'd never talk about his deeds, yet he had a lifetime of them. He knew hordes of folks as famous as Agee. Father Flye was not a name-dropper. He would go out and have drinks with Tennessee Williams, for instance, but he would never tell anyone about it."[4]

With much fanfare, "James Agee Week" was held in the fall of 1972 at St. Andrew's School. The speakers generally fell into two categories: those who knew James Agee or David McDowell personally, or those who had been inspired by Agee's prose.

On the morning of October 14, 1972, approximately 200 guests, dignitaries, scholars and Agee family members (Agee's widow, Mia; her son, John; and a few of Agee's cousins), met inside the St. Andrew's chapel to begin James Agee Week. The opening day speakers were the Headmaster, Father Franklin Martin; Charles Carr, President of the Board of Trustees at St. Andrew's; Father Conner Lynn, the Father Superior of the Order of the Holy Cross; Bishop Robert Campbell; and David McDowell, who was the chairman of the festivities.

On the following days, panel discussions were led by notable scholars, including: Dr. James Lee, a St. Andrew's graduate, editor of the *Journal of the American Novel* and an English teacher at North Texas State University; Dr. William Stott, James Agee authority from the University of Texas; St. Andrew's alumnus Charles Angermeyer, of the University of Minnesota; Andrew Lytle, editor of the *Sewanee Review;* Arthur Ben Chitty, University of the South historiographer; Allen Tate, poet and novelist; Frances Cheney, chief officer of the joint Vanderbilt-Peabody Libraries; Robert W. Daniel, head of the English Department at Kenyon College. Also there were William Peyton and Edmund Phillips, St. Andrew's graduates, who had attended classes with James Agee.

On hand for the occasion were: Huntington Hartford, producer of *The Bride Comes to Yellow Sky*; John Huston, director of the Oscar-winning *The African Queen*; Dwight MacDonald, staff critic at the *New Yorker*; Louis Kronenberger, editor at *Fortune*; Robert Saudek, producer of Agee's *Omnibus* series about Abraham Lincoln; Also authors Brainard Cheney, Warren Eyster, Margaret Long, Madison Jones, Walker Percy, Frederick Manfred, David Madden and Peter Taylor.

Representatives from Kenyon, Vanderbilt, Harvard, Louisiana State and University of the South came to the event, as well as book editors from the *Nashville Tennessean* and the *Louisville Courier-Journal*. Television stations from Chattanooga and Nashville filed reports from the campus.

James Agee Week was a public relations bonanza for St. Andrew's. Agee was not a graduate of the school, but his connection to St. Andrew's and Father Flye was well-known. Dedication of the Agee Memorial Library was an opportunity for St. Andrew's to get national news coverage, and school officials took advantage of the occasion as best they could.

Then in his late 80s, Father Flye was present, and he naturally received a great deal of attention. Though he was suffering from arthritis, he enjoyed the social activity. His health forced him to nap every afternoon. He could not be at all of the seminars, but he appeared at many of them.

Headmaster Martin reported: "Father Flye was a bright star that week. Oh, what a great man. Of course, I had heard about him long before I ever met him. He was legendary. I first met him in the late 1960s, and convinced him to revisit St. Andrew's, which he did. I lived in the same house where he lived for many years. I remember he came to the front door, and stood still with his eyes closed for a long time. It was such a moving experience for him to return. He stayed with us three days. He talked to the student body and visited some classes. Everywhere he went he was surrounded by students, especially the younger kids. It was amazing.

"No politician ever had Father Flye's charisma. Youngsters can detect falseness right away; they also spot genuine love immediately. They saw what a beautiful man he was, and that he was interested in them. He had so many things to say that stuck with you. Many of the alumni told me how much they loved him and what a great teacher he had been. Just a wonderful person and priest. All of us felt Father Flye being there for Agee Week was icing on the cake."

Bowen Ingram said: "Being there was momentous for me. Besides talking to people who knew James Agee, there was another bonus. For years I heard the name Father Flye spoken by men in a tone of respect that made me wish I could have know him. Meeting him was delectable. His courteous demeanor was an echo of times past."

David Madden admitted he had second thoughts about attending. He felt the Agee mythology, enhanced by the printing of Agee's letters to Flye, had produced an unreal sugar-coated romanticism. Madden had not liked Agee's poetry, claiming it was too pretentious, and found *The Morning Watch* tedious, but the atmosphere at the school that week was such that Madden reconsidered his ideas. He later wrote: "Jim Agee's presence was felt during that uncannily felicitous time on the mountain."

Some writers who came to St. Andrew's that week were not necessarily Agee fans; friendship compelled them to accept David McDowell's invitation. But like Madden, by the end of the week, a few of them acquired a new appreciation of Agee's work. Walker Percy said: "Agee has brought back poetry into modern prose."

In many ways, literature is like art—beauty lies in the eyes of the beholder. Agee's writing didn't generate worldwide acclaim, and some of his work baffled readers. Stanley Hole said: "I talked to Father Flye about *The Morning Watch*. I just didn't get it and asked him to clarify. He tried to explain, but I couldn't understand where Agee was coming from. Much of *The Morning Watch* didn't make sense to me."

Hole's puzzlement was not unique. Reviewing a passage where Agee used four pages to describe men's overalls, critic Al Stapleton wrote: "It is the question of overkill. I'm reminded of *Ivanhoe* where the forest is described ad nauseam. Ernest Hemingway leaves something to your imagination, but not James Agee."

The students at St. Andrew's were prisoners of the Agee Week mania. They had no choice. Upon the direction of the Headmaster, every English class during the fall semester was assigned to study Agee's poetry, criticism, short stories, novellas, scripts and correspondence. During James Agee Week, all classes were immersed in his product. The school was awash with his words.[5]

Some of the faculty thought the Headmaster had overdone it. One history teacher said to a colleague: "This week is ridiculous. Too much attention has been paid to a drunk who didn't make it as a writer when he was alive. The best career move Agee ever made was dropping dead at an early age." Another teacher voiced his contempt about Agee's immoral lifestyle: "Do these supercilious asses really think James Agee should be a role model for our boys?" Another said: "The way people are acting this week, it wouldn't surprise me if they suggested we name the school Saint Agee's." A chemistry teacher, weary of trying to analyze the nuances of Agee's writing, asked his class one afternoon: "Will you be happy when this week is over?" The class erupted in a loud cheer.

Biology teacher Walter Chambers remembered: "There is one scene in *The Morning Watch* about several boys sneaking off to go swimming, and in the process they kill a snake. One professor from Sewanee was waxing about the symbolism in Agee's writing, claiming the snake story was a metaphor on good and evil. I was disgusted after three days of hearing nonsense about hidden meanings, so I told the professor he was full of crap."

The climax of the week was an address by Dr. Robert Fitzgerald at a Saturday night banquet. Fitzgerald, poet and translator of Latin at Harvard, had first met Agee while the two were students at Harvard, and later they were co-workers in New York City. Fitzgerald commented: "We came here to see a library dedicated in his name at an institution that he attended, and we have to face questions as how he would like this. His works are the objects of our piety. Given his sense of this aspect, he was sensitive to the pretense institutions claim for themselves, openly or by implication. His skin crawled at manifestations that were phony. Saint Andrew's has not only named a library for James Agee but has, deliberately and with ceremony, paid attention for a week to what he actually said."

James Agee Week was McDowell's idea. He spent three years on the project, collecting originals or copies of almost everything Agee had written, plus film clips and other memorabilia.[6] He had the daunting challenge of getting commitments from important individuals, asking them to travel and interrupt their busy lives. The fact that so many prominent people agreed to participate was a tribute to Agee's memory, and to McDowell's friendships. St. Andrew's had never before hosted such a gathering of celebrated personalities.

Mathematics teacher Kenneth "Speedy" Speegle reported: "I was mostly a chauffeur during 'Agee Week,' shuttling folks to and from the airport. Most of the big hitters, the famous writers and poets and movie producers, didn't stay for the whole week. Their participation was only for a day or two."

By any measure, James Agee Week was a success, and no person enjoyed the experience more than David McDowell. He had accomplished what he set out to do: to remind the literary world of Agee's singular talent.

There was another reason behind his celebration. Fourteen years had elapsed since the Pulitzer Prize had been awarded for Agee's novel, and McDowell's life had deteriorated since then. He desperately needed reaffirmation. James Agee Week was a counterbalance to the fact that he was 53 years old, unhappy with his career prospects, and increasingly depressed. The festivities in the fall of 1972 were the high-water mark of his closing years.[7]

□ □ □

What happened to McDowell? A perfectionist, he cared deeply about literary quality, and he became a victim of the changing times. His arrival on the New York City literary scene coincided with the beginning of the decline of quality publishing. Respected magazines had begun to emphasize the sensational. A new liberalism was advocating "freedom of speech" to the extreme. Obscenities were creeping into print in books and magazines. Television had started to make its impact (the 1949 inauguration of Harry S. Truman had been televised, giving only a hint of the future influence of the medium). It did not occur overnight, but the print media, especially magazines, would become desperate to stay alive commercially. McDowell wrote to Father Flye in 1950: "This vulgarization is degrading the publishing business, and this makes me ill." As time went by, McDowell felt more isolated as he held on to his literary standards.

Madeline reviewed her husband's work history in New York City: "David was at Random House, and he impressed everyone when he got Whittaker Chamber's book *Witness*. Random House thought David walked on water at the time. David was on speaking terms with every important person in the city. For example, he was a friend of former president Richard Nixon. David went to drink martinis at Mr. Nixon's fancy apartment in Manhattan. But David was never happy. He complained Random House didn't publish the better authors, so one day he came home and announced he had quit his job. I was totally surprised, but he told me not to worry."

David Madden remembered: "McDowell was riding pretty high at one time. Bennett Cerf once called David the 'Golden Boy' of publishing. However, David had a loud disagreement with Obolensky, who originally had the small publishing house for tax purposes. The business has had its share of wealthy owners who use their publishing houses for pet projects. Ivan stuck his finger into the operations, and told David what books to print. David knew the work wasn't up to professional standards. One day David finally said he wouldn't be associated with a vanity press for Obolensky's socialite friends. Their relationship ended with a venomous flavor."

Madden did not mention the crucial part that McDowell's personal life played in his fall from grace. McDowell had a private bar in his office at McDowell-Obolensky, and the close proximity to Johnny Walker and Southern Comfort was too tempting. Sometimes McDowell and his secretary, Martha Murphy, who drank heavily with him, failed to show up for work for days on end. McDowell eventually married Martha, but their union was doomed from the start, and did not last long.

Madeline continued: "When David has his falling out with Ivan Obolensky, he had been drinking on the job for four years, and it was getting worse as time went by. In those days, the word alcoholism wasn't used. People would say things like 'tipsy,' or 'he had a little too much,' and chronic drinking was treated as a joke. Nightclub comedians used to build their whole act around a man being sloshed. But, for me, living with an alcoholic was never a laughing matter."

After Agee died in the spring of 1955, Father Flye conducted a Requiem Mass at St. Luke's Chapel in New York City. His words included: "It is not the custom of this church to eulogize its dead. I can only say that those who knew James Agee will never forget him." The priest had lost his beloved Grace, his teaching position at St. Andrew's, and Agee, all within a period of 15 months. It was a time that sorely tested his soul.

Agee was buried in Hillsdale, New York. As he walked away from the grave, Flye said to McDowell: "I can't go through this again. I love you as much as I did him. Promise me you will outlive me. Please promise me this." Stunned and momentarily speechless, McDowell finally replied: "Yes, Father Flye, you have my solemn word that I will stay alive longer than you." As events unfolded, McDowell's graveside vow became his anchor in rough seas.

As the years passed, McDowell lost his esteemed reputation. He lost the respect of colleagues. His decline was tragic, laced with whiskey-soaked fanciful ideas. One of his daughters, Beverly, remembered: "Dad's promise to Father Flye kept him alive. I know this to be a fact. Dad constantly talked about Father Flye. He was the most meaningful figure in Dad's life. Father Flye was the man who was always there for guidance, understanding, and I guess, forgiveness."

Beverly McDowell continued: "Dad ended up hating New York City, I mean he despised the place. In his heyday he had loved it, but all that changed. He moved to Nashville in the late 1970s, and he took me with him. We moved into an apartment on Belle Meade Boulevard, noted for its mansions and bluebloods. Dad and I used to joke about our moving up in the world."

McDowell tried to stay active in literary circles, staying in touch with authors and editors and occasionally editing projects sent to him by friends. He began to call himself a consultant. Little by little, he started selling his literary valuables: letters, papers, first edition books, correspondence with famous people. One by one, his volumes were purchased by rare book dealers.

He sold his grandfather's stamp collection, owned by his mother's side of the family for nearly 100 years. He sold a letter with Ezra Pound's signature, and had tears in his eyes when it was handed over. He gave away a series of first edition books and autographed books, as collateral for a loan from Craig Oxford, a long-time friend. To make matters worse, fire destroyed his Nashville apartment, and his precious book collection was essentially ruined. Before he left Nashville, he sold what few books were left at bargain basement prices. It was a frightful time for McDowell, a nightmare of disheartening circumstances.

McDowell's other daughter, Claire Friedenberg, said: "Dad was not the same after the fire ruined his Nashville apartment. It had a sun porch which he dearly loved. The great loss, of course, was the thousands of books he had collected. The fire was a catalyst; after that, his outlook darkened. He thought his life was cursed, and I suppose it was.

"Dad had one thing in common with Father Flye; he also knew poetry as well and told great stories at the drop of a hat. He was always spinning a yarn and reciting poetry. Even though he had his faults, Dad tried to be a good parent."

The early 1980s saw McDowell traveling alone from state to state, visiting writers he had helped when he was an editor in New York City. Many of his visits parroted *The Man Who Came To Dinner*. McDowell proclaimed he was only "dropping in for a few days," then stayed weeks or months. Inevitably, he was asked to leave. Frederick Manfred, Warren Eyster, David Madden and a number of other writers were involuntary hosts to McDowell's gypsy lifestyle.

Warren Eyster recalled: "He stayed with me and my wife twice in those days, for four months each time. McDowell had aged terribly. He was losing his memory and had some trouble talking. It was sad. He went to live with Doc Santee, and then Peter Taylor. All he had was a small check from Social Security. His cash situation was desperate."

McDowell then went to live with his youngest son, Brian, who was the head football coach at St. Andrew's-Sewanee School. Brian McDowell recounted: "I graduated from St. Andrew's in 1970, so I was tickled pink to be on the faculty at a school I loved dearly. I kept in touch with my sisters, Beverly and Claire, along with my half-brother, Alan, so I knew of Pop's problems. I was apprehensive about him coming to live with me, but what could I do? He was my flesh-and-blood.

"Somehow Pop got the idea that he wanted to be a teacher at SAS. He might have been a good teacher what with his knowledge of French, English, good writing, good editing, but he couldn't stay sober. Having him live in my apartment at the school was an embarrassing catastrophe. He was seen several times sprawled on the floor, unconscious in his own vomit. He was a pathetic drunk. There is no question that Pop's behavior was the reason my contract wasn't renewed. I taught at SAS for two school years, 1981 through 1983.[8]

"We managed to get Pop into the Veteran's Administration hospital in Murfreesboro to dry out. It is known as a family intervention. It was a tough period for everybody. Pop then started his traveling act again. He would go and stay with friends, sponging off people, until he was asked to leave. He told everybody he was writing, but it was all a lie. It was painful for all of us. The sauce had taken over his life completely."

One of McDowell's few friends at this time was Archie C. Stapleton, Jr. , a Monteagle-based Episcopal priest. Stapleton's style was such that that he preferred counseling people over a cup of coffee at a local cafe rather than at his parish office. His relationship with McDowell was one of "live and let live."

Brian McDowell continued: "When he died, Pop lived alone in a small cabin at The Assembly in Monteagle. It was several days before anyone found his body. Someone had noticed water running from under his cabin, and they had to break in. A faucet had been left running. They said he probably had a heart attack."

David McDowell died on April 7, 1985, at age 67. He kept his promise to Father Flye. He knew he could finally let go. McDowell and Father Flye died within days of each other.

From his home in Luverne, Minnesota, author Frederick Manfred wrote to Claire Friedenberg in a letter dated April 10, 1985: "It was so sad to learn about your father. He called me about one month ago asking me if he could borrow some money. I told him that I'd try to send him some.

"It's almost thirty years now since I first met David. I'd gone to New York to find an editor. I first asked Francis Brown, editor of the *New York Times*, who recommended Roger Straus. I left word at Straus' office, and went to New Jersey to visit William Carlos Williams and Clayton Hoaglands. When I told them that I needed an editor, they recommended your father. Williams called your Dad immediately. He had been out late the night before, a Saturday, but he got up, shaved and showered, and came right over. I gave him a copy of my *Lord Grizzly*—my *Morning Red* was on its way to Alan Swallow, so he missed that—and from that Sunday morning on, we were always good friends.

"After getting your sad news, I called Andrew Lytle. He knew why I was calling. Both of us remarked that if David hadn't been so prideful, he might have become a great power in publishing. We both agreed he was superb editor, the best. However, he drank too much, and couldn't get the monkey off his back. Lytle said: 'Literature suffered when he didn't achieve his full stature.'"

Manfred concluded: "Thinking back on those days, my life was so rich when I flew in to see David at Alice Astor's townhouse, and also her home up in Rhineback. David and I had so much fun together. Who of us could have predicted that things would turn out the way they did? What webs we mortals weave. I will miss your father."

❏ ❏ ❏

Why did Father Flye tolerate Agee's and McDowell's destructive habits? First and foremost, he was a priest who naturally "hated the sin, but loved the sinner." No clergyman was more pardoning of human nature. [9]

Beverly McDowell wrote: "Father Flye understood that alcoholism, which struck so many close to him, is a disease. He knew that the devastation it brings to those with the illness and their loved ones is not merely bad behavior. I know from Father Flye's own words to me that his tolerance of my Dad, came not from pastoral obligation, but from heartfelt friendship and genuine love."

Agee's and McDowell's lives were parallel in many ways: Both were already writing prose at an early age; both could be charming; both traveled in Europe with Father Flye; both loved him as a parent; both had dangerous drinking problems; both had self-inflicted marital difficulties; and both failed to fulfill their promising potential.

❏ ❏ ❏

[1] Mrs. Flye painted a double portrait of James Agee when he was ten years old. In a 1920 letter to her father, A. C. Houghton, she wrote: "When Rufus was over, I painted a study of him. It's on the wall in the sitting room. I wanted a spot of red on the wall, and his small red cassock showed. In a few days after the first study, I then painted another one. It is a rough sketch, and an entirely different boy. Yet both to me were so just like him. I will show you sometime. Quick studies catch something that go so fast they fly out the window."

[2] Laura Agee published a pamphlet of religion poems in 1922, which came to the attention of the Bursar at St. Andrew's, Father Erskine Wright. Born into a rich Philadelphia family, Wright was proper and smug to a fault, the opposite of Laura's first husband. She married Father Wright in 1924. Both were buried at the St. Andrew's cemetery.

[3] Madeline McDowell reported that she and David and Father Flye: "... had a great trip in 1948. We left Paris and went to Italy where we visited Rome, Capri, Naples, Sorrento and Pompeii. Father Flye really enjoyed seeing the Coliseum and St. Peter's. Much of the time we stayed with my relatives, so our costs were kept to a minimum. I remember discovering how light Father Flye traveled. One afternoon, while he was out with David, I thought I would iron his clothes. In his battered suitcase there was very little: crumpled newspapers, a priestly collar, a toothbrush, some socks and underwear. That was it. Nothing else."

[4] Father Flye first met Josephine "Jo" Healy at St. Luke's Church in New York City, and it was she who introduced him to Tennessee Williams. Jo, a Theater Guild employee, befriended the playwright long before he became famous. The Flye-Williams friendship was centered around

poetry. Both had started composing verse as small boys. The "Tennessee Williams Center," a modern performing arts complex, was formally dedicated in May, 1999, at the University of the South. The playwright left his estate to a university he never visited. He had learned of Sewanee through his grandfather, the Reverend Walter E. Dakin, who was a student at the university's School of Theology in the late 1890s. Tennessee Williams' will specified he wished to underwrite the program to promote creative writing and also honor his grandfather.

[5] Despite the emphasis on Agee's work, James Agee Week did not leave a lasting impression with every student. A few weeks later, the Headmaster was talking about James Agee Week with a visiting parent, and asked a boy about to enter the dining hall: "Tom, tell us what was the most important event in recent St. Andrew's history." Without hesitation, the boy said: "It was beating Sewanee Academy 6-0 at their Homecoming football game."

[6]CHRONOLOGY

1957: David McDowell and Ivan Obolensky form a partnership. McDowell-Obolensky publish *A Death in the Family,* which generates critical acclaim and wins the 1957 Pulitzer Prize for fiction.

1958: McDowell-Obolensky publish *Agee on Film: Reviews and Comments* in 1958. Respected as the classic of the genre, it is required reading for any serious student of film.

1960: McDowell-Obolensky publish *Agee on Film: Five Film Scripts by James Agee,* with an introduction by John Huston. The book includes *Noa-Noa, The African Queen, The Blue Hotel, Night of the Hunter,* and *The Bride Comes to Yellow Sky.* Houghton Mifflin reissues the almost-forgotten *Let Us Now Praise Famous Men,* complete with photos by Walker Evans. In stark contrast to its initial reception, the book soon becomes a best seller. Tad Mosel's theatrical adaptation of *A Death in the Family* becomes a Broadway hit. Titled *All the Way Home,* the stage play also wins a Pulitzer Prize.

1962: Publisher George Braziller issues *James Agee's Letters to Father Flye.* Gleaned from 30 years of correspondence, the book elevates Agee's status, and puts Father Flye in the literary spotlight.

1963: The film version of *All the Way Home* premieres, produced by David Susskind, directed by Alex Segal, and starring Robert Preston and Jean Simmons.

October 14, 1972: The James Agee Memorial Library is dedicated. The Agee Room at St. Andrew's School becomes a repository for Agee-related materials.

[7]Seven months after James Agee Week, the 1973 St. Andrew's School Yearbook was dedicated to Father Flye. The dedicatory page read: "During James Agee Week last October, Father Flye returned to participate in this event and offer his knowledge to help create a more vivid picture of the past at St. Andrew's." Three years later, the school again honored the former history and civics teacher. During May 1976, Father Flye was given a document that read, in part: "One of the most beloved and committed teachers of our time, noted for his rare scholarship, his articulate prose, his love of learning, his compassion for students, his commitment to his Church and his God, it is with a sense of thanksgiving and gratitude that the Board of Trustees hereby presents the first Saint Andrew's Medal for a non-alumnus to Father James Harold Flye." In May, 1980, the St. Andrew's chapter of Alpha Beta Kappa of the National Honor Society declared

Father Flye to be an honorary member. Juanita Barry, a long-time St. Andrew's School employee, said: "One positive thing about Father Franklin Martin, the Headmaster from 1960 until 1980, was that he adored Father Flye. He said the history teacher had not been treated right by the Order of the Holy Cross. Though it was late in coming, he saw to it that Father Flye was honored at St. Andrew's."

[8] Brian "Coach Mac" McDowell became a well-liked physical education teacher and wrestling coach in neighboring Grundy County, Tennessee. He brought the Grundy County wrestling program to new heights in 1999 when it competed at the national level.

[9] Father Flye believed there was a distinct difference between personal and institutional sins. He tolerated Agee's and McDowell's misbehavior, but was critical of St. Andrew's officials. In his thinking, some administrators committed grievous institutional errors. Decades after the incident, Flye spoke with emotion about the Headmaster who censured a boy for wanting to light a candle to honor his mother.

CHAPTER 9

Football—Toilet Troubadours—Student Hazing

The credit belongs to the man who is actually in the arena; whose face is marred by dust and sweat; who strives valiantly; who at the best knows the triumph of achievement; and who at the worst fails while daring greatly, so that his place shall never be with those timid souls who know neither victory or defeat.
—THEODORE ROOSEVELT (1858-1919)

FOOTBALL WAS CARVED on the Mountain's culture when a University of the South team accomplished an incredible feat in 1899. Within a six-day period the traveling football squad from Sewanee defeated Texas, Texas A&M, Tulane, LSU and Ole Miss. A sports reporter wrote: "After six days of battles, on the seventh day the University of the South football team rested."

The 1899 "Iron Men" had a 12-0-0 season—322 points versus 10 points.

October 21, Atlanta:	Sewanee 12	Georgia 0
October 23, Atlanta:	Sewanee 32	Georgia Tech 0
October 28, Sewanee:	Sewanee 46	Tennessee 0
November 3, Sewanee:	Sewanee 54	Southwestern 0
November 9, Austin:	Sewanee 12	Texas 0
November 10, Houston:	Sewanee 10	Texas A&M 0
November 11, New Orleans:	Sewanee 23	Tulane 0
November 13, Baton Rouge:	Sewanee 34	LSU 0

November 14, Memphis:	Sewanee 12	Ole Miss 0
November 20, Sewanee:	Sewanee 71	Cumberland 0
November 30, Montgomery:	Sewanee 11	Auburn 10
December 2, Atlanta:	Sewanee 5	North Carolina 0

Famed football coach Vince Lombardi said: "The accomplishment of the Sewanee football squad in 1899 will probably never be equaled." The proximity to this level of football accomplishment and lore had an inspiring impact on the football program at nearby St. Andrew's School.

True to his nature, Father Flye hated violence. He disliked the school having a boxing team, but his feeling about football was one of complete loathing. He wrote in 1930: "No one disputes the benefits of exercise, but I question the fanaticism for football that I see here. The argument that this game builds character is built on loose sand. Integrity is in a boy before he ever plays football."

During those years, before helmet face guards, tackling and blocking left their mark. It was not uncommon for a St. Andrew's football player to come to class Monday morning with a bruised and swollen face. A broken finger or broken nose, scabbed-over shins, loose teeth and abrasions were seen as normal wear-and-tear of the game.

Flye wrote in his journal during the 1930 football season: "138 boys taken in. This means overcrowding. Administration's refusal to face facts. 100 would be plenty to handle. The football madness has started. Pierce was dropped from school but has been reinstated because he is such a good football player. Fr. Harrison wanted Pierce here, as did Clarence Lautzenheiser. Everyone here excited that St. Andrew's beat Bridgeport 39-0. The emphasis here is always contrary to my beliefs."

His antipathy to football forced him to write in 1936: "The game is barbaric and shameful. Football is a collision sport. Parents would never think of crashing their automobile into a tree, yet they send their children out to be at risk. St. Andrew's teachers scream at players during close games, but these same men don't say a word if the boys have failing grades. There is tacit approval to ignore studies if they excel in football." St. Andrew's athletes were expected to have minimum scholastic levels; however, Father Flye was accurate when he wrote that most faculty members were avid football fans. They undoubtedly gave athletes some slack in the classroom.

At another time he wrote: "Ours is the only country which directs its seats of higher education to provide the general public with sports entertainment. It is inconceivable that Oxford would tolerate having illiterate oarsmen, yet here in our country we see empty-headed athletes treated like royalty. What does the under-educated gladiator do after his brief time of glory? Newspaper clippings won't pay his mortgage."

A page from the St. Andrew's School Yearbook, 1926

Tennessee sports editors had favorite nicknames for St. Andrew's football teams. Over the years, the football squads were alternately called: Mountain Lions, Lions, Saints, Padres, Maroon Marauders (the school colors were maroon and white).

The football team in 1922 was probably the best in St. Andrew's history. The school played Decherd for the Mid-State Football Championship that year and lost 6-0. The success of any football program should be measured by its competition. The school did not schedule games against junior varsity teams or weak opponents. Before parity was required, the Mountain Lions competed against public schools that enrolled ten times more students than St. Andrew's. Father Bonnell Spencer wrote: "When you consider we were half the size of the next smallest school in the Mid-South League, we did remarkably well in sports."

In 1936, a Nashville sports columnist referred to the St. Andrew's football team as the "Cursing Saints." Offended by this characterization, the Prior told the football team that the school's reputation was too important for the players to use profanity. His admonition was ignored. Ed Yokley, a member of the 1936 squad, said: "Father Parker was right about swearing being wrong, but he wasn't out there on the football field. We were always taunted across the line of scrimmage, with other teams calling us mountain hicks. It was hard not to get angry."

St. Andrew's enjoyed great success in varsity football. The first Saints football squad appeared in 1916. An exciting tradition started that year: the night before a football game the student body held a "war dance" around a roaring bonfire. The evening's hoopla ended with the singing of the official school song:

> Where the mountains rear majestic
> To the sky their noble heads
> Where the southern sun benignant
> All its softest radiance sheds
>
> There the school we love was founded
> There it stands for God and right
> May its colors long be waving
> Colors fair, Maroon and White
>
> We will live for thee St. Andrew's
> We will live for thee each day
> As the years go by in memory
> We will honor thee for aye

Going to a game on the school bus, the team yelled the unofficial school song:

> We are the boys from old Saint A, and we don't give a damn
> We go to school to break the rules, and flunk the damn exam
> To hell with the east, to hell with the west, and the whole damn crew
> If you don't go to our dear old St A, to hell, to hell with you

St. Andrew's varsity football team, 1935

Patrick Kennedy, a 1922 St. Andrew's graduate, said: "Playing football against us was like standing behind an angry mule in honeysuckles. It was not where you wanted to be. I know other teams dreaded playing us."

William Peyton, a 1925 graduate: "We had other sports, but the emphasis was on football. When our team played away from school, we traveled by train as there were no roads to speak of. Our biggest football rival was Sewanee Military Academy, located a few miles away. Clarence Lautzenheiser was a football legend on the Mountain. Besides "Lautzy," there was his brother, Ernest, Red Simmons, Fuzzy Green, Pat Kennedy, Dewey Long, Joseph Riddle. All were very tough characters. St. Andrew's had mean football teams in the 1920s."

The Prior at St. Andrew's, Father Liston Orum, mentioned football when he wrote "Ode to the Class of 1926." The second stanza read:

> Here where the mountains rise
> Here where the mist wraiths creep
> Here have you mastered the words of the wise
> Pondered on problems deep
> Often in mimic football fight
> Wearing the cherished Maroon and White
> Straight down the field with all your might
> Thunderously did you sweep

The November 13, 1931, edition of the *Mountain Lion* student publication carried these football inserts: "St. Andrew's team will meet its toughest foe when it plays Tennessee Industrial School of Nashville next Friday. T.I.S. is strong this year. Last year's students are making good in football at other schools. Thomas Cathey is first string halfback for Chattanooga High School and doing it well. It looks like he will be All-City. Dainty Garland is playing first string tackle at South Pittsburg. Mr. Warr lost his temper at the Branham-Hughes game Friday, and was injured in a tussle with a policeman. He spent the rest of the weekend in jail."

The same edition printed this poem written by a St. Andrew's English teacher:

> Ship me somewhere in the autumn
> Where the fullback hits the line
> And the halfback does the tango
> Up some right tackle's spine
>
> As the punt goes sailing swiftly
> As the spiral cleaves the air
> A flock of cleats land deftly
> In the quarterback's tangled hair
>
> Ship me somewhere in October
> When you hear that howling mass
> Where the flashing ends sweep outward
> To receive the forward pass
> Run or dive through center
> For a dozen yards to go
> A husky tackle nails him
> And the halfback lays him low

In appearance, the football squads in the late 1920s looked down-and-out. St. Andrew's could not afford to buy new equipment, and players took to the field with helmets and uniforms that were discards from other schools. Thomas Gorman said: "We looked pathetic. My helmet drove me crazy; it never fit properly. I used to stuff rags inside to make it comfortable. But we fought hard and got respect the only way we could. Football was important to us."

The following notation was found among the effects of David McDowell, who graduated in 1936: "We were on the road against a fancy school where everybody treated us with snotty purse-proud condescension. There was a Packard convertible parked near a corner of the end zone, and I deliberately ran into the damn thing on a pass play and dented a fender and broke a headlight. God, how I hated what that car represented! We won by a touchdown, which gave me a great deal of satisfaction."

Sports writers routinely use colorful descriptions. This comment appeared in a Nashville newspaper during the 1936 football season: "St. Andrew's lineman Elisha Tate is the one to watch. His opponents often look like they tried to take a

Elisha "Smokey" Tate

bath in a bucket of rusty nails." Floyd Garner, a 1937 graduate, recalled Tate: "He was tougher than leather. He would invariably set me on my butt during scrimmages. I saw stars every time he hit me. He excelled at football."

Edward Yokley, who graduated in 1937: "We never had more than 25 boys go out for football. I can't remember ever being relieved for injuries, on offense or defense. You played if you were hurting. We had football games against McCallie, Columbia, Baylor, Castle Heights, Sweetwater, Battle Ground Academy, Darlington, all larger schools. We went against the Tennessee State Reform School in Nashville. The competition was rugged, but we still had guys who made All-Southern. Some of us earned football scholarships to universities, including myself. The newspapers called me 'Stonewall Yokley.' How to describe St. Andrew's football in those days? We went on the field angry, and we left the field happy."

Chattanooga and Nashville newspaper clippings from the 1930s show that the St. Andrew's football teams competed against public high schools in: Maryville, Winchester, South Pittsburg, Manchester, Decherd, Tullahoma, Shelbyville, Huntsville, Centerville. During this same era, the Mountain Lions played in a conference of private schools (mostly military schools): Darlington, McCallie, Baylor, Notre Dame, Wallace, Father Ryan, Tennessee Industrial (TIS), Battle Ground Academy (BGA), Duncan, Castle Heights, Tennessee Military Institute (TMI), Morgan, Sewanee Military Academy (SMA).

The school dropped football after Pearl Harbor was bombed by the Japanese—the 1942 football schedule was canceled. There were not enough boys to field a team; too many juniors and seniors had enlisted in the military services. Football was reinstated for the 1949 season. The layoff did not affect the school's traditionally tough schedule or diminish its winning ways. The neophyte 1949 football squad defeated Dunlap 48-0 and Huntland 67-6.

Father Flye wrote in 1949: "Playing a football game in Manchester is reasonable, but to schedule a football game in Elizabethton, past Knoxville near the Virginia border, is another case of bad planning. The team didn't get back until two in the morning. Can I logically expect a player at the sunrise service?"

Wirt Gammon of the *Chattanooga Times* reported: "1949 will be remembered as the year when the boys from St. Andrew's returned to the gridiron. Besides sausage, eggs and grits, what are they feeding the boys on the mountain? The Saints 6-0 victory before a Woodbury home crowd of 1,000 fans is the prep upset

Halftime snapshots of St. Andrew's football team at the 1949 win (6-0) over Woodbury

of the season. Doc Litkenhous, the guru of state prep rankings, had Woodbury listed as a 35-point pre-game favorite! In a defensive struggle where both teams had crunching, ear-ringing, goal line stops, the Saints prevailed when fullback Lloyd Baker threw a slight-of-hand 15-yard pass to halfback James Seidule for the game's only touchdown."

On September 23, 1950, Father Flye wrote in his journal: "It is the custom here in recent years to carry on the spirit of the day's football games at Saturday suppers. Last night, soon after the beginning of the meal, Fr. Turkington rose and said he wanted to thank Novice Steele who made a list of the scores, which was then read aloud: Duke beats South Carolina (applause) Georgia beats Maryland (cheers). I sat there bored, wondering what possible concern it should be to this particular student body whether West Virginia defeats Western Reserve."

Floyd Garner: "One of the most memorable members of the faculty was Father Flye, a certified eccentric, who despised football. He couldn't stand to see you kill a bug or any creature. It just tore him to pieces. I once saw him take a mouse and let it scamper off into the woods. A boy had put the mouse inside a jar and brought it to class. Piffle took off on a long lecture claiming all of God's creatures, large and small, were here for a reason, and they shouldn't be molested. We knew he felt that way, because he and Mrs. Flye always kept little critters in their house.

"His hands were really huge. He was the most energetic man I ever met. He had a determined walk, not stopping for anything or anybody. Father Flye always walked fast. Despite his bizarre ways, he was a fabulous teacher; however, he didn't care one bit for sports, and he didn't associate with most of the faculty. He kept to himself and his books. I never saw him when he wasn't carrying a book."

Vernon Ragland, a 1938 graduate, recalled: "Father Flye was the most gentle person I ever saw. He hated bullies. He hated cruelty of any kind and for anyone to harm anything that was alive. One day in class he spotted a boy holding a moth.

He berated the boy and made him release the bug out the window. Then he lectured us about respecting all life, be it a rabbit or a tree. I thought he was silly, since it was only a moth which set him off. I've changed my mind since then."

Phillip Cook, a 1950 graduate: "It was natural that Father Flye disliked football. The one thing that sticks out in my memory was his intolerance of anybody causing pain or injury. He detested taunting and bullying; he wouldn't put up with such behavior in his presence. He was kindhearted and good. You'd better pity the dumb kid he saw molesting one of God's creatures. At least emotionally, he could have been a member of the Audubon Society or other conservation clubs, long before it was fashionable like it is today."

Father Flye's journal entry of January 9, 1944 shows his sensitive nature: "The hazing of the newer boys has begun by rolling them in the snow, rubbing it in their faces and putting it down their backs inside their clothes. This sort of thing always leaves me with feelings of moral disapprobation with feelings of anger, disgust, sadness. I regret my inability to do anything about it. Most adults accept these things as natural and to be expected. With this point of view I am in sharp and eternal disagreement. This is the spirit of the pack, which I loathe."

The history teacher usually felt it was not his place to intervene in what he saw around him, even if it did upset him. In 1936 Flye made an exception. He overheard students talking about a frog being put in a toilet bowl in the school building's basement, and bets were made as to how many flushes were needed to make the frog disappear. The outraged Flye ran down to the basement and rescued the imperiled amphibian. The six boys who took part in the cruelty were themselves terrified when they saw how angry he was.

Father Flye uncharacteristically asked the Headmaster, Allious Reid, to allow him to decide the boys' punishment. In front of a giggling audience at the quadrangle, the six boys had to stand and recite poetry for the next three Sunday afternoons. After that, they were called "the toilet troubadours." Father Flye chose a censure of mild embarrassment.

He wrote in 1944: "I'm interested in techniques which get results with a minimum use of penalties. To do so has been the most gratifying thing in my experience. One of the most searching tests of a person is how he uses authority or power. An orator said of Abraham Lincoln that 'having been entrusted with almost absolute power he never abused it except on the side of mercy.'"

The history teacher detested the Letterman's Club initiation. It is unclear when the ritual began, but before a St. Andrew's athlete could wear his varsity sports "letter" on a sweater or jacket, he had to endure the ordeal. Sometimes the initiations were rough affairs. In 1951, Grace Flye wrote to her niece, Mary: "Yesterday I chanced to meet the Prior and Hal is very bitter about him. Last year he condoned hazing at the Letterman's Club initiation. Cruelty makes a fury in Hal, a blinding cold fury."

Father Flye acted on his rage. He wrote scathing letters about the Letterman's

Club inductions to prominent educators: Dr. Bruce B. Robinson, Director of the Child Guidance Department, Board of Education, Newark, New Jersey; W. Carson Ryan, Professor of Education at the University of North Carolina; Dr. Thomas L. Hopkins, Professor of Education at Columbia University.

His April 21, 1951, letter to Dr. Hopkins was graphic. "... membership in the Lettermen's Club is not actually obligatory for those who have won their Letter, but the assumption is that they will join. The pressure of opinion would render the boy unpopular if he did not join.

"... the club's initiation, over two days, is where a current Letterman orders a new Letterman to carry a huge rock around everywhere he goes, kneel on command. You know of this kind of cruelty, the purpose is to cause embarrassment and discomfort.

"... the final proceedings, lasting for two hours or more, take place at a distance from the school about 9:00 p.m. and are never witnessed by the rest of the student body. The new Lettermen are blindfolded and beaten with belts and forced to run through woods where they are cut and bruised by tree branches.

"... bonfire is where the final ceremony takes place. Boys are forced to swallow raw eggs or other distasteful things, nauseous and disgusting potions being given which cause gagging and vomiting. More beatings. Wet soot and earth being rubbed on their faces and bodies. Old slop from the kitchen garbage is poured over them. From year to year the torture varies. Some boys have had broken arms. The eating of live worms has been reported to me. There is loud shouting next to a boy's ears.

"... the conclusion comes when the blindfolds are removed and an address is made to the boys in which they are told they are now Lettermen, and it is hoped they would put next year's new Lettermen through what they had been put through. They are then told to stand in place until they hear the chapel bells ringing; then the older boys return to the dormitories and shower (using all the hot water available) and then, after about thirty minutes, ring the bells. The initiates then have to clean up as best they can in cold water. What is your opinion as to these practices?"

In a letter dated May 3, 1951, Dr. Robinson replied: "I am prejudiced against such rough initiations dating back to my high school days. The rough initiations I saw in high school made me determined to never join a college fraternity where such rough initiations were also practiced. Paddling seems to be a regular part of most school initiations and is so widely accepted that I presume we have to accept this as normal procedure ... faculty control is necessary to prevent extremes."

On May 15, 1951, Dr. Ryan wrote: "It is puzzling to me that supposedly Christian schools can tolerate the sort of thing you describe."

Dr. Hopkins did not respond to Father Flye's letter until October 4, 1951. After explaining he had been ill and unable to correspond, the Columbia University professor wrote: "I feel administrators should discourage all forms of rough activities by helping pupils find better outlets for their sadistic urges."

Father Flye then waited. Finally, during the second week of March 1952, he walked into the office of the Headmaster, Father William Turkington, confronting him with the mail responses he had collected. Not surprisingly, the Headmaster was infuriated that the Letterman's Club initiation rites had been exposed to a national audience of prominent educators. The Prior, Father Bonnell Spencer, was summoned from the classroom where he was teaching Church History. The three men became involved in a shouting match—contrary to their normal behavior—and Father Flye was ordered to leave the Headmaster's office.

Incredibly, Father Flye was not terminated that day. However, he walked on thin ice after the loud exchange. He was already beyond the normal retirement age.

In any event, his action brought results. The Letterman's Club initiations became milder, less punishing. The history teacher had accomplished his goal. However, the St. Andrew's administrators never forgot his "back-stabbing disloyalty."

The next decade saw a decline in the school's football fortunes. St. Andrew's lost the gridiron reputation it once had. The football coach since 1949, Eugene Towles, resigned in 1954. His successor was Harold Kennedy, a 1939 St. Andrew's graduate who suffered from ulcers and habitually carried a thermos bottle of milk to ease his pain. The Prior told Kennedy to stop drinking from his thermos as he walked the sidelines during games. Why? Spectators might get the idea the football coach was a drunk! The astonished coach told Father Spencer not to be concerned, because from now on, the entire coaching staff would drink from thermos bottles on the sidelines.

The school's athletic program was not immune to the anti-establishment virus that swept through the country in the 1960s. It was a time of college student upheavals, race riots, anti-war protests, draft card burning, and political assassinations. For the first time in St. Andrew's history, traditional values were challenged, and this caused attitudes to change. St. Andrew's maintained the football program, but the days of the entire student body and faculty crowding the sidelines, screaming until hoarse, faded into the haze of history.

❑ ❑ ❑

St. Andrew's athletes were competitive in tennis, track, basketball, soccer, baseball, wrestling, boxing and football. They competed with teams from public and private high schools in Tennessee, Alabama and Georgia. Some of the "away" games and matches meant traveling long distances on twisting two-lane roads. Especially in icy weather, the trips were a test of endurance.

Athletes sometimes had to "make do." The author of this book remembers, "We had warmup outfits in the late 1940s, but our track team didn't have an official uniform, so we wore whatever we could find. I once ran in swim trunks at

Left: St. Andrew's basketball squad, 1937

Above Left: St. Andrew's tennis practice, circa 1960. Right: William Hampton (St. A '51) winning the 100-yard dash on St. Andrew's track, April 1951

St. Andrew's baseball team, 1937

a track meet at Castle Heights. My trunks split down the middle in a 100 preliminary race. Smokey Tate and I went to the school bus where he put in some safety pins. I won the final 100 and 220, but it was painful, because the pins had popped loose. I was humiliated. Father Flye heard about it, and the next day he drove me to Winchester to buy white cotton shorts. Mrs. Flye sewed maroon piping around the edges. They looked spiffy."

Throughout his life, Flye ate a proper diet—he was a lifelong vegetarian—and he exercised regularly. Throughout his tenure at St. Andrew's, maintenance men and pupils spotted him jogging around the school's athletic field in the morning. The man had enormous energy. He rarely walked anywhere; he almost sprinted from one place to another. The sight of him, head down with an armful of textbooks, hustling across the quadrangle was part of the local folklore. It was a foggy day in December, 1943, when he walked straight into one of the campus's big pine trees. For several weeks he sported two black eyes. When the Headmaster, Father William Turkington, inquired about the accident, Father Flye explained: "I was thinking."

The wiry priest (his 1935 Tennessee drivers license showed Father Flye was 5'9" and weighed 165 pounds) frequently played tennis with Brother Dominic on weekends. Their tennis skills were not superior, but their matches were entertaining. One match was described this way by James Hollingsworth: "It was the funniest thing I ever saw. Brother Dominic was not fleet of foot and huffed and puffed all the time, but he had a superb backhand slice. His returns took some weird bounces, and this drove Father Flye insane. I don't know why, but Father Flye had the tendency to swing his racket with all his might. There was this gray-haired fat man placing soft lobs over the net, and a skinny little guy knocking the tennis ball to Huntsville. I laughed so much that my stomach ached."[1]

One incident in the 1950s illustrated Father Flye's lack of knowledge about sports. Eddie LeBaron, a quarterback with the Washington Redskins from 1952-59, visited St. Andrew's. LeBaron strolled to the football field where he thrilled awe-struck boys with his passing ability. Seemingly without effort, the National Football League star threw the football 70 yards.

LeBaron was told he had a long distance telephone call, and as he walked toward the administration building, he struck up a brief conversation with Father Flye, who was walking in the same direction. Bystanders, at a distance, noticed both men looking up at the treetops in the quadrangle. The history teacher was later questioned about his chat with the NFL quarterback. Flye's reply made it clear he did not know or care about Eddie LeBaron's status as a sports figure: "He was a friendly young man. We discussed our hairy woodpecker population. They are noisy this time of year, and one of them was making a commotion."

The most renowned athlete to set foot on the St. Andrew's campus was world champion tennis player Bill Tilden in 1935. He played on the tennis courts located 20 yards southwest of the Flye bungalow. No local tennis player was able to handle Tilden's over-the-net serves, so he competed against two players at the same time. Grace Flye watched the exhibition, and later wrote in a letter: "Mr. Bill Tilden was extremely charming. I served tea to his entourage under our willow tree."

❑ ❑ ❑

One of Father Flye's most memorable traits was his opposition to inflicting physical pain. This is why he deplored both the boxing and football programs at St. Andrew's. He was known for his protectiveness of other creatures, even of insects. The teacher probably drew the line at flies, roaches and ticks (but this was never proven); otherwise, he loved everything alive. No man loved life more than he did.

❑ ❑ ❑

[1] Brother Dominic and Father Flye were friendly tennis opponents for nearly 30 years. They had a camaraderie despite their educational differences. Born as Sidney Taylor in New York City, Brother Dominic went to high school in Brooklyn, and worked as a telephone repairman for eight years. He then worked as a file clerk at a department store. He entered the Order of the Holy Cross in 1920, and took his vows six years later, becoming Brother Dominic at the age of 42. He taught Sacred Studies at St. Andrew's, and was the chapel organist. Legions of St. Andrew's graduates had warm memories of the always cheerful Brother Dominic. He died on March 2, 1960, one day short of his 76th birthday.

CHAPTER 10

Father Flye's Teaching Philosophy—Birdwood— Poetry and Prose

Educating children, essential to any society, never gets the regard it should.
—FROM A LETTER WRITTEN BY FATHER FLYE, OCTOBER 8, 1924

FATHER FLYE WROTE "Reflections on St. Andrew's" in 1921, and the article was re-published 20 years later in the *Holy Cross Magazine*. In this commentary, Flye described some of the students in 1921, and made references to the firm educational precepts that prevailed at the time: "Most of our boys come from homes and from among people where although one finds a natural nobility, there is, nevertheless, of reading, literary knowledge, of art, of enlivening influences, almost nothing.

"And so we get our material—childhood, boyhood—those that come to us, many of them quite young, away from home if he has one, away from the fostering home care, often sensitive and shy, striving not to show it, capable of being influenced to a great degree either for good or bad. A child —of whom our blessed Savior said: 'of such is the kingdom of heaven.'

"Of such, to take concrete examples, are Billy Lewis, George O'Dear, Buford Finney and Raymond Kersey. Of such, in their best qualities, is the kingdom of heaven. Can this still be said of them after a few more years? Various influences at St. Andrew's will help determine that.

"One sees instances of unselfishness that are beautiful, of patience, forgiveness, good spirit, devotion, and good sense. Such boys as Austin Allen, Mark

Hannah Sullivan, John Stewart, Robert Stewart, Pat Kennedy, Sam Willis, all so sensitive, easily hurt, keenly responsive to friendship.

"We find among them, to be sure, ignorance of many things commonplace to adults. But to ridicule them for this, to be scornful of their ignorance, is narrow-mindedness on our part. Were we not also so ignorant of many things? Everyone is ignorant until he has had the opportunity to learn, and who of us are expected to know the leading jurists of Paraguay? Our own knowledge can be ridiculed by Mr. Thomas Edison, for example. Common sense bids us not to expect the impossible; and real charity means, at any rate, a kindly appreciation of people's best.

"Our aim surely is not the cold dreary one of creating a rigid system and then forcing human beings to fit it, but of helping each individual boy. Not merely of helping St. Andrew's students as a group or class, but of making life happier and richer for Willie Huntsman, Dave Mooney, George Kelly and Jack Church.

"General Lee, when the president of a Virginia college after the Civil War, was noted for his direct and personal rather than standardized methods. Some faculty member said to him once in regard to a student brought up for official consideration: 'We can not respect persons, but we must have regard for precedent.' Robert E. Lee replied: 'I always respect persons, and I care nothing for precedent.' Coming from someone who knew all that could be said in favor of the rigid system and rules which are the army's ideal of discipline, these words seem to me to show unmistakably the greatness of the man and his kindliness and reason.

"In this matter, as well as others, we should use every care, it seems to me, to show the children at St. Andrew's School examples of adult dealing which is at least just, swerving from strict justice in the direction of mercy. Every boy is keenly sensitive in the matter of fairness, and nothing will tend to shake his faith in us, and perhaps his fellow-man generally, more than the belief that we acquiesce in injustice.

"I have not meant to imply that there should be absolutely no rules and never any punishment. Some rules and punishment are necessary. It is only that I have seen rules and red tape overdone. I would like to see all such reduced to the necessary minimum and the greatest possible liberty accorded. Someone said of the school of the great educator Pestalozzi: 'Why, this is not a school, it is a family.' Surely that is a good ideal."

Father Flye concluded his 1921 article: "What the future will be at St. Andrew's I do not know. I wish that it may be a place where young men should rise onto their feet less dreadfully crippled, a great deal more capable of living well, a great deal more aware of their own dignity, a great deal better qualified, each within his own limits, to take part toward the creation of a better world."

Educational pioneer John Dewey started an experimental school in 1896 with

Road repair crew near Sewanee, 1937

just 12 pupils and two teachers. Departing from the traditions of the day, Dewey envisioned a school where children grew mentally, physically and socially, where they would be challenged to think independently. Subjects would expand on a child's curiosity. The idea was for a student to develop a love of learning and think critically. Dewey wrote: "An education is something that should not be imposed from without, but should be drawn from the endless possibilities from within the child. Education is life and not merely a preparation for life."

John Dewey also wrote: "Many an ordinary school disregards the present needs of the child; the fact that he is living a full life each year and hour, not waiting to live in a period defined by his elders. Nature has not adapted the young animal to the narrow desk, the crowded curriculum, the silent absorption of complicated facts. His very life and growth depends upon motion, yet the school forces him into a cramped position for hours at a time, so that the teacher may be sure he is listening or studying books. Short periods of exercise are allowed as a bribe, but the relaxations don't compensate for the effort he makes. The disease of indifference attacks his sensitive soul before he has fairly started on the road to knowledge."

Flye read Dewey's book *Democracy and Education* in 1925, and it had a lasting impact on the history teacher. He recognized a kindred spirit in the author, who believed, as he did, in "progressive education." While traveling to summer duty in Milwaukee in 1926, the priest visited one of John Dewey's experimental schools in Chicago. After that trip, Father Flye was consumed with the concept of having his own school that would emulate Dewey's theories. He had seen too much "conformity in the rote way of teaching" at St. Andrew's. He could do better.

In September of 1926, Flye presented "Some Ideas for a School" before a

James Ragland scores in 1940 as St. Andrew's defeats Rossville (Ga.)

Kiwanis meeting in Chattanooga. His speech revealed his views about progressive education. In part, this is what he said:

"The faculty is an important factor and selected with care; would have to qualify not only in education, but in character as well as temperament. No neurotics or 'peculiar' persons. They must understand and like young people.

"There is to be a general atmosphere of friendliness; no cant, or patronizing. None of the superior-adult attitude, but mutual respect between teachers and pupils.

"There will be a minimum of rules and prohibitions. Many school rules are arbitrary and the student feels that in breaking them he is just that much ahead if he doesn't get caught. We want the whole attitude in our school to be different from this, to have no rules that will seem useless or burdensome.

"There will be a minimum of punishments; it is to be hoped none at all. I am very suspicious of the whole practice connected with this word. If some wrong has been done and a compensation can be made, let this be made. The boy will, as a matter of honor, wish to make compensation where he can do so. Some wrongs can be righted, things stolen can be restored, work not done may be made up, damages repaired. I have little or no faith in the efficacy of punishment as a deterrent.

"Judge John Lindsey wrote: 'Fear with children is the father of lies. I found that when a boy was brought before me, I could do nothing with him until I had taken the fear out of his heart.'

"Stress on vocabulary. Spelling matches and 'spelling baseball' where teams contest, an error counted as a strike ... doing this language work easily and leisurely, not in the nerve-racking way of most language teaching.

"Considerable science, some of it informal [such as] botany, to know of flowers and trees. Astronomy. Familiarity with stars and constellations. Knowledge of birds and animals, regard for all of them, appreciation of their nature, circumstances of their life and sufferings. Principles of the American Humane Society.

"Elementary geology, earth history, practical knowledge of rocks and minerals. Some idea of the world revealed by the microscope. Cells, protozoa. Facts about bacteria.

"There is to be cultivation of the spirit of enlightened reverence ... the symmetry of a seed-pod, the play of light on tree trunks, the beauty of mist, the enchantment of the moonlight, the iridescence of an insect's wing, the beauty of color, form, and life.

"No expression of the creative impulse is ever to be made fun of, but encouraged. No forcing of children in these matters, but on the other hand, they are to be given the opportunity to know of various means of self-expression.

"Pupils will get acquainted with the best things in literature, music, and other fields of culture ... readings of poetry and prose ... songs learned and sung ... recitals where someone plays the piano so students may get acquainted with the best music.

"Anglo-Catholicism at its sanest. Every effort to get frank, natural, and unaffected type of religion. The superficial type of religion guarded against as pernicious. We want to foster what is wholesome, sincere and charitable. Smugness and bigotry in religion will not be tolerated."

Flye's speech lasted about 45 minutes. The Chattanooga audience gave him a polite, but not enthusiastic, applause at the end of his presentation. His endorsement of a school with few rules and student freedom of expression was an alien concept to the mid-1920s businessmen. Father Flye told Grace that one angry man accused him of having "radical ideas." The St. Andrew's history teacher was a man ahead of his time.

Flye wrote in his private journal: "If there is anything lovelier than the wholesome development of childhood, mentally, physically, spiritually, I do not know what it is. Why could not education be made joyous instead of grim?"

Father Flye was an early member of the Progressive Education Association. In 1938 he was awarded a Fellowship by the Carnegie Endowment for International Peace, as one of 40 teachers of history and Social Science. The other 39 were university professors. The award presentation was held at Ann Arbor, Michigan. Among his academic peers, Father Flye was known as a modern Socrates.

❑ ❑ ❑

Father Flye's journal entries in October 1926 reflected a deep malaise: "I realize I'm in a rut here which I should get out of. There has been no steady and consistent policy, and various things done by the school have been at variance with my ideas. There have been things done which seem to me stupid and short-sighted, based on wrong ideas.

"When I first came here the religious ideal was greatly emphasized. I felt we might accomplish much by not only teaching actual secular information, but also inoculate boys with the practices of the Anglo-Catholic church. Piety was strongly stressed; a good many confessions. An effort was made to encourage prayer and devotion. The school's spiritual tone is now rather low. There are few confessions and communions. The changes began when Fr. Campbell left in 1922. Frs. Campbell, Wright and Lorey had strong influences in maintaining the spiritual atmosphere.

"One would think the Order would have a fixed policy and aim for this school, but no, it all depends who is Headmaster and therefore subject to radical change at any time. A thing is tried here, works out badly, but later tried again under the successor who knows nothing of the previous bad practice. Oh, the stupidity of working out things de novo. There is no accumulated experience carried on.

"I ought to be using my life to better advantage. I think a great deal about founding a school that would have a quality student body, and the teaching would be of a high ideal. I don't know if I could manage such a thing, but others feel I could and that it would be worthwhile. At present I don't know how this could be done. I don't know of a place for a school, and I have almost no money."

In 1928, Father Flye discovered what he considered to be the perfect location for his proposed school. The property was southwest of Sewanee, off Sherwood Road, three miles south of Highway 64 (41-A) with a panoramic view of Lost Cove Valley. The site was at the end of what is now known as Carriage Lane.

The property had originally been a boys' summer camp in the early 1900s; however, by 1928 the buildings were long-deserted and needed extensive repairs. Despite the obvious renovation demands, both he and Grace saw the property as the answer to their prayers. Mr. and Mrs. Malcolm M. MacDowell owned the land and indicated a willingness to sell. The Flyes privately named the site "Birdwood."

For the next seven months, Grace Flye's letters communicated excitement and urgency. Following are excerpts from June through November 1928:

June 27, 1928: "Harold went to Sewanee to see Father Luke and talk over the matter of having a school. Fr. and Mrs. Luke are interested in Harold's future."

June 28, 1928: "Harold went out to see Mr. MacDowell. I wish that Harold could have that place. It is the very first time I have ever seen him filled with an inspiring enthusiasm. But it is a costly undertaking to start a school, and unless Fr. Luke wants to go in with him, he will have to give it up. Fr. Luke is so bitter about St. Andrews.

"There is a movement on now all over this country and in Germany, England and France for these new types of schools, where the grouping is not institutional, which is deadening and distasteful to the young. The studies are carried on in an informal and creative way, giving a young mind initiative in carrying out his line of studies. The movement of these new type schools has risen rapidly because of the great need for them and because of the brilliant result of those now flourishing. Harold follows their progress with keen enthusiasm.

"As you know he went to New York a year ago as soon as school was out to study the methods of a famous school in New York City. He studied them in Chicago and in Washington and for years has subscribed to *New Education*. That is why he pines for Mr. MacDowell's. It has the noble look of a home and near to Sewanee. His chance, as I can see now, is whether Fr. Luke will be interested in working out the situation with him. Fr. Luke has nothing in the world to do and has such ample means that he does not need to do anything. He is discontented over the fact that he has nothing to arouse his energies."

July 2, 1928: "I've talked with Mrs. Luke and she is interested. If they want to join with Harold it could be done. They are impressed that Mr. Claiborne wants Harold to stay on the mountain and start a school of his own. The Lukes have admiration for Reverend Claiborne, as everyone else has. Our ten years here have rooted us firmly in this region. Saturday we strolled the beautiful grounds with that view of Lost Cove Valley in front of our admiring eyes."

July 17, 1928: "Fr. and Alice Claiborne have a house close to Sewanee left to her by her parents. They told Harold that they would let him use it for a school. It is on a poor road, but Harold was so touched with their generous thought."

July 19, 1928: "I cannot leave Harold [to visit relatives in Florida] in this crisis when he is so discouraged. He is in his prime of life and should not stay where his energies are of no avail. Hal is not anxious to begin another school year here. Fr. Lorey left in opposition. Fr. Whitall too. Fr. Wright resigned and the Order never thanked him for his years of service. So it is time Hal left. He is so humiliated by staying on."

August 2, 1928: "Fr. Wright wrote that they expect to cast their lot in with us in a common aim. It is Harold's ambition to have the Goodwins with us. I hope he won't have to stay here. It is humiliating. I will be glad when this uncertainty is over. My life here has been one of joy. This Noah's Ark, where I can paint to my content, has been my heaven on earth. But I see we will have to go. This uncertainty is enough to try the patience of anyone."

August 8, 1928: "I had a lovely note from Mrs. Wright. She is so sympathetic. I had counted all summer on knowing something definite by the first of August.

And when it arrived with a blank my own expectancy wilted away."

November 9, 1928: "St. Andrew's has never cared for contacts with Sewanee or DuBose. It was a delight when our friends were here: the Wrights, Goodwins, Lukes. They are gone, we are lost as if in a desert. My world is inside this bungalow, but I see we must go. Rev. Claiborne is done with this place. So is Hal."

In the late 1920s, Father Flye's life was one of ambivalence and frustration. Along with Mrs. Flye, he wanted to stay on the Mountain. He had friends at the University of the South, the EQB Club and the DuBose School. He reveled in the intellectual give-and-take of their shared camaraderie. The vision of having his own school was an emotional magnet; he constantly talked about it with friends.

On October 7, 1929, Father Flye purchased 40 acres from Mr. and Mrs. MacDowell for $500. The idea of a small progressive school was now beyond the talking stage. A financial commitment had been made. The Flyes now owned the Lost Cove property they called Birdwood. The purchase money had come from the sale of bonds left to Grace by her mother.

The transaction occurred one month before the Wall Street Crash. Father Flye was a victim of incredibly bad luck and timing. The 1929 disaster propelled a financial tsunami across the country. Except for the extremely wealthy, it was a tough period for everybody. Communities and individuals saw bank accounts vanish. Flye knew Grace's inheritance had become worthless. He suggested they might as well buy real estate rather than keep bonds which were sinking in value. Some of Mrs. Flye's bonds were sold, and they returned 3 percent of their original face value. Flye wrote in his journal in 1931: "I didn't get paid until July, three months late. A maintenance man, Mr. Smith, was also paid late. His check was half what he expected. What is going to happen to us?"

Franklin County records show Flye bought another nine acres from Mr. MacDowell for $100 in 1931. At the time, both men believed they were getting a bargain. In a letter dated July 8, 1932, Father Flye wrote Grace from Ayer, Massachusetts: "I think we might do something with Birdwood if we ever get it fixed up; maybe in two years or so. It is a beautiful place and worth having for a home." Four days later, on July 12, he wrote: "However things work out for us, it is good to have our Birdwood. I wish it were in a further stage of completion. Some of the bonds we sold to put in the place would have been worthless by now."

On February 16, 1933, the Flyes bought an adjoining four acres from Mr. and Mrs. Alexander Green for $100.

During this period, Father Flye's anguish became so acute he considered getting out of teaching altogether. He fantasized about being a parish priest. From 1928 through 1934, he wrote at least 100 letters to parishes from New Jersey to California, but his inquiries were futile. His Tracy City friend, James Hollingsworth, commented: "The deck was stacked against Father Flye leaving St. Andrew's. The depression kept the lid on everything. Plus, and this is important, who in their right mind would hire a priest who had picked a fight with a Bishop?"

Grace Flye had been prophetic in 1928 when she wrote her father: "Hal is talking about an opening in Philadelphia. If he does succeed in getting an offer, I'm not too sure he would really act on it. He loves the Mountain and these boys too much. Is it preordained that we will stay here in our bungalow forever?"

By the mid-1930s, as he reached his 50th birthday, Father Flye probably knew he would be staying at St. Andrew's. His journal notations were still critical of the way the school was administered, but a boggy resignation had set in. He maintained his cheerful countenance in the classroom, keeping his disappointments private. Weather permitting, he would drive to Birdwood on weekends to "do repairs." The buildings at isolated Birdwood were occasionally vandalized and this depressed Flye. It is doubtful he actually made any repairs; however, the solitude of Birdwood provided him a refuge from the rest of the world.

He still had his summer duties to look forward to. Starting in 1921, every spring he anticipated leaving the Mountain. He knew his summer duties would not require a big workload. He would have the opportunity to do the things he relished: reading, visiting museums and libraries, meeting interesting people. He made friends easily; his repertoire of witty poems served him well. His personality was such that he was liked by almost everyone he met, especially those in the artistic community. In New York City, he socialized with artists, poets, writers. He made lifelong friendships and correspondents during those summer interludes.

Andrew Lytle remarked: "Father Flye would not have survived without his summers in the larger cities, where he rubbed shoulders with the erudite, and had his mental battery recharged."

Flye worked summers in Chicago, Washington, Milwaukee, Atlanta, Philadelphia, New York City, St. Paul. One summer he stayed in the Bahamas. Several summers were taken up with trips to Europe. He spent part of one summer in California.

Grace never went with him. The truth is that she did not want to go. Her letters show she was always glad to see him leave. She welcomed the three months of not having to adjust to his demands, his moods, his schedule. Summers were a time when her relatives could visit her at the St. Andrew's bungalow with some privacy. The Major liked Father Flye, but he was not very popular with most of the Houghton family, so his absences were welcomed by the summer visitors. The Houghton women loved to get together and talk about family matters, enjoying each other's company. It was common knowledge, however, that Grace's husband detested gossipy "small talk."

Grace wrote in one of her letters: "The weekend of June the first, second and third is the school's commencement, a difficult time for everybody, and me too. So much excitement in the air. Then Hal leaves for New York in his final rush, trying to do the things he's had no time for, in a panic of packing at the last minute. I gasp like a fish thrown up by a tidal wave on the seashore when it is over, sinking into a nirvana of infinite calm."

Father Flye expanded the Birdwood property in 1940. He bought an additional six acres from the widow of Malcolm H. MacDowell for $50. The concept of having his progressive school at Birdwood was moot by then, but he still believed the site might somehow be used, perhaps for a retirement home in his final years.

Living at Birdwood was a persistent idea with Grace Flye. In a letter dated April 20, 1948, she wrote: "My apprehension about our future is tied to David McDowell, who has dreamed of living with us at Birdwood. He hoped he could be with the *Sewanee Review*, but so far there is no opening. Two weeks ago the head of the magazine came out and discussed David, and said he wanted an assistant, so my hopes sprang to the heavens. If David and Madeline do come here, I want them to stay with us until we can fix up our Birdwood. Madeline and I want to have a flower and vegetable garden, vineyard, a horse and a Lotus pool to reflect the sky. Hal and Madeline want to make casks of wine. David and I want to tunnel into the cliff to store them."

In a letter dated October 7, 1948, she again wrote about Birdwood: "Hal's heart is bound up in teaching, but it is much too late. He cannot bear the idea of retiring, but nothing remains but Birdwood to us. He is excessively intense in an intellectual way, but he is utterly alone for the companionship he craves. Hal is dampened by the idea of pioneering, which is the breath of life to me. My plan is to have our friend, Alec, go with us to our Birdwood. He loves Birdwood the way I do, so his enthusiasm will bolster us up. I am so anxious for him to be with us. He has such an atmosphere of vibrant living, and that is what we have been without since our early years in this spot."[2]

In a 1948 letter, Mrs. Flye described her apprehension about an intimidating forest fire: "The last two weeks of October were ominous, the smoke of burning forests and the air heavy and blue. All the fire wardens were called to Winchester as word came the fires were out of hand. An urge of terror took hold of me that Birdwood would go. I went out every day, frantically raking away around the buildings. My feet began to swell; it didn't matter. The Cove near Birdwood was a sea of white smoke. A crew of six men came and burned a fire guard. Flames leaped to the sky, but Birdwood was saved." For three days in October, 1948, the St. Andrew's student body manned fire lines on the Mountain. Despite the inherent dangers, the boys saw the experience as an exciting vacation from the classroom.

Grace wrote to her husband on June 16, 1950: "Our friend, George Mackleheron, came by with his family, driving from Fort Worth to Cincinnati. He was anxious to see you, but as a second choice, I got on famously. I wanted to tell George about our future at Birdwood, but I didn't.

"To listen to George one would think there were few to equal you in this hemisphere, with all your knowledge and magnetic quality as a teacher. His three children love to study. The two boys are sixteen and fourteen, and the girl twelve. The oldest son is keen on languages, especially Latin, and he wants to take up French. He is halfway between Oliver Hodge and James Frazier. The sixteen year old noticed the book on Italy by Count Sforza and stopped as if hypnotized; he opened it and could hardly put it down. To have such a boy study with you at Birdwood would be God's answer to our prayers."

In March of 1953, Father Flye sold a permanent easement at Birdwood (694 feet long and 75 feet wide) to the Tennessee Valley Authority for $600. The TVA needed the clearance for transmission lines. That same month, he sold another two acres of the Birdwood property to James and Louise Merrit for $200.

A Grace Flye letter dated September 23, 1953, showed her anxiety: "A TVA lawyer came to the bungalow. He talked to me about more of our Birdwood set aside for power lines. He was from the Chattanooga office and friendly, but I was terrified to learn the northern part of our precious property may be appropriated. Hal praises me for having the mind of a lawyer, but I wish he would be more active in this matter."

In another letter, one month later, Mrs. Flye wrote: "I'm writing letters to obliterate our wicked opponents. Nothing will come out of trying to shove the Giant Electric Line (TVA) off the north section of our land. The dumb court-house in Winchester can't get a routine matter straight. Those people stupidly put a piece of our land for sale for unpaid taxes! We held all the tax receipts, and the county had to buy it back for us after it was sold to a couple from Kentucky. There is now some crazy argument over assessments."

The Flyes would continue to visit Birdwood, sometimes together, sometimes alone. It was their sanctuary of hopeful dreams. As time went by, their visits were tinged with an increasing melancholy. Tears would be shed for what could have been. The place was symbolic — it represented the Flye Academy, where talented students could have received a classical education.

St. Andrew's faculty wife, Ethel Louise Simmonds, knew about Birdwood and said it was a sad component in her friendship with Grace: "She always talked about the idea of having a school for boys who had an aptitude for higher learning, a place with less than a dozen boys. Mrs. Flye told me that, at one time, Father Wright was going to be the school's business manager. Every spring she would go out to their property to clear weeds. She always talked about getting the school ready. It was unreal. We all knew it was just a fantasy.

"The heartbreak piled-up for the Flyes. A friend of Father Flye, an English teacher at the University of the South, told me about the time he drove Father Flye out to his Lost Cove property, and how Father Flye just sat there and sobbed."

Andrew Lytle remembered: "The roofs had caved in, the well was dry, the door jambs were rotted, as was half the floor spaces. The property at Lost Cove looked neglected and forsaken. We went there several times together, but all Father Flye talked about was how boys needed the proper atmosphere to learn. He never discussed what it was going to take to get the property up and going.

His ideas about the school were odd in that he planned on having no more than ten boys, and they had to be exceptional to go there in the first place. I'm talking about boys with high IQs and already versed in the classics. It was a utopian concept, not very realistic."

Robert Costa reinforced Andrew Lytle's elitism impression: "Two of Father Flye's favorite quotations regarding education were St. Paul's 'there is a diversity of gifts,' meaning not everyone should be forced to have the same education, and the other was from *History of the Decline and Fall of the Roman Empire*, where Edward Gibbon wrote: 'Instruction is seldom of much efficacy, except in those happy dispositions where it is superfluous.' Father Flye often said Gibbon's wisdom was superior to all the books written on education. Plato would have felt comfortable at Birdwood."

Father Bonnell Spencer, Prior of St. Michael's Monastery at St. Andrew's from 1947 through 1955, wrote: "The Order of the Holy Cross knew of his dream for having his own school. He made no secret what his plans were. But, in my opinion, he was an idealist with no grasp of reality. He had no idea what went into running a private school. He was a great teacher, but he lacked practicality. He was caught-up in his own theoretical world of ideas."

Even if the Great Depression had not taken place, it is unlikely Father Flye would have raised the funding to get his school started. There are no records to indicate he ever asked anyone for money. He never created a business plan; never put on paper what it would cost to renovate Birdwood; never projected the school's income or overhead. Even unsophisticated investors expect a minimum of planning before they write a check. Ivory tower theories do not inspire bankers or investors, yet all Father Flye ever offered were his ideas about progressive education. This is puzzling when one looks at his family background; his grandfather and parents were knowledgeable about profit and loss columns.

Mrs. Flye was as naive as her husband when it came to business. During a visit to the bungalow by Mary Boorman, Grace showed her niece a sketch of the buildings at Birdwood, explaining: "This is where Hal will teach Latin, over here we will have an art room, here is where geography will be taught, here is where the boys will sleep. Hal will show our plans to our friends after supper. He is so excited about this place of ours, that he can't hold it in." After studying the outline for some time, and being afraid to offend, Mary cautiously asked: "Aunt Grace, where is the kitchen?" "Oh, we hadn't thought of that," was Mrs. Flye's reply.

In a letter-to-the-editor published in a Tennessee newspaper in 1962, Arthur Ben Chitty stated: "Hereabouts we consider Father Flye to be the greatest correspondent since the 18th century. His life was dedicated to gifted children. On the edge of our mountain here stand the ruins of Father Flye's great dream, a school, never opened, for exceptional boys. His wife, a Houghton, lost her inheritance in the depression. The doors and windows of the main building were not framed. For years, packets of roofing shingles mouldered; what a pity it is that the Flye Academy never opened."

At another time, Dr. Chitty said: "The overriding factor about Father Flye's status quo was his timidity. He was an aggressive bear of a teacher, but the instant he left a classroom he reverted to an embarrassed shyness. He considered self-promotion to be indecent or dishonest, so there is no mystery as to why he failed to get his school up and running. The practical, the useful, the place where the rubber hits the road, did not enter his thinking. He lived in his own sphere of lofty concepts.

"At one time, the Claibornes offered their acreage close to Sewanee for the so-called Flye Academy, but that notion was turned down. The Flyes rejecting the offer of free land is inexplicable. Additionally, there was a wealthy branch of the Houghton family in New York and New England, but the Flyes never asked that side of her family for any financial aid. It was common knowledge that both Arthur and Amory Houghton were very approachable, and gave away millions for worthy causes."

James Hollingsworth: "When I think about Father Flye's personal history, and the property called Birdwood, I'm reminded of something written by Prime Minister Benjamin Disraeli: 'Youth is a time of blunder. Manhood a time of struggle. Old age a time of regret.' Father Flye's educational ideas were too advanced for that time in American history. His notions are being used in your better schools today, and this is why Birdwood was a sad paradox."

❑ ❑ ❑

What if Father Flye returned today to the campus where he taught for many years? He would find a co-educational institution that has excelled. Members of the 1999 graduating class at St. Andrew's-Sewanee School were offered one million dollars in scholarships, and were accepted at 42 colleges and universities. Father Flye would be impressed.

The geographical location is the same, but comparing St. Andrew's School in Father Flye's time with today's campus is like comparing night and day. He would love the current St. Andrew's-Sewanee School, because it is a laboratory where the future of education is being developed. Today's SAS students are active participants rather than passive listeners in class. Regarding this approach to teaching, one can imagine Father Flye clapping his enormous hands, and saying: "Yes, yes, yes."

Today's SAS classroom atmosphere is relaxed but busy. The individual freedom given each pupil to develop at his or her own pace, would indeed be sweet poetry to Father Flye. This is what he had in mind when he dreamed of his own school at Birdwood.

Affirmation that the school is on the proper path comes from test scores and college admissions. In both categories, SAS students consistently rank much higher than the national average. Father Flye would be proud of this fact.

St. Andrew's-Sewanee is the second-oldest Episcopal school in Tennessee, and the ninth-oldest Episcopal boarding school in the nation. The foundation of the current school began with the 1981 merger of St. Andrew's School and Sewanee Academy, two schools linked to the Episcopal church. There is no doubt that Father Flye would love the historical continuity and Christian ethics represented at today's campus.

❑ ❑ ❑

Father Flye encouraged any pupil who showed an inclination toward creative writing, and he used poetry as his lever. Lyrical poetry is usually short and has a rhyming quality. Narrative poems tell a story that is usually lengthy. Dramatic poetry tells a story through the speech of one or more characters. Father Flye knew that the writing of poetry forced the author to use language in a special way. Over the years, a number of St. Andrew's pupils submitted their poetry for his appraisal. Regardless of the quality, he was not judgmental about the poem, limerick or jingle. The following was composed by student Lee Medley, a 1935 St. Andrew's graduate:

> At first he is an infant small,
> And does not seem to grow at all
> There on his mother's breast he lies
> And only very seldom cries.
>
> And then he starts out into life
> And thinking only of a wife
> But later time will change that way
> From dreary night to sunny day
>
> He is not now a righteous man
> But he is reaching for God's hand
> And when they meet He gives him grace
> And tells him how to win the race.
>
> Then when his God gives him the sound
> And his poor body is in the ground
> He sleeps there in his cold, cold grave
> Until he becomes strong and brave.
>
> Then up he goes into the sky
> Where his dear King will never die,
> And waits there on that golden strand
> To join God's happy royal band.

And this poem about World War I is Father Flye's, written September 1, 1938, exactly one year before World War II began.

Flanders Fields Twenty Years After

In Flanders Fields no sleep we know,
Although the crosses, row on row,
Still watch above us where we lie,
And poppies blow, and through the sky
The larks sing and the soft clouds go.

Ominous sounds of shame and woe
Disquieted our rest below;
Was it for naught we had to die
In Flanders Fields?

Cringing before our brutal foe
Whose paths o'er freedom's ruins go,
The torch that we held so high
To earth let fall, for peace you cry.
Remember us who lie so low
In Flanders Fields.

Father Flye wrote commentaries and poetry all of his life. On September 24, 1965, at age 80, he wrote the following. He titled it "The Tree."

"In the soft, fading light of a September evening after a cloudy, somewhat humid day, with light rain now beginning to fall, about six o'clock, I sit looking out through the open door and across the little terrace at 19 Perry Street, in Greenwich Village, above and across the enclosed court and garden just in the rear of St. John's Church.

"A bit of wind has begun to come up in gusts. Above the level of my eyes, as I look through to the rear of the church, is the top of a maple tree, some 40 feet, perhaps, above the ground, the branches now swayed, now still. The top is not console thick but that one can see through to the rear of the Church; these extended branches, with their gentle lines. Now they stand almost still; no day sway, dense by the gusts of the wind. The vital green of the leaves from the summer's growth; no trace yet of the colors of fall; the wonderful, soft green branches and twigs with leaves, thousands of them.

"None of those leaves knows of its own existence, of its own individual and beautiful form, or of the branch of the tree of which it forms a part. No cell in any one of the leaves knows of the leaf of which it is a part, or of the tree. Each intent, so far as it can be said to be intent, on its own being. These leaves are living, vital, supplied by the watery sap which comes up to them in tiny channels through the trunk, the limbs, the twigs, the little stems, the delicate leaf-structure, from the earth below. None of these could conceive of the tree, but the tree is an entity; yet shall we say inherently, or only to an intelligence capable of perceiving it as such?

"This tree stands, its top far above the ground, the branches supported by the trunk, and this anchored in the earth by roots, sinews of wood terminating in filaments with tender, delicate tips burrowing down into solid earth and forming the great root-system capable of solidly supporting the visible structure of the tree above ground, tons in weight.

"In a few weeks those leaves will have lost their green vitality. They will have become brown, dry; they will fall; and there will be the bare branches to be seen against the sky. But the life of the tree goes on, and with the recurring northward course of the sun, buds will form on the twigs and the tiny beginnings of leaves will put forth and grow, and by summer, again the tree as one looks at it will be clad in green leaves, branches growing, extending, more twigs and leaves forming, the tree enlarging. And the tree itself a part of a greater entity, and this of a greater, and this of a greater.

"And what shall we say of the cells which form the organs and parts of the entity of our own body? And our body, is it a component of a larger entity? What is that?"

❑ ❑ ❑

[1] Another reason Grace did not travel with her husband in the summer was the menagerie living in the bungalow. Most of the new-born or injured animals that were brought to her house were eventually released back into the woods. However, in some cases, a rabbit or cat, whatever, became a pet. Grace Flye could never leave "her little creatures."

[2]Alec's surname is unknown.

The St. Andrew's curriculum improved with the passing years. This schedule of courses was printed in a 1960s school catalogue:

ENGLISH	THEOLOGY	LANGUAGES
English I, II, III, IV	Old Testament	Spanish I, II, III, IV
English V (honors)	New Testament	French I, II, III, IV
European Literature	Church History	German I, II
American Literature	Contemporary Living	
Classical Literature	Ethics	
Public Speaking		
Journalism		
Creative Writing		

MATHEMATICS	MUSIC	CLASSICAL LANGUAGES.
Algebra I, II	Fundamentals & Appreciation	Latin I, II, III, IV
Geometry	Chorus	Greek I, II
Analytic Geometry	Rejoice Band	
Trigonometry		
Probability & Statistics		
Senior Mathematics		

SCIENCES	HISTORY	ART
Biology	U.S.A. History	Basics
Chemistry	European History	Advanced
Physics	Ancient History	
Forestry	Russian History	BELLEEK
Ecology	English History	(porcelain)
Aeronautics	Oriental History	Beginning
	American Government	Advanced
	Western Thought (tutorial)	
	Latin American History	

CHAPTER 11

New York City Memories

A merry heart doeth good like a medicine, but a broken spirit drieth the bones.
—PROVERBS 17:22

*I*N 1941 FATHER FLYE began his summer respites in New York City as a vacation-relief priest at St. Edward The Martyr church, at the northeast corner of Central Park, and the Church of St. Luke in the Fields in Greenwich Village. From 1943 until 1954 his summer duties were exclusively at St. Luke's. He became a fixture at the church in 1960, and for the next 23 years he was at St. Luke's permanently.

In 1970 he moved from 19 Perry Street to 96 Barrow Street, in the same block as St. Luke's. He collected his mail at 487 Hudson Street, the St. Luke's parish office. In 1971, he moved to an apartment on the St. Luke's property.

Flye loved New York. Ever since he had visited the city as a young boy, he thought it was one of the most stimulating cities on earth. Grace did too. She enjoyed her days in New York as an artist, and she had warm memories of "being with Hal during our magical courting days."

He was near graduation from the Union Theological Seminary when on February 22, 1915, Grace wrote her father: "Hal took me over to Staten Island today to see a home for the destitute blind. It seems good to sit and look into the blind faces, with such character written over them, their hair and dress so neat and tidy. It makes you fall over to behold their contrast to seeing folk. Later they all held his hands and said their thanks to him. Hal preaches simple, strong words."

In those days, Flye privately visited burial sites for the homeless. It took several men with picks and shovels up to an hour to dig a grave, lower a wooden coffin and then cover the grave with dirt. With no mourners present, this was a lonely and depressing business. As only a divinity student, his presence carried no official weight, but he thought society's exiles deserved his unspoken benediction.

The cantankerous, awesome, dirty, proud and magnificent New York City is the ultimate urban experiment, where all races, religions and schools of thought try to co-exist. Statistics about the city are overwhelming. In each of the city's five boroughs, there is a small part of everything the world has generated: the smells of Canton, the din of Turin, the beer of Berlin, the Creole of Port-au-Prince. Basques, Kurds, Tibetans, every oppressed group on earth, have chosen New York as the place to voice their agony. The city has more than 3,000 places of conventional worship, and one for every cult and sect invented by man in his search for spiritual belonging.

New York has been the nation's fashion model, bank, designer, artist, photographer, publisher, advertiser, publicist, playwright. The concert halls, jazz clubs, and off-Broadway stages have been the incubator for the nation's artistic maternity ward. In Manhattan people can buy anything: diamonds from a black-robed Hasidic merchant on 49th Street, stolen household appliances at a fencing operation as elaborate as any department store, chocolate-covered ants from Uruguay.

Despite the upheavals that marked the city in the decades of the 1960s and 1970s, Father Flye took the historian's long-range view, keeping events in perspective. When a friend complained about the city's crime rate, he reminded his friend the city had suffered from a much worse crime rate 100 years earlier.

Flye was aware of the city's myriad problems, but he chose to remain optimistic, a virtue fondly remembered by St. Luke's parishioner Catherine Maldonado: "Once I was griping about the awful streets, the potholes. I don't know how he did it, but when I walked away from him that day I was feeling very rosy, very proud of New York. The man was remarkable."

In a letter to Henry Talbert, the priest wrote: "Despite the hysteria you hear, you'll not find any opium dens here. Editors like their high ratings, so don't be fooled into thinking people here are cringing behind bolted doors. Not all New Yorkers are rude, any more than all Dutchmen wear wooden shoes. The media is guilty of stereotyping and malicious puffing. New York is a wonderful place to live."

Residents of New York City have always spoken their own language. Depending on where you live, the designation "New York" means Manhattan, New York City or the state of New York. Father Flye never had any trouble speaking the language. The list of people he knew there was a kaleidoscope: publishers, street vendors, bums, poets, artists, store clerks, taxi drivers, actors, the homeless. His pastoral outlook enveloped everyone he greeted. In turn, everyone liked him.

Television personality Dave Garroway said: "Father Flye was the friendliest man I ever met. He had a bubbling enthusiasm for living. He did the nicest thing for me at a party one night. He wrote down a catchy poem, which I later read on the *Today* show." The poem was "A Kind of Love Letter to New York," by Phyllis McGinley, one of Father Flye's favorites. Part of it reads:

Ah, some love Paris,
And some Purdue.
But love is an archer
With a low I.Q.
A bold, bad bowman,
And innocent of pity.
So I'm in love with
New York City.

In 1978, Flye heard that McGinley was ill. He tried to visit her, but was told she was too ill to see anyone. She died a few days later.

Part of Flye's optimism came from the fact that he had traveled the city's streets for years and he was a keen observer of the human condition. As a clergyman, he saw the potential for good in all people. His positive outlook was aided by his knowledge of the city's promise for the future. He reminded everyone that New York City had the nation's safest drinking water, the United Nations, and the Statue of Liberty.

He had many friends at St. Luke's. Mostly better-educated, well-traveled and social, the congregation appealed to him; in turn, churchgoers treasured his friendship. In the garden next to the church's Rectory is a bronze plaque that reads:

A garden is a lovesome thing, God wot!
Rose plot,
Fringed pool,
Ferned grot —
The veriest school
Of peace; and yet the fool
Contends that God is not —
Not God! in gardens! when the eve is cool?
Nay, but I have a sign;
'Tis very sure God walks in mine.

In memory of
Father Flye
Priest, Teacher, Friend —
a man who loved beauty
and had the touch of a poet

Even though he was never a full-time priest at St. Luke's, the plaque bears witness to his extraordinary influence.

Amy Clampitt, a St. Luke's parishioner, remembered his fluttery friendliness: "I met him at a party and handed him my new book of poems and he had this big smile. I look back with a great deal of fondness on that moment. I regarded

Father Flye and children in Harlem, circa 1941

Father Flye as a friend, right from the start. He didn't come across with the kind of priestly mumbo-jumbo that so many priests can put on. There were people who said he was a saint. I don't know about that, but I do know he had a happy awareness of this world.

"He was bony. He was thin. Very large hands. Expressive hands, which were part of his personality. They were happy hands. Eccentric? Yes, I suppose so, but in a very nice way. Only someone very unusual would have loudly said: 'Look at those lovely oranges!' inside an A & P store. I was there when he did it. Child-like wonderment; yes, that's what it was. He had a childlike awe of everything around him.

"Years later I wrote a poem, 'Nothing Stays Put,' about supermarkets and exotic flowers suddenly showing up on the shelves. When the poem appeared in a book, I dedicated it to him. He didn't know it at the time, but he was the one who gave me the original idea. It is a happy memory when I think about Father Flye."

Clampitt, author of the children's book, *The Horse Who Lived Upstairs*, continued: "One of my recollections was his excitement about classical literature. I got excited the evening I heard him recite the first line of the *Iliad* in Greek. He said it in Greek! That was a new experience for me. He had a never-never mythical quality about him. On the other hand, he giggled a lot. He found humor in everything. He didn't look like an elf, but he behaved like one."

Anne Compton, a Perry Street neighbor, remembered: "He didn't live in a cloistered bubble. He read several newspapers every day. He listened to the radio and got upset about what a shady politician said or did; however, he was always sure the charlatan would sooner or later be voted out of office. He once said history's rear view mirror teaches you to be patient."

Beginning in the 1940s, an impressive number of former St. Andrew's students, some with wives and children, visited him in New York during the summers. He once said jokingly: "In all fairness, I should ask the mayor for a medal. Look at all the tourist trade I've created around here." Countless young, and not-so-young, men climbed the steep stairs at 63 Perry Street to see their beloved Father Flye.

In his later years, when he lived permanently on the premises at St. Luke's, the ritual of "seeing Father Flye in New York" continued. It seemed there was an unspoken yet firmly held maxim among the men who had known him at St. Andrew's—he spoke the truth when he whispered to James Hollingsworth: "I am blessed. I have many sons."

Until the 1970s, when illness began to take its toll, he was available, almost on a moment's notice, to show visitors his adopted city. He was consistently a cheerful tour guide to Central Park, Chinatown and the city's museums. Over the years, the priest spent innumerable hours entertaining out-of-town visitors.

Charlotte Lorna met Flye when she was a student at Columbia University in the 1940s. She eventually moved to Illinois, but they corresponded regularly.

She recalled a 1965 visit: "His hectic pace drove me ragged. We went to the Museum of Modern Art. Then we went to the public library, where those two huge lions are out front. Father Flye and I saw an original Gutenberg bible. Many of the museums were free or cost only a dollar or two. We sat at a sidewalk cafe and had three hours of conversation, which I really enjoyed. He knew where those interesting nooks and crannies were, especially in Greenwich Village. He was the perfect host. For example, he knew about the exciting free lectures in town on any given day.

"Once we were at Washington Square and we watched a young woman playing the cello, the big fiddle between her knees. There was a sign which read 'music student' and folks were dropping coins in a bucket at her feet. She was playing a classical bit, and Father Flye put a dollar bill in the bucket. Once we saw a young violinist in the subway. His sign read Juilliard and he was doing something bouncy. Father Flye and I got caught up in the spirit of it all, snapping our fingers and tapping our feet.

"He told me how he used to stand on the corner in New Haven, while he was at Yale, and play the harmonica for tin cup tips. He chuckled as he told me about being so proud the day he collected $1.50. He waited on tables, sorted catalogue cards and proofread items in the school library, sold pots and pans door-to-door during his college years. He quit playing the harmonica after he was hurt in a car wreck."

Lorna continued: "I visited him in New York about five times over a 20-year period, and we went out and mixed with engaging folks. Once it was a neighbor's wedding party; another time it was a party where someone had written a book. I was in my 20s when I met him. He was always like a grandfather to me, always hovering, always making sure I enjoyed myself. My visits with him always left me breathless. He had more energy than anyone half his age.

"I vividly recall us going down the four flights of steps at his Perry Street apartment, and when we got to the subway turnstile, he made certain I knew his door would always be open to me."

In the late 1950s, Father Flye was a devoted fan of New York City radio personality Carlton Fredericks, an expert on nutrition. He reminded visitors to his tiny apartment: "Don't forget, Carlton says to take your vitamin C today."

Father Flye was a steady customer at Wright's Book Store in Greenwich Village. He befriended Thomas Martinez, the store manager, who recalled: "Sometimes I thought he was a bit naive in his abiding optimism. On second thought, this wasn't all bad, was it? Once, in the winter, I was griping about the snow not being removed. But he said the lousy weather was not such a bad thing, because it would force people to help each other. I thought he put an unusual twist on it.

"Later that same day I saw a teenager stop, turn, come back and help an old woman get across an intersection down where the World Trade Center was later built. It was obvious they didn't know each other. The wind was really vicious.

The boy put his arm around her and held her up all the way across the street. Then they went their separate ways. It was a scene which stuck in my mind. I later told Father Flye about it, and he just smiled and said he wasn't surprised. He always had the ability to see the brighter side."

Erik Wensberg, New York editor, had sunny memories of Father Flye: "I never knew a man more whole in himself, equally kind to children and adults. This was true with St. Luke's parishioners, his neighbors on Hudson Street, or poets, writers, university students, or others who sought him out. He knew scholars, grocers and mechanics. It isn't really odd that Father Flye could discuss politics and literature in both a grand and humble setting. He was flexible. One's social circle is determined by whom one knows. An interesting person has a way of meeting other interesting people, and he had a knack for cultivating friendships.

"His politics were what could be called conservative; derived from his 19th-century background, reinforced by his adoption of southern individualism. Having said this, I must add that in his conversations political differences would always slip from sight in favor of Christian charity. For the most part, he exuded an inner joy, a happiness which would seem inexplicable to ordinary people. Father Flye believed that man had an obligation to reflect the qualities of a forgiving God.

"I recall him telling me in the summer of 1970 that he had just performed a marriage ceremony for a young couple of distinctly hippie bohemian style. He allowed as how he would probably disagree with them on many of their ideas; he was always strongly opposed to the more rambunctious forms of student rebellion. But then he went on to describe the sweetness and friendliness of this boy and girl, and his real pleasure in performing their marriage ceremony."

Petite New York pottery artist, Anna Zachary, recounted: "I first met Father Flye at a book store. He was the one who introduced me to Eastern philosophy, a subject that I found curious for some priest to be interested in. The last time I was with him, we talked about sexism. I complained that women didn't get enough credit in history.

"He brought up such notable women as Joan Of Arc, Madame Curie, and rattled off other names, some which I didn't recognize. He acknowledged that world cultures have held women back from equality, that he understood my attitude. He mentioned cowboy movies were based on the code of the West where women were protected, I argued this was chauvinistic, and women didn't need protecting. He gave me the oddest look when I said that.

"Father Flye said historians weren't anti-female, but most of them had been men and they wrote about war and politics, areas dominated by men. He said women rarely had the chance to make history. He assured me that women would soon be center stage in politics, business, science, you-name-it, and that made me feel better. Father Flye admitted men of his age felt uncomfortable about the changes taking place.

"The Vatican had just issued postage stamps honoring Galileo Galilei, acknowledging the church had been wrong to imprison the astronomer in 1633 for claiming the sun was at the center of the solar system. I asked Father Flye if Rome was going to wait another 300 years to modify its ideas about women priests? He gave me an oblique answer, explaining Jesus had traveled with women, and that women had been present at the first Pentecost. He went on to say that Jesus appeared first to Mary Magdalene following his resurrection, and the apostle Paul had picked Lydia to establish the first Christian church in Europe. In other words, Jesus and his followers treated women as equals; however, he personally didn't think women should be ordained. We agreed to disagree, and let it go at that."

Zachary concluded: "He talked about his mother having such an influence on him when he was a child. He said she read stories and poetry to him when he was a boy, always introducing him to good literature. I could tell he loved his mother. Father Flye was delightful, with an old-fashioned courteous refinement."

Father Flye's duty during his twilight years at St. Luke's was as a substitute priest for morning Mass. The Rector, Leslie Laughlin, remembered meeting him for the first time in 1971: "He was living in an apartment not far away from St. Luke's, but it was on the fourth floor. He had trouble getting up and down stairs, so I suggested he move to St. Luke's, where there was a vacant ground floor apartment. I had heard of the legendary Father Flye, and was curious why he was so popular with everybody. As it turned out, I also became one of his devoted fans."

Father Laughlin continued: "He chose to celebrate the Holy Communion, and I was glad to have him do it. It was not some duty, except he felt to celebrate the Eucharist was internally connected to his relationship to God and the church. He wasn't under anybody's authority to be so involved; he chose to put himself there. He refused to do the new liturgy, and this is why he was liked by the parishioners who thought the church's rhythms and language should be left alone. It was not a theological issue, as such, but it was an aesthetical fineness for Father Flye that had a lot to do with his capacity to worship. There were plenty of parishioners who believed as he did.

"When I think of him, I see his face and his wonderful hands. He had piercing eyes, very intelligent eyes, and absolutely fascinating and large gnarled hands. His gestures with those hands captivated your attention. When he said Mass, it was like watching a dramatic play. He was full of intensity. I once had a conversation with a nun who had served at St. Mary's School near Sewanee, and she told me that Father Flye was noted for his theatrical way of celebrating Mass. He had this same intensity when I saw him perform at the altar.

"He did not believe God came into a person's life creeping silently, but that he burst in with a thunder clap and lightning bolt. He demonstrated this during a service at St. Luke's. He was elderly, barely able to walk, yet he lifted a wooden chair up over his head and dashed it onto the floor with a crash, saying: 'That's how God comes into your life.' This episode is part of St. Luke's folklore.

"To watch him, at his advanced age, set off across Hudson Street between 8th and 9th Avenues, major thoroughfares, was something to behold. He never crossed at the traffic light; he jaywalked like a crab with his arms out, pulling himself sideways. God was looking out for him on those occasions."

Father Laughlin added: "I was awed by Father Flye. He would have been startled by such an attitude, and that is just why I had to say it. He carried his own erudition so lightly and his religious faith so gracefully! He enjoyed the company of shopkeepers and scholars, and was interested in everyone and everything about him. My favorite memory is of him on the sidewalk, bent over, intently studying a column of ants carrying the remains of a shattered cookie back to their nest. He was excited and I marveled how anyone his age could be thrilled about something the rest of us took for granted. His sense of nature was something impressive.

"He was sitting alone in the Rectory garden, and a crying girl appeared, saying she was looking for Father Flye. The little girl was about eight years old. She wanted to talk to him, because her father had died. It is hard for me to explain how children were attracted to him. I saw it many times, but I can't explain it. It was his honesty and expression; any child could see that. Children knew they could trust him. Father Flye didn't have any barriers to youngsters, the way most adults do.

"People who cared about quality were drawn to him. He was surrounded by poets and playwrights. He had friends who were agnostics, and maybe even a Hindu mystic thrown in for good measure. This really didn't surprise me. He had so much devotion for literature that provided bridges to other people who shared an enthusiasm for life. He had no imperialism in his faith. His intellect was extremely versatile. His sense of humor drew folks to him. To say the least, he wasn't your typical clergyman. We will probably never see the likes of him again."

At her home in Florence, Italy, Father Laughlin's wife, Roxanna, remarked: "Father Flye's magnetism was extraordinary. I think of him with great affection. He would walk into a room and be quite gracious. He was great company; there was always a splendid conversation with him present. He often talked about things he had recently read, and somehow got you involved in the subject. Getting your input was a primary thing with him. He was held in great esteem at St. Luke's. He was familiar with the neighborhood, and the people who went to his services were always pleased when he was there. He was a great reader, and he had a gift for making our language be alive and wonderful."

William Jackson, a 1951 St. Andrew's graduate, said: "I visited him in New York City several times. He lived on Hudson street. He took my wife, Liz, me and my little daughter, around the city for a whole day in 1968. We had a lovely time. He was a little crippled with arthritis, but once he got moving he was okay. He knew New York City like he had been born there. He was the most knowledgeable person about history you could meet. He said the Frenchman, Alexis de Tocqueville, should be required reading in every American history class. One of the paradoxes about him was he could keep up with anyone on an intellectual basis, yet he would act like a giddy child. Everything was so exciting to him, whether it was seeing a pigeon eating popcorn in Central Park or a new building under construction. He was a romantic realist. That may be a contradiction in terms, but that's what he was."

Timothy Barton lived in the same Perry Street building where the priest rented an apartment for many years: "I was just a kid when I met Father Flye. I was skeptical and full of vinegar, questioning everything adults believed in. The thing I recall most was his ability to reduce complicated subjects to the level where a boy, like myself, could understand. When I first met him I was at that stage where I was curious about almost everything. I bombarded him with questions. He wasn't sanctimonious, like I had expected. Once we sat on the front steps, and though our conversation was many years ago, I remember what was said. I asked him: 'How can you prove the existence of God?' He used the analogy of a man finding a wristwatch on the sidewalk. He said logic told the man the watch, with its gears and springs, was made by another person. The man couldn't know where or how the timepiece was made, or who made it, but he would know the mechanisms inside the watch weren't there by random chance. It would be obvious there was some design and purpose to the watch.

"He said the universe might appear to be random matter, but it has order and was designed by a vastly superior intellect. He said the survival instincts of a newborn gazelle, which can walk around in minutes after birth, was a mystery of nature. He told me the more scientists learn about what was so miraculous to our forefathers, the more they become reverent of God, not less.

"I then asked him what was the greatest miracle he had ever heard of. I expected him to say something out of the Bible. But he didn't. What Father Flye did do was gently put his finger against the middle of my chest, and whisper: 'The greatest miracle of all, Timmy, is what changes you here.' I never forgot that moment."

The author of this book remembers, "In the summer of 1952, during the Korean War, the Air Force was shipping me overseas from a debarkation base in Brooklyn, so I called Father Flye when I arrived in New York. We sat for hours at a sidewalk cafe in Greenwich Village, and he had me laughing with his humorous poetry. His memory was unbelievable. No matter what we talked about, he remembered a poem that was appropriate. I had missed him, so I was pleased to see him again.

"We went to Jim Agee's for supper. I had heard of Agee, of course, but had never met him. He was friendly. He showed me the screenplay he was writing about the French artist, Paul Gauguin, who moved to Tahiti in the latter part of his life. However, the proposed film, *Noa-Noa*, was never produced. Agee was a jazz aficionado, and he suggested we all go see a popular drummer, Buddy Rich, currently appearing at a Harlem jazz joint. Agee said jazz is good for your soul. We were in a taxi on our way to Harlem when Father Flye recited a Shakespearean soliloquy, and a few minutes later he was using table forks to keep time with the jazz band. He eased from Shakespeare to "Lullaby of Birdland" with no effort at all.

"Agee didn't look healthy. He had bloodshot eyes, no muscle tone, a heavy smoker's cough. I wasn't surprised to hear several years later that he died. It wasn't until 1963, when I was in the St. Louis airport and saw *James Agee's Letters to Father Flye* in a bookstore, that I learned of Agee's connection to Father Flye. I realized that my old St. Andrew's teacher had a history I knew little about."

Dr. Arthur Ben Chitty told this story about Flye and a Chinese boy: "I was living in New York City in the late 1960s. Father Flye had a small place on Perry Street. To the despair of my suffering wife, I picked up strays who had no direction. And such a boy was Mon Sing Eng, whose parents were both dead.

"He was 11 and hyperactive. His public school teacher said he was a lad with superb potential. He became 'John' Eng and I took him to see Father Flye. John presented a real challenge to the 75-year old retired priest.

"In a couple of months, Father Flye called and asked if I could come by to see him. He told me he had detected John stealing money from him, but he had not talked to him about it. His strategy would be to continue teaching, which was reading classics to each other, with Father Flye providing the commentary. Things went well for the next year. Father Flye kept his trinkets and cash in a safe place. But then Father Flye noticed John was flashing more money than a schoolboy should have. With discreet questioning, he got John to confess that he was delivering illegal drugs for hoodlums in Greenwich Village.

"John had a bicycle and the local dealers were using him as a courier, knowing the police would probably overlook the boy's activities. Their reasoning was also that if he were caught, the court would go easy and treat him as a juvenile offender. Hoping it might break his living pattern, I arranged for a friend of mine to pay for John to go to a fancy school, Deerfield Academy, for which Father Flye prepared the boy. Sadly, John was later expelled from Deerfield for stealing.

"In due course, John notified us that he was in jail for drug dealing. He dropped out of sight, and we never heard from him again. This particular story does not have a happy ending. I can only tell you what a forgiving man Father Flye was. If only John Eng had given Father Flye a chance, maybe a 'tree would have grown in Brooklyn.'

"Along Father Flye's path there were many John Engs, most of them with happier endings. The point is that he was always the forgiving priest, ever ready to start again anew, when his experience should have made him a bitter man. He was a person who always offered friendliness and optimism. I don't know how he did it. I pray God will give us more like Father Flye."

Father Flye caused a stir in the 1970s when the *New York Herald Tribune* published a review of his "Pacifist in Athens." He wrote: "More than thirty years after my paper on Pacifism was written, my views have not changed. With a condemnation of war's heinous cruelty I'm in full accord, and also with something that General Sherman wrote to the Mayor of Atlanta: 'You cannot qualify war in harsher terms than I will. War is brutality and you cannot refine it.' If the men of Athens at the time of the Persian invasion in 490 B. C. were pacifists, we would never have heard the name of Euripides, there would have been no writing of *The Trojan Women* or other notable works produced in that flowering of Athenian civilization after the defeat of the Persians, and the expanded opportunity for freedom of the Greek mind and spirit."

In a letter dated January 24, 1973, the St. Luke's Rector, Leslie Laughlin, wrote to Father Flye: "Thanks for your sensitive and controversial essay on pacifism. What I like most is the depth of your feelings for both sides of the argument. I was struck by the fact that James Reston and you both dealt with the problem of the bomber pilot and artilleryman who carry out their destruction without actually seeing the work of their hands. There are many people in this congregation who would enjoy your essay, because of what you have written and because it was 'you' who wrote it. Would you let me Xerox copies and offer them to anyone who would like it? I know of numerous folks who want to read it."

Robert Costa, who as a young man met Father Flye in New York City, remembered: "Father Flye relished the art, the culture, the mixture of people found in the Big Apple. He liked to talk to the writers and poets he met. He was so congenial with everyone. Here was this great intellect trapped inside a sinking ship. In his advancing years, as his hearing and eyesight worsened, he had bouts of depression so common for the elderly. But well into his 80s and 90s, he had tons of visitors and this pleased him very much. During his last years at St. Luke's he had a devoted team of caretakers who made his life comfortable. His quiet and green enclave at St. Luke's was his private oasis, and we can only thank God he had it. If he had lived anywhere else, he would have died many years sooner."

CHAPTER 12

Robert Costa and Frederick Santee

That I make poetry and give pleasure are because of you.
—HORACE (65-8 BC)

A S HE WAS ENTERING HIS TEENAGE YEARS, Robert Costa met Father Flye, and it turned out to be a fortuitous encounter for the young man.

Robert Costa earned a B. A. at Hunter College of the City University of New York in June 1969, in Greek, Latin, and English. He taught at Bushwich High School in New York City from 1969-71. From 1972-75, he studied at Magdalen College at Oxford University, reading Literae Humaniores, including Latin and Greek literature, ancient history, philosophy and classical philology. He is now a classics teacher in the New York City school system. Following are excerpts from a long interview with Costa, who recounted his friendship with Flye:

"I met him while I was working at my family's grocery store, across the street from St. Luke's Church, in August of 1961. I was 13 and about to enter the ninth grade at Brooklyn Technical High School. He modified my future, to say the least.

"He walked in the store one day, and we began chatting. When he found out I was interested in learning Latin and Greek, he erupted in a wave of excitement. It was the start of our special friendship. When he learned I liked books he just flipped out, and he began to bring me newspaper and magazine articles. Before long, I started visiting him at his Perry Street flat, and he opened up a world of scholarship. The next year he began coaching me in Latin, and later he introduced me to the Greek alphabet.

"I did the deliveries for the grocery store that had been there ever since my parents immigrated from Italy in 1919. Being Italian, my family was Roman

Robert Costa at age 13

Catholic, but this didn't affect our warm feelings about the Episcopal churchgoers at St. Luke's.

"Many priests who wear the clerical collar are not that friendly, that approachable, but Father Flye had a bubbly and smiling personality. He was the most popular priest who ever served at St. Luke's. Parishioners gushed when they mentioned his name. The ladies at St. Luke's were especially fond of him. They told my parents the way Father Flye did the Eucharist service was dramatic and entertaining.

"During my high school years, we visited Father Flye's niece, Eleanor Talbert, who lived in Washington, D.C. He wanted me to see his enormous personal library that was kept there. He always complained that he missed his books, but there just wasn't enough room inside his small Perry Street flat. From what I saw, a thousand Perry Street apartments couldn't have held all his books! We had a field day going over the many titles on a wide variety of subjects.

"Father Flye's politics were conservative. He read the *National Review*, and he had met its publisher, William Buckley. From the onset in our friendship, we didn't talk politics. As Father Flye put it to me: 'James [Agee] and I didn't discuss politics, so we remained friends. You and I should also keep this subject out of bounds.' He knew I didn't agree with him. He voted for Barry Goldwater, and I was exasperated when he voted for Richard Nixon. I thought he took too many politicians at face value.

"I recall being at his place when the secret Nixon tapes were released; they bothered him. He found it hard to consider the President of the United States using such foul language. It was a crisis for Father Flye. Here was someone he had looked up to, and he felt disappointed. His Victorian sensibilities were bruised by Nixon's four-letter words. He voted for Ronald Reagan, so I gave up trying to argue with him.

"He was a 19th Century man. He liked the British sense of deference. I wouldn't go so far as to say he would have been a Tory in the Revolutionary War, but the idea of a monarchy appealed to him. He was attracted to that elegant class structure, as so many people are. He subscribed to Aristotle's concept of justice as a proportional thing. He never would have thought that everyone should go to college—that would have horrified him. On the other hand, he would treat a cab driver the same way he would a college professor. He just thought all people have different gifts.

"Some aspects of the civil rights movement bothered him. He said racial and gender hiring quotas only diminished standards. He equated it to supplying every student a passing grade, regardless of the test results.

"He was very keen about me going to Oxford, and I remember he went to Columbia University to see the playwright, Quentin Anderson, about me. He also saw Jacques Barzun, distinguished professor and author at Columbia. My studying at Oxford was Father Flye's original idea, and he was the person who made it possible. He was like a mother hen to me.

"One of his friends was the famous poet, W. H. Auden. I'll tell you the story how he helped me get into Oxford. Auden had left New York to live the last part of his life at Oxford. I wrote to Auden saying I want to meet you, because we both know Father Flye. Auden wrote back, saying: 'By all means, come and see me. Any friend of Father Flye is a friend of mine.' Robert Fitzgerald, who worked with Jim Agee at *Fortune* and *Time*, was also helpful. Father Flye introduced me to Fitzgerald. I later met Fitzgerald at Perugia, Italy, and he wrote Oxford on my behalf.

"Robert Temple was also instrumental in my going to Oxford. He was a former St. Andrew's student [a 1961 graduate] who had heard so many incredible tales about Father Flye that he decided, on his own, to go see him in New York. Naturally, Temple and Father Flye hit it off, both being eccentric, both sharing a love for exotic literature and languages. For example, Temple had studied Sanskrit, the ancient language of India, while he was an undergraduate at the University of Pennsylvania.

"I was 16 years old when I first met Robert Temple. Father Flye had arranged for me to go to this party of well-known literary figures, and for a teenager this was quite a thrill. One evening, Father Flye, Robert Temple, Tennessee Williams and myself went bar-hopping, an unforgettable treat for a boy my age. When *The Glass Menagerie* was playing on Broadway, I went as Tennessee's guest. I showed the ticket to my mother, and she almost fainted. Tennessee invariably contacted Father Flye when he came to New York City, and they'd talk for hours about poetry. Tennessee Williams told me he started writing poetry before he went to kindergarten.

"Robert Temple went to live in England, and he married a wonderful woman, who was a granddaughter of ex-Prime Minister Neville Chamberlain. Temple graduated from the University of London, and wrote science fiction books, plus he became a television producer. He pulled strings for me at Oxford, and he came to see me several times while I was at Magdalen College.

"Father Flye used to come over to my parent's house in Brooklyn for dinner. One night at their house he met the Vatican City's Latin Secretary, Reginald Foster, who wrote all the official Latin correspondence for the Pope. After that, Father Flye and Father Foster corresponded regularly, in Latin, of course.

"Speaking of my parents' house, I'm reminded of one of the few times I saw Father Flye really angry. He had taken a taxi to come for supper, and apparently the taxi driver had deliberately gone in circles, running up the meter. I watched from the front door, and saw Father Flye angrily jump out of the cab, slam the door, and yell at the cabby: 'I hope you don't have a nice Easter!'

"The only other times he showed irritation were when drunks came to his door at his St. Luke's apartment. He was always bothered by lushes. He was an easy touch for the homeless who lived near St. Luke's. He would shout: 'Get out of here. This is the last time I will give you money.' In the summer we would be sitting out front and every half hour somebody would come to panhandle. He was well-known among the Greenwich Village boozers. He once said to me, 'I'd rather they be honest and admit they want the cash for wine.'

"Father Flye selected his words carefully, and more often than not left you with a bit of wisdom to ponder. He once said to me that you should never trust a person who says he loves everybody, as he undoubtedly hates individuals. In other words, trust those you know for certain are kind to everyone. He said many 'lovers of humanity' were actually cruel to their own families and co-workers.

"He kept values that most Americans have abandoned. In that sense, he lived in a time that had different proprieties. He didn't go shopping. He was honest. He said you should be saving and never be wasteful. He wasn't part of the consumer culture. However, he loved his few gadgets, such as his camera and audio cassette recorder. He often recorded people's voices. He valued technology if it was useful. He marveled at those things. He commented what a remarkable life he had lived. When he was born, there were no airplanes, no automobiles, no telephones, no television, no radio, no electric lights, no computers. All these advancements came during his lifetime. Incidentally, he had the opinion that space exploration would have a great impact on the world, with satellite communications, and so on. I recall him saying: 'Science fiction is now science fact.' He would have enjoyed today's Internet and e-mail.

"He was eccentric. He subscribed to strange periodicals. There was some crackpot club that sent him anti-Darwinian magazines. The articles stated: 'This is impossible! How could you believe this?' There would be this animal, and the article would ask: 'How could it have evolved this way?' Father Flye said aloud to himself: 'You idiot. God created this animal's features.' He got agitated when he read the nonsense, but he continued to get the periodicals in the mail.

"*L'ombre de la Croix* [*Shadow of the Cross*] was one of his favorite books about North Africa. He had a fascination with Arabic history and culture. He loved books like Marguerite Yourcenar's *Memoirs of Hadrian*. She was the first woman to be elected to the French Academy, by the way.

"We used to talk about that famous passage in Lucretius, where he wrote that people ask for miracles, but all they had to do to find miracles is look up at the stars. Father Flye didn't take anything for granted; everything was a wonderful miracle to him. He thought great writing, music, life itself, were all miraculous.

"A poem which I remember Father Flye reciting in Latin, and which also moved him to his depths, was the epigram Emperor Hadrian [A.D. 76 –138] wrote for his own famous Mausoleum, which still stands in Rome, and is called the Castel Sant' Angelo.

> *Animula vagula blandula,*
> *Hospes comesque corporis,*
> *Quae nunc abibis in loca*
> *Pallidula rigida nudula,*
> *Nec ut soles dabis iocos!*

> Ah! gentle, fleeting wav'ring sprite,
> Friend and associate of this clay!
> To what unkown region borne,
> Wilt thou now wing thy distant flight?
> No more with wonted humour gay,
> But pallid, cheerless, and forlorn.

"Another epigram he loved was by the Alexandrian Greek poet Callimachus [305-240 B.C.]. He knew it by heart from the celebrated translation by the classics master at Eton, William Johnson Cory [1823-1892]:

> They told me, Heraclitus, they told me you were dead.
> They brought me bitter news to hear and bitter tears to shed.
> I wept as I remember'd how often you and I
> Had tired the sun with talking and sent him down the sky.

> And now that thou art lying, my dear old Carian guest,
> A handful of grey ashes, long, long ago at rest.
> Still are they pleasant voices, they nightingales, awake;
> For Death, he taketh all away, but these he cannot take.

"After reciting this, he'd wave his huge hands to reflect the transcience of life. We sat for hours discussing poetry and literature, since I didn't have anyone to talk to about these subjects. This was the case, until I went to Oxford and met other like-minded folks. But, even then I didn't find many. Through the 1960s and 1970s I visited him at least once a week. My mother packed some pasta or ravioli, with a bottle of wine, which made our meetings congenial. God, how I miss Father Flye! It was pure joy to have known him.

"Father Flye loved anecdotes about the classical scholars at Oxford and Cambridge or the ancient universities of the Continent. For instance, Gilbert Murray, the regius professor of Greek at Oxford, Maurice Bowrs, as well as Sir William Osler, the regius professor of medicine at Oxford, who was a writer and bibliophile. He was ecstatic when I would come back from Oxford and tell him of the scholars I was studying with, and anecdotes about the university, current and past.

"A quote I heard Father Flye use was from the 17th Century Oxford scholar, Sir Thomas Browne, who wrote in *Urn-Burial*: 'The long habit of living indisposeth us to dying.' He loved *Religio Medici* too.

"T. S. Eliot's essays on religion, *Homage to Lancelot Andrewes*, will give you a good idea of what Father Flye's Anglo-Catholic tenets were. He had met T. S. Eliot through his association with Jim Agee. Incidentally, one of his favorite stories was when Jim Agee was in the middle of getting a divorce, his second or third, and Agee turned to Father Flye and said: 'The trouble is, I want to be married to all of these women at the same time.' From what I've gathered, Agee's morality was on shaky ground. This is why I had trouble putting Jim Agee alongside Father Flye; the two men were undoubtedly a mismatch in terms of doing what was right and wrong.

"Father Flye thought highly of Cardinal Henry Newman, the founder of the Oxford Movement, who converted to Catholicism in the last century. One book he admired was Cardinal Newman's *The Idea of a University* [1852]. He would quote Newman's celebrated statement: 'The definition of a gentleman is one who never inflicts pain.' I sincerely believe Father Flye would have made a superb Buddhist.

"To understand him, you should know that he always called himself a Catholic, never a Protestant priest. The Catholic concept of the Apostolic Succession had a genuine emotional pull for him. He told me he had traced back to the Middle Ages the names of all the Bishops in his own succession, starting with the one who had ordained him. He made it clear he was a part of the Order of Melchizedek in the ordination rites.

"I recall writing him from France, when I described being at an Abbey where there was a long list of every man who had been Abbot there since the year 600. My letter sent him into ecstasy. He was just so deeply moved by that sense of continuity. The concept of the laying on of hands moved his historical consciousness. He marveled at the idea that a 20th Century priest could have actually been consecrated by someone who had been consecrated by Jesus.

"He loved the volume of poems, *A Shropshire Lad*, by A. E. Housman, teacher of Latin at Cambridge. He enjoyed hearing the famous anecdote about when Housman went into a lecture hall to recite Horace's poetry in Latin, but was unable to talk, holding back tears, and merely said to his audience that this was the greatest poem in ancient literature. Then Housman walked out. Father Flye loved that story.

"As I've said, Father Flye was a Victorian. You must recall that he was just 16 years old when Queen Victoria died at the turn of the century. He told me the Queen's death moved him and his mother, with emotions too deep for tears. I suggest that if you want to get an idea of the measure classical literature played in his intellectual life, then you should read Gilbert Hightet's *Poets in a Landscape*, a charming book on Latin poets. You could also read *The Greek Poets* by Moses Hadas, plus *The Classical Tradition* and *Man's Unconquerable Mind*.

"He loved French poetry, like those by Verlaine, Baudelaire, Lamartine, whose poems he had written out in his commonplace book. He had the *Oxford Book of French Verse*, which he recited from when he had an appreciative audience. He was fond of Mary Renault's haunting tale about Socrates and his circle during the Peloponnesian War, *The Last of the Wine*, which he persuaded me to read when I was in high school. I vividly recall his reading the lyrical opening to me in his small flat on Perry Street, and how entranced I was at the time.

"This brings up something that should be said. Father Flye was a born teacher. I now understand why he was respected by so many of his former students at St. Andrew's. My association with him was generally limited to weekend tutoring, so I didn't have the chance to see him operate in a classroom. I envy those people who saw him when he taught at St. Andrew's. What an experience that must have been!

"Father Flye kept an open mind. When I began reading Bertrand Russell, I brought *Why I Am Not a Christian* to discuss it with Father Flye. *History of Western Philosophy* was another book we went over. He had the wisdom of gentleness, and was willing to hear another person's viewpoint. He was a priest and a teacher, and he loved the dual role. Perhaps, most of all, he was the world's greatest listener. He had the rare gift of making you feel that what you were saying was the most important thing he had ever heard. I have concluded that Father Flye was a damn good psychologist.

"I had a difficult adjustment when I was assigned to teach ghetto kids in that part of the city called Bedford-Stuyvesant. It was only natural he would listen to my tales of woe and commiserate with me about teaching. He occasionally had visitors drop in, mostly former St. Andrew's students, but he always found the time to see me.

"It was clear to me Father Flye had ambivalent feelings about St. Andrew's. He said what caught his imagination in those earliest days was the Order of the Holy Cross coming to the Tennessee 'wilderness' to run a much-needed school. I think he liked it when he and Mrs. Flye first arrived there after World War I, but, as time went by, he didn't like the school's direction. I never asked him to explain, so it was always a mystery to me why he stayed at St. Andrew's those many years.

"He never went into any details, but I had the impression he thought his life at St. Andrew's had been useless. I knew this was silly, because I saw hordes of grown men, former St. Andrew's students, visit him. Their love for him was obvious, so he was never useless to them. Additionally, he received invitations to go back to the school to receive recognition for his past duties. I believe Father Flye was no different from many men of advanced age who question their life's efforts. However, Father Flye's popularity was based on many years of good deeds, and I was only one of thousands of people he influenced in a positive way."

❑ ❑ ❑

Dr. Fred Santee with Father Flye

At the age of three, Frederick Lamotte Santee spoke English and German. At the age of five, he was in the fourth grade. At the age of eight, he translated Caesar's Gaelic War from Latin to English, and then retranslated it into Latin to match his own prose with that of Caesar's. He graduated from high school at the age of 12, and entered Harvard University. He graduated from Harvard at 17, then enrolled at Oxford University to continue his studies in Latin and Greek. He next earned a degree at a Berlin university; then yet another from a university in Rome. The young genius told his mother at the time: "All I want from life is to teach Latin and Greek." At the age of 20, he began teaching at Lehigh University. One year later, he transferred to Vanderbilt University, where he taught Latin and Greek. He was there for four years, the youngest associate professor on the faculty.

However, the Great Depression abolished Fred Santee's position. His bank account vanished when his Nashville bank failed; he was flat broke. Fred's father, Dr. Charles L. Santee, offered financial help on one condition: his son had to go to medical school. The Santee men had been physicians in the town of Wapwallopen, Pennsylvania, since the Revolutionary War. As far as the elder doctor was concerned, the family tradition had to be continued. Fred would become a doctor, like it or not.

Fred Santee began his medical training at Johns Hopkins University. With medical degree in hand, he became a teacher at Kenyon College in Ohio. David McDowell was one of his students at Kenyon, and this is how Father Flye came to meet the eccentric physician-author-scholar, Fred Santee.

Robert Costa recalled the outlandish Flye-Santee friendship: "David McDowell had kept in touch with the Doc, and he really wanted Father Flye to meet Doc Santee, because he knew they were joined at the hip with their intellectual interests.

"Santee was a character. He was a real prodigy like Mozart, and he had the weirdest characteristics imaginable. Despite his medical training, his heart always stayed with his love of classical poetry, Latin, Greek, history. He took over the family's medical practice in Wapwallopen when his father became old and feeble. Santee always had a tongue depressor in his shirt pocket, and called himself 'just a village doctor,' but the truth was that he was a poet and a philosopher first; any doctoring he did came in a distant second. He only practiced medicine to keep bread on the table.

"Father Flye had been to Wapwallopen a number of times with David McDowell. I was in high school the first time I traveled there with Father Flye and my class friend, Dale Finos, who now teaches at Amherst. It was an unforgettable experience. During the 1920s, Santee studied with all the great scholars in Berlin, and he told stories of crazy Nazis getting drunk in Berlin beer halls. He spoke fluent German.

"Doc Santee, Hitler, Goebbels and Goering were on speaking terms at one time. As a matter of fact, Santee showed me a set of dishes Hitler sent to him after he became Chancellor of Germany. Each plate and saucer was edged with tiny Nazi swastikas. Santee was sort of a chauffeur in one of Hitler's campaign swings back in the 1920s, and he heard Adolf Hitler blame all of the world's problems on the Jews. After the insane ranting and raving, he made it a point to stay clear of German politics.

"Santee was a great hero of Father Flye's, because all the Doc wanted to do was to sit and read Latin and Greek poetry. He had a photographic mind. You could open up Homer anywhere and read a line or two and he would go on from there. He could go through just about the whole of German literature by heart. Sometimes he and Father Flye would recite in unison poetry from antiquity. They were like a duet from some Broadway vaudeville act. It was phenomenal. Father Flye was mesmerized when he was with this mental giant.

"Doc Santee messed up his life completely, in my opinion. This village doctor came across to me as some sort of mystical warlock, surrounded by his castle witches. I'm talking about his medical assistants, his secretaries, his housekeepers. Santee insisted they always had to wear high heels, 'dress like ladies.' His place was like some sort of surreal asylum. He had all these women hovering around him, all wearing high heels, I called them the witches, not a one of them with any comprehension of what was being said. They didn't know Latin or Greek, or appreciate the nuances of what Socrates meant about the eternal human condition. Meanwhile, Father Flye would sit in front of the fireplace, sipping his wine as if in a coma, eating up every word that came out of Santee's mouth. The doctor was a

Dr. Fred Santee

mixture of madman and genius, and Father Flye adored him."

Fred Santee was a naval officer in the South Pacific during World War II. After the war, he worked at Johns Hopkins Medical Center and other clinics in Maryland, and then settled in Wapwallopen, where he operated his medical practice out of a big three-story house. There was a reception room, an examination room, and a medical storage chamber.[1]

Costa continued: "Doc Santee's big house was overrun with books, cats, witches, and his many guests. It was a charming place. The Doc was an exceedingly friendly man. The Doc loved Father Flye. I remember we were once snowed in. Father Flye used to say: 'Let's go see Santee,' so we'd take the tortuous bus ride down to Pennsylvania. We went about four times a year. Doc Santee had so many books he had his own 'book house.' It would have taken someone a lifetime to go through all his volumes. The same could be said about Father Flye's private library at Eleanor Talbert's home.

"Father Flye used to get excited about reciting poetry, in any language. He would get all excited and clap his hands. He knew thousands of lines of poetry. Doc Santee was the same way, and when he started reciting poetry from ancient times, Father Flye went into a trance. It was hysterical. The witches were all walking around in their high heels, and a dozen cats were shredding the furniture, and there were at least 20 outdoor cats living there, but none of this mattered. The ambiance at Doc's was one of a friendly laissez faire, where anything was discussed. [2]

"I vividly remember Father Flye and Santee talking about the longevity of the Roman Catholic church, and how valuable this was to Father Flye. He had told the doctor he had traced his priestly confirmation bindings back to the fifth century. Santee, who wasn't a religious man, but had studied church history extensively, said: 'I've always thought the Catholics had a point. Since you have pulled your ecclesiastical rope as far back as the fifth century, I'm willing to give you the other four or five centuries.' They both had a chuckle over that.

"Keep in mind Father Flye was well into his eighties at the time, and at the end of the day I would gently help him to his bed with him muttering: 'We are in the presence of a genius.' I would agree with him, but sometimes I had my doubts. You see, the problem was that Doc Santee didn't look the part. He wore old boots, a plaid shirt with wrinkled pants, held up by suspenders. He had a beer-belly paunch, a bald head, and a slow mountain twang. He smoked cigarettes and drank like a fish. He didn't fit the traditional image of a scholar. He wasn't hired by central casting.

"Father Flye and the Doc sometimes talked about politics. Santee would ask: 'Who did you like at the turn of the century?' Father Flye replied: 'My mother liked Mr. McKinley.' Santee answered: 'Well, my father did also.' Their conversation would continue along these lines: 'I voted for Teddy Roosevelt.' 'I did too.' 'I hate to admit I voted for Franklin [Roosevelt] the first time around, but not again.' 'Yes, I never did have good feelings about him.' And so on.

"Father Flye loved to hear Doc Santee talking about the prominent scholars. His father, Charles L. Santee, had studied with Sir William Osler at Oxford, a regius professor of medicine, and probably one of the heroic doctors of the 20th century. Osler was a great literary scholar, and wrote many provocative essays. As I've said before, Father Flye relished hearing about the esteemed professors at Oxford.

"When you love someone, you enjoy seeing them happy. And this is why I enjoyed taking Father Flye to visit Doc Santee. It was an honor to see their extraordinary camaraderie. I seriously doubt I'll ever see the likes of those two gentlemen again. They broke the mold when they were made. By the way, Father Flye and Doc Santee used to send postcards to each other, written in Greek or Latin. Their literacy was impressive."

Frederick Lamotte Santee wrote a book, *The Devil's Wager*. The theme is a Faustian fable: the selling of souls to the devil. The volume lambastes bureaucrats, atheists, communists, and chiselers who want government to keep them financially afloat. Santee's book also rips into "educational theorists" responsible for the failure of the nation's public school system.

It is easy to see why Father Flye and Dr. Santee savored each other's company.

❑❑❑

[1] During this period, Doc Santee had an unusual marriage. His wife's name was Elizabeth, and she was a recluse who lived in nearby Hobby, Pennsylvania. Santee tried to visit her every day. Fred and Elizabeth Santee are buried next to each other.

[2] After her divorce from David McDowell in the early 1960s, Madeline worked in Santee's medical office in Wapwallopen. It was there she met her future husband, Gerald Grodzicki. She is now again called Mara, her favored childhood name.

CHAPTER 13

Grace Houghton Flye

There is nothing so powerful as truth.
—DANIEL WEBSTER (1782-1852)

D AVID LOCKMILLER, former St. Andrew's student, said: "There was a manual training shop at the school. I made a what-not box out of hard maple in 1919, and Mrs. Flye painted a beautiful butterfly on it. She was a sweet lady."

One day in 1921 Father Erskine Wright was driving by the bungalow and saw Mrs. Flye lying face down in her yard. Her eyes were closed. He stopped his car, rushed over, and asked her if she was all right. She replied: "Yes, Father Wright, everything is wonderful. I'm just feeling the ground, getting the feel of our Mother Nature. You know, spring will be here soon."

John Seymour Erwin: "My mother was a watercolor painter who thought Mrs. Flye was the greatest portrait artist of the 20th century. I recall going to St. Andrew's when I was a little boy, back in the 1920s. My mother would pack a box lunch for us before we drove up from Chattanooga, and she would chatter away about Mrs. Flye's talent. Two things stand out in my mind about Mrs. Flye's house: books upon books, all the way to the ceiling, and the smell of easel paint."

Stanley Hole, a 1949 St. Andrew's graduate: "I won't say that Mrs. Flye was a substitute grandmother for any of us, because she didn't impose herself on anyone. But if you were upset or crying she would quietly appear and put her arm around you. She would never ask why you were crying, just be there with a comforting hug."

Leon "Bud" Sutherland was a St. Andrew's student during the 1950-51 school year, but he had earlier spent summers doing odd jobs at the campus. He recalled being frightened the first time he met Grace Flye in 1947: "I was using a very loud gasoline lawn mower in front of the Flye house, when someone tapped me on the shoulder. I looked down at this tiny woman who was no bigger than a

Grace Flye in front of the bungalow at St. Andrew's School, mid-1930s

bar of soap after a hard day's wash. Her complexion was so dark I thought she was an Indian. She apologized for scaring me and asked me what time it was. After that, whenever she saw me she offered me a glass of iced tea."

Dale Doss: "Mrs. Flye would be literally unheard from, busying herself about their house when Father Flye and I would talk. I'd be aware she was around, but she was so quiet I didn't pay attention to her. I recall she once silently placed a glass of milk next to my chair. She was unobtrusive and very kind. She carved a small mahogany jewelry box and gave it to me as a Christmas present. Her paintings were all over their house, tucked behind boxes, even hanging from the ceiling."

❑❑❑

Grace Houghton Flye was ultimately recognized across the nation as an exceptional portrait artist. Posthumously, her name was placed in the Registry of Renowned American Artists by the Smithsonian Institution. Early on, she developed a technique that resulted in truly haunting oil canvases. Her portraits of children were exceptional. She painted close to 500 portraits; a goodly number of them were of boys at St. Andrew's, or of children who lived nearby. Her canvases are now family heirlooms, passed from one generation to the next.

Art experts have praised her skill at portraying her subject's eyes, capturing on canvas the person's inner self. In her painting of a child's face, Grace Flye was able to show a hint of the future adult. She never considered herself a commercial artist. Only occasionally did she receive money for her work—money was not what motivated her.

Grace Flye's talent was not restricted to creating oil portraits or pencil sketches. She sculpted clay likenesses, she carved wooden objects, and she was an exquisite seamstress. Her letters had a bouncy lilt. She wrote in August 1925: "It is now blueberry picking time and the entire mountain population is in for a thick tornado of activity. One sweet student, Edmund Morrison, has promised me he will deposit two buckets of berries at our door. These summer excursions with nature give my heart a lightness of delight, and my spirit soars like an albatross."

Her written descriptions were sometimes priceless. She wrote in a letter dated January 7, 1930: "The fog has arrived, and an opaque cloud surrounds us. We are inside of a Japanese print. There is only one dimension to the landscape, as flat as a pale pancake, little pencilled figures against a ghost-like gray; but not as thick as a London fog. I love my existence here in the backwoods, like a Queen Bee in a hive, surrounded by layers of admirers."

Grace Flye wrote to her husband on June 22, 1950: "Your envelope just came. The zoo sounds marvelous. Those penguins are well suited in their special zoo house. One couldn't drag our Fishie [her cat] away if he laid his eyes on them. I'm pondering on modern art. If one sees it quite close to classic painting, it shows a dynamic quality which is arresting, a vibrating shock, as Frank Petty said when he told me about jazz. It does something to you. That's how I felt when I looked at the painting by LaFarge of the Muse, as well as the cubic style of the 'Woman Cutting Bread,' one stationary, the other dynamic."

An irony in her life is that while her fame as an artist spread, she deliberately avoided publicity. In 1940 a *New York Times* art writer asked for an interview, but she refused. One of her nieces, Mary Boorman, said: "Aunt Grace lived in terror that the *New York Times* reporter would suddenly appear unannounced." On several occasions, relatives tried and failed to get Grace Flye to agree to be interviewed by newspaper journalists. Her motives were often baffling to those who knew her.

Mrs. Mildred Watts wrote: "My husband, David, was a member of the St. Andrew's faculty in the 1940s. My strolls over to the Flyes' cottage were rare, but rewarding. Mrs. Flye was a very talented artist and she kept her paintings, many framed, some not, several layers deep and not on display. It seemed to me her pleasure came in the act of painting. I was told that she only had one public exhibit of her work years ago in Sewanee, and she once conducted art classes for the local mountain women. Her art was exceptionally good, really phenomenal.[1]

"She was an excellent portrait artist. She painted a picture of a school boy which was very unusual. It was three pictures in one: one was how she saw him, one was how his mother saw him, one was how he saw himself. You could tell all three versions were the same child, but the three were different too.

"She was always modestly dressed in clothes that bespoke earlier years, the 1920s and such. She wore huge hats and flowing dresses, which made me think she had not always been skin and bones. Her doctor had her freeze ground beef in ice cube trays, and I concluded raw frozen beef was her main diet. How I wish we had known her in those earlier years. What I heard is that she had once participated in the busy social life of the Mountain. This is frequently the case with reclusives, talented and loved though they may be. All kinds of bizarre rumors ran with the school gossipers. Only someone who had been part of the early years could separate fact from fiction.

"Of course, we discussed books. She was always straightforward, not putting on airs. Although we never discussed anything personal, when I left her presence I felt a fresh outlook on the tangle of my own life. My impression of Mrs. Flye remains that of a shy, delicate, unselfish person who loved all things beautiful, even the many varieties of beauty found in the events of the world."

John Steiger, a 1941 St. Andrew's graduate, recalled when his portrait was painted by Grace Flye: "I was so flattered by the experience. She told me to bring two separate shirts to the sitting, as the lighting would determine which shirt I wore. What a talent! She caught me exactly as I looked. We only had two sessions of about 45 minutes each. I still have that portrait hanging in my dining room."[2]

Ann Tate, who was a faculty wife and later a school employee, remembered

The Rev. Harvey A. Simmonds

the time in 1943 she was invited to tea by Grace Flye: "I'd check the mail two or three times a week, and each time I passed the Flye house I would wave to Mrs. Flye who worked in her garden. She always waved back and smiled. This went on for quite some time. I never expected to ever be inside the Flye house, because it was common knowledge you had to make an appointment beforehand. Much to my surprise, Mrs. Flye waved me over one morning and asked: 'Would you like to have tea someday?' We agreed on a time four days later.

"I enjoyed myself immensely. We talked of general matters, nothing really serious. It seemed that when Mrs. Flye talked to me, her inner beauty shined through, therefore eliminating her physical appearance. I also didn't notice her lack of housekeeping; it didn't matter. Besides being a talented artist, she was a nice woman."

Mrs. Tate concluded: "From the sidelines, I observed Father Flye and Mrs. Flye for many years. They were compatible. They had a happy marriage."

Ethel Louise Simmonds: "We first met the Flyes when we moved to St. Andrew's in 1947. My husband, Father Harvey A. Simmonds, had been stationed at the Order's mission in Liberia for 13 years, before he became the Bursar at St. Andrew's. The Flyes loved each other in their peculiar fashion. He was a vegetarian, but she never ate vegetables. To say their marriage was unusual is an understatement, but their marriage worked. You could see their fondness for one another. I recall Mrs. Flye saying to me: 'Hal has always been my best friend.' Small-minded women at the school spread horrible rumors about Mrs. Flye, and I never understood why. Mrs. Flye never said an unkind word. I guess her biggest sin was her peculiarity.

"One thing the Flyes shared was their gentleness for all creatures. They wouldn't kill a spider! My husband once told me that he began to tell the students to bring any captured mouse or whatnot to his office. He knew from experience that Father Flye would only release any critter caught by the boys, or maybe even nurse it back to health if it was injured. They not only loved animals, but all natural things. Father Flye was curious why bees didn't fall over from exhaustion. He told me they were consuming more energy than was possible. For hours on end, he studied bees through his window.

Oil portrait of Mary Helen Goodwin by
Grace Flye, 1919

Unfinished Grace Flye portrait of unknown
mountain child

Oil portrait of Jean O'Leary, St. Andrew's
faculty wife, by Grace Flye, 1931

Charcoal drawing of aspiring actress
Nancy Drew by Grace Flye, 1906

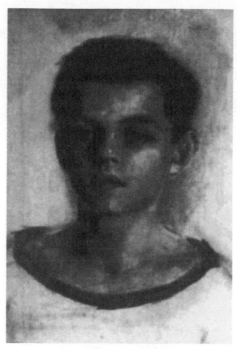

Oil portrait of unknown St. Andrew's student   *Oil portrait of unknown St. Andrew's student*
by Grace Flye, 1926   *by Grace Flye*

"We heard many stories about Grace Flye when we first arrived at St. Andrew's; she was the school's mystery woman. We were told that years ago she would be hostess for up to 20 people, who came over from Sewanee for Sunday night Benediction. But, when I met her, she stayed to herself. She was a nice lady, but she had her likes and dislikes. If you wanted to visit her at her house, you had to place a note inside her mailbox asking permission. She was very introverted.

"They both were odd. One thing I remember about Father Flye was that he would never leave the antifreeze in his car overnight. He drained his engine every evening during the winter. It was humorous and insane at the same time, but that was the way he was. Another peculiar thing is that he sniffed snuff. He had a small snuff box, and he'd get a pinch and inhale it up his nose in a micro-second. He did it so quickly, you almost didn't see it. His teaching was legendary, but he was strange.

"During the summer months, when Father Flye was away for his summer duty work, Mrs. Flye lived alone, and the rest of the faculty worried about her welfare. Knowing how reclusive she was and not wanting any drop-in visitors, a simple plan was devised to satisfy all concerned. A broom kept on the Flye's front porch was a signal flag; if it was parked at a different spot on the porch each day, this meant she was active in her own quiet way, and we could all rest easier.

Oil portrait of John Steiger (St. A '41) by Grace Flye

"The faculty wives also worried about her not eating when Father Flye was gone for the summer. She was so tiny, so thin. Meal trays from the kitchen were brought to her house, but she went days on days without eating anything. We were worried she would faint, or something worse, if we didn't check on her. She would paint for days on end without eating a bite."

Father Bonnell Spencer, who served as both Prior and Headmaster at St. Andrew's from 1947-1955, wrote: "One night, as I was walking with a faculty member, we heard a moaning, and we found Mrs. Flye collapsed on the ground near the entrance to the chapel. She was wearing a clerical collar and she had an oversized pair of boots on. We dashed her to the hospital, where it was discovered she had scurvy, since she ate nothing but meat. She recovered all right, but Father Flye stayed at St. Luke's in New York, and did not return to the campus until school opened six weeks later. This was the summer of 1949. The Sewanee hospital put her on a sensible diet. I don't think she was in the hospital for more than a day or two. Father Flye may not have even known of it unless she wrote him about it. We had the impression he was indifferent, so we didn't call him. Strange couple that they were, their behavior was nothing short of enigmatical. Nobody understood them, least of all myself."

Grace's health practices became more eccentric with the passing years. It appears that her odd eating habits began around her 65th birthday, in 1940. Starting at that time, when her relatives visited her at St. Andrew's, she never ate meals with them. She ate alone in the middle of the night, if at all. Her habit of eating alone denied her those sociable benefits of sharing meals with other people. Over a span of 36 years, records show she was taken to the Sewanee hospital eight times, suffering from malnutrition, anemia and a host of other ailments. Father Flye apparently made an effort to get his wife to follow a reasonable diet, but to no avail.

One incident in the summer of 1947 spoke volumes about Grace's attitude. She had spent two weeks at the Vanderbilt Medical Center, suffering from beri-beri, caused by a thiamin deficiency. She was also treated for impetigo. Her attending physician was Thomas Frist. Mary Boorman recalled: "We were driving back to St. Andrew's, and Aunt Grace scanned Dr. Frist's diet list. She turned to me and said: 'You know I can't follow these dumb instructions,' and tossed the list out the window. I watched, in the rearview mirror, the piece of paper fluttering on the highway."

Grace Flye was afflicted with Addison's disease, a failure of the adrenal glands, and this is why her skin darkened. She was anemic, so she ate meat for the iron — she probably craved it. One symptom of Addison's disease is the suppression of appetite, and anorexia occurs. It is amazing that Mrs. Flye coped as well as she did.

David and Madeline McDowell visited the Flyes in 1948. Madeline recounted: "I was shocked. There were books, paintings, and old newspapers everywhere, covered with layers of dust and dried leaves. Mrs. Flye's appearance startled me. I wasn't sure she was a woman when I first saw her. I immediately felt sorry for her. David and Father Flye were talking to each other, and I was trying to keep up with them when I then noticed that Mrs. Flye had disappeared. She never made a sound.

"You knew Mrs. Flye was there in the house, but she moved around like a ghost. You saw glimpses of her, nothing more. She had only one conversation with me, and that was when we all drove to see some property they owned at the edge of the plateau. She and I talked about putting wine casks in caves. We visited them for four days."[3]

Grace's letters to Mary Boorman in the late 1940s showed, among other things, that she was ill, yet she kept busy: "I haven't written Hal that I was sick in June. I don't want to worry him. I'm busy sorting innumerable boxes, books and letters, mechanical junk, stored for years in the school shop. Now they line our porch stacked alongside my poor washer. These alien boxes belonged to a teacher who was here 18 years. He died under sad circumstances and Hal is still bitter about it.[4]

"Hal is going to Decatur, Georgia, for Christmas services. I am not up to traveling across the campus, much less anywhere else. I must stay inside my Noah's Ark. Now that winter has set in, it makes me want to hibernate like a furry animal. I would like you to purchase some port wine, as much as you can conveniently get. Hal goes twice a year to Chattanooga to get me a supply, but he had no free Saturdays this year. He had to work at Birdwood because someone stole windows, then examinations and the school functions kept him busy."

"I've written this in the wee hours of the night, often I only sleep about five hours, so I get up and usually just think. By and by, I eat my oatmeal, take a nap, and then sip some coffee and sit still some more out on the porch, looking at the towering trees, intoxicated by the fresh sunlight."

"I tried the sherry Saturday and found out the difference between the two wines. The sherry is a small stimulant, and might be better for me most of the time. But I'll keep the Port for one has to go on nerves, and the Port is more of an instant nourishment. I've heard it goes right into the blood, energy without vitamins; what chocolate is for explorers and soldiers who need some accelerated energy. I don't know how much the sherry costs, but I am putting a check in this envelope for some more."

Like most couples who had been married for a number of years, the Flyes adjusted to each other's personalities. An accommodation had been reached between them. New York City playwright, Kevin Kennedy, wrote: "Father Flye's relationship with Grace was compatible, necessary to his personal being. Both interpreted reality, and needed privacy. They complemented each other in ways an outsider could never understand. Kahil Gibran knew lasting relationships always require a degree of privacy. He wrote in his poem *The Prophet*: 'Let there be spaces in your togetherness. Let the winds of the heavens dance between you.' The Flyes understood this."

Harvey Simmonds, a 1956 St. Andrew's graduate, wrote: "It was through the eyes of a nine-year-old child that I came to know Mrs. Flye in 1947. By now, she had grown increasingly reclusive, and although the bungalow was only a matter of a few yards from the school chapel, it had something of the quality of a moated castle. Whatever may have been earlier, by the late 1940s the house and its dense enclosure seemed altogether apart from the ordinary. We children had been told not to play noisily about, or intrude upon, that hallowed space. The Flyes and the house they lived in had slowly darkened over time. Mrs. Flye's appearance, which apparently was striking in her youth, moved toward the astonishing with advancing age. Her wardrobe took little account of the changing fashions, and her attachment to the large hats of the decades before World War I did not lessen."

Simmonds continued: "Delight sparkled through Father Flye's telling of the friendships he and Mrs. Flye had with teachers and students through the decades at Saint Andrew's, each with its special note. I think of the photographs of Grace Flye which Father Flye turned to with pleasure. Out of them she smiles, that remarkable face given a sweetness that had a gentle coquetry of long love and light."

The *Washington Post* printed an article written by Father Flye in 1965. The headline read "A Churchman Looks At Marriage." In the Sunday feature, the priest wrote: "Individuals differ in feelings, tastes and temperament. Some of these may render impossible the harmony there should be—traits like cruelty, selfishness, suspicion and excessive irritability. No contented marriage could survive such circumstances. But there are other differences and divergences, recognized and accepted on both sides in understanding and good will, which do not cause alienation or distress."

❑ ❑ ❑

Eleanor Talbert spoke of her "Aunt Grace" with deep emotion: "She was the dearest soul I've ever known. Her art made her a solitary person, and unlike the other wives at St. Andrew's, she didn't believe in idle gossip. Women can be such bitches when it comes to that. Her appearance was a constant source of gossip. Her health was never good, and this affected her appearance. I overheard one of the St. Andrew's faculty wives call Aunt Grace 'the ugliest woman on the Mountain'—mean words out of a Victor Hugo novel. I wanted to scream, but Aunt Grace had too much civility to harbor any hostility.

"When I was a little girl, my parents told me Aunt Grace was engaged to be married when she was much younger, but her bridegroom was killed in a road accident one week before the wedding. That would have been the marriage that had children, not like the situation she had with Uncle Hal. That would have been the marriage with love in the house, and all that goes along with it. It was too bad, for she loved little things, be it children, birds or rabbits. Considering her disappointments, to keep sane, she lived in her own world of enchantment.[5]

"My family's sewing circle said the only reason he married her was that he needed a wife to be a parish priest, and she married him to escape being an old maid. Many people said they had a marriage in name only, the French term is *mariage blanc*, but whatever the case, nobody can know why people stay together. Can you imagine what it was like being married to Uncle Hal? I would never in a thousand years have called him happy. There was a dark intensity about him much of the time, and she had to live in that environment. And like all the other men of his generation, a part of him was a male chauvinist who didn't think women were able to handle serious subjects.

"I visited Aunt Grace and Uncle Hal at St. Andrew's during my childhood, but there was a gap of about 12 years before I saw them again when I was 29. Due to horrible circumstances involving my husband, I went to live with them and they helped me survive a dreadful ordeal. Along with my friend, Dorothy Mulligan, we lived in their house at St. Andrew's for close to six months. Our living there was ignored by the school administration. Our meals were brought over in heated aluminum containers by someone from the kitchen. Uncle Hal always ate in the dining hall.

"For the most part, Uncle Hal had little to say to Dorothy or myself. He would come in the back door and head straight to the little room he called his study. It was where he did his reading—he did a great deal of reading—and where he slept. He constantly had visitors and the study is where those conversations took place. If the weather was nice, he'd sit on that big swing and talk to folks on the front porch.

"I have pleasant memories of the three of us, Aunt Grace, Dorothy and me, spending a lot of time together talking about women's interests, subjects that men could never understand. I don't wish to sound unappreciative, but Uncle Hal had a casual outlook about any day-to-day maintenance. If a light bulb needed changing, somebody else had to do it. His outlook was imperial, as if this was beneath his station in life. This infuriated me, but Aunt Grace never complained. She adjusted to his way of doing things over their many years together, and I'm sure he had learned to live with her quirks.

"My comments should not be misunderstood; Uncle Hal was there for me when I needed him. I wanted a car and he made the down payment on a Dodge that had only 3,000 miles on the odometer. It was a lovely maroon car, exactly what the doctor ordered. Having that car made life bearable. Dorothy and I then moved to Monteagle, where we worked at the Monteagle Court Motel. She had the night shift and I worked days for the next five years until the middle of 1954. This arrangement gave us enough spending money to get by.

"Uncle Hal was a brilliant conversationalist. He had baptized me as a baby, and one night in the kitchen he said: 'There have always been two things I believed in, one is the U.S. Post Office and the other is the Roman Catholic Church, and would you look at what has happened to the Post Office?' His conversations were filled with great repartee. Incidentally, I later converted to Roman Catholicism, and he accepted this. He said the really important thing was to believe in something, and then go on from there. Aunt Grace sometimes sat with us and joined in, but she usually didn't say much when Uncle Hal was holding court."

Mary Boorman wrote this insightful article: "Any effort to capture the life of Grace Houghton Flye in a compact sketch bears a resemblance to the explanation in two words of the aerodynamics of the hummingbird. An attempt is justified, however, by the distinctive quality of life found in this great lady who, it was once said, blended the appearance of a Gandhi with the soul of an angel.

"Artist, recluse and mystic, Grace Houghton was one of the most distinctive Sewanee ladies of the first half of the 20th century. While her paintings are now found mostly in private hands, her position as one of the most talented American portrait painters of her period is certainly secure. She came to St. Andrew's in 1918, three years after her marriage to the Rev. James Harold Flye, and there over a period of more than three decades created for herself a unique position on the school campus. Shy by temperament, she gradually became almost a complete recluse, with eccentricities both in clothing and in behavior that became local legends.

"In her personal contacts with students, and most sharply in her painting, the spirit of Grace Houghton came magically alive and achieved its most significant expression. Most of her best portraits depict members of the Houghton family and those of the St. Andrew's community.

"During her years on the Mountain the untidiness of her housekeeping was balanced by the purity of her instincts and by the elemental Quaker integrity of her spirit. In her being she combined the traits of a Francis of Assisi along with the imagination of an Emily Dickinson of Amherst, the mixture leavened by an elusive blend of control and artistic perception which must charge the brush of the superior portrait painter. Never robust to begin with, her physical condition declined steadily, in huge part to her neglect of elementary health rules; she suffered from malnutrition for years."

Grace Houghton Flye died on February 13, 1954, at the age of 79.

□ □ □

Eleanor Talbert: "The day Aunt Grace died was very strange. Uncle Hal brought me and Dorothy into the room where she was stretched out on a board. Without saying a word, he simply left us there. An hour passed and we finally concluded it was going to be up to us to get her ready for the undertaker. Rigor mortis was beginning to set in, and I found the atmosphere terrifying, but Dorothy knew what to do. We dressed Aunt Grace and walked into the next room where Uncle Hal was sitting and we said: 'She is ready.' All he could do was nod his head.

"Her death really hit him hard. I've never seen a man carry so much pain. His grief had a tangible presence. Dorothy and I were worried about him. His eyes were so bloodshot. We once tried to treat his eyes with drops, but he stumbled out of the room. Someone must have called the Flyes' friends, because they began showing up at the house right away. They were an enormous help."

Sewanee pottery artist Jean Tallec was among the first to arrive: "I rushed over when I heard of her death, and I helped Eleanor and her friend prepare Mrs. Flye for the ambulance. She had on Father Flye's white clerical collar; her choices in what to wear were always eccentric. She was very thin, not weighing more than 100 pounds.

"Father Flye was overcome with private guilt. You see, he told me the circumstances around her death. Mrs. Flye was in their kitchen and quietly said: 'Hal, please come here.' He answered: 'I'll be there in a minute,' but he continued to read a newspaper article he was looking at. Several minutes went by and she again called to him, but he went on reading the newspaper. This happened several more times, her quietly asking him to come to the kitchen, and him ignoring her. He finally got up and walked into the kitchen where he found her dead on the floor.

"Father Flye was inconsolable, convinced he could have saved her if he had paid more attention to her calls for help. We told him he couldn't have known she was dying, and that he was totally blameless. However, he was in a state of shock and our words weren't really registering with him. He sat for the longest time in the rocking chair, rocking back and forth, his arms clasping his chest. His eyes couldn't focus, as if he was staring at something miles away.

"As I left St. Andrew's that sad day, I thought back to my childhood when Mrs. Flye painted my portrait when I was 12 years old. I remember she then wore her hair in a bob, and she was a friendly little bird who relaxed me completely. My father was also an Episcopal priest, Reverend Erle Merriman, and he taught at the DuBose Seminary in Monteagle, and that is where he first met

Father Flye. My parents really liked the Flyes. There was a great deal of laughter when the two couples got together. Paul and John Merriman, my brothers, were St. Andrew's students in the 1920s.

"When I was a girl, the Flye house at St. Andrew's was a beehive of social activity. It was a wonderful place for a child, filled with musty books and the smell of painting oil. It gave me a feeling of genuine friendship and acceptance. Reverend Claiborne, a giant of a man with a booming voice, was often there with his wife. I remember the adults having spirited discussions about literature, poetry, music and politics. Jazz, bootleg gin, and liberated 'flapper girls' were hot topics in those days."

Jean Tallec concluded: "As the years went by, it seemed Mrs. Flye became more shy and introverted. I never knew what caused her to be that way. Father Flye continued to be bouncy and active, but Mrs. Flye slowly dropped out of sight."

Father Flye obviously knew his wife had been sickly for many years, yet her death stunned him. She had been part of his life, his silent anchor, for almost 40 years. Now, death had put an end to their alliance which had started one glorious day in Winter Park, and which now seemed so long ago. The man who had countless friends had lost forever the best friend he ever had.

Grace Flye left a legacy of superb oil portraits. She was fondly remembered for her kindnesses. She was also recalled as a tragic figure, as her final years were ones of self-imposed isolation. She had many disappointments: the Great Depression reduced her inheritance to nothing but worthless bonds; she never recovered from the loss or her beloved father who died in 1931; her fantasy dream of Birdwood never materialized; her appearance was horribly altered by Addison's disease.

As the years went by, her dietary habits became increasingly unhealthy. Her reliance on alcohol became more acute. Her life had a Alice in Wonderland quality, as she withdrew into a reclusive shell. Amazingly, she remained cheerful and uncomplaining until the end. Grace was a gentle, brave, and very talented woman.

Did the Flyes have a good marriage? Except for Grace's father, A.C. Houghton, the rest of Grace's relatives disliked Father Flye, thinking he was intellectually arrogant, and that he treated Grace as a second-class person. But were these valid criticisms? It all depends on your point of view.

Father Flye never complained about his wife's poor housekeeping, which was rare for a man of his generation. He never interfered with her artistic activities. Grace lived for her art; it was the passion of her life. James Harold Flye gave his wife complete freedom to pursue her artistic dreams.

One interviewee claimed she never saw the Flyes kiss or hug each other; however, the Flyes were raised in a Victorian environment where only public affection for children was allowed. Granted, the Flyes rarely traveled together, but they had no need to be constantly at each other's side. They were never lovers, in the traditional sense. He was 30 and she was 40 when they married, and they already had become independent personalities. Their marriage was one of compatibility. In the final analysis, this guaranteed an enduring relationship.[5]

A study of the letters between the Flyes over more than 30 years shows a pattern of genuine affection. Most of their letters to each other began with "Sweetheart" or "My Dearest Friend." Father Flye's letters to Grace were filled with descriptions of what museums he had visited, who he had talked to, the people with whom he had dined. Almost day-to-day, he shared with Grace his thoughts and activities.

In turn, she wrote him about her observations. On their wedding anniversary, July 15, 1930, she wrote: "This is St. Swithun's Day! What do you think of that? It is our day. This morning when I looked out the window I saw a rabbit sitting with his ears standing up. The katydids have arrived and give a concert every night. You should spend some time in New York every year—it is just the thing for you, with all the contacts you make, but I would rather be here. I have a thousand things I'm so eager to get accomplished. The tiny chipmunk and I plan our time balancing energy with immobile meditation. Sweet kisses for St. Swithun's Day."

Grace Flye was buried at the Sewanee cemetery on a clear, cold and windy February afternoon. One of the pallbearers was St. Andrew's senior Dale Doss: "It was bitterly cold, and the grave service went on for the longest time. I saw Father Flye visibly age, become older and stooped. He was suffering deeply." Father Flye insisted on doing the Eucharist service himself, and it was a shattering experience for him. There were moments when it appeared to the spectators he could not continue. He paused many times. He performed the entire service in Latin, speaking extemporaneously for 45 minutes. He later said that Latin was the appropriate language for such a solemn occasion.

Forty-six people were present at the burial—20 St. Andrew's students; Mary and Herbert Clark; James Agee; David McDowell; Eleanor Talbert; Dorothy Mulligan; Herman Green; and 19 other local residents.

Part of Father Flye's despair over his wife's death was connected to his telling Grace he had been fired at St. Andrew's. His termination took place one week prior to her death. The reality that she would be evicted from the bungalow, her private cocoon for so many years, her own Noah's Ark, probably was a contributing factor in her death. One can only imagine how devastating it was for her to learn that her days in the bungalow were literally numbered.

The St. Andrew's Prior, Father Bonnell Spencer, wrote: "Fr. Flye had reached the age of retirement some years earlier, but the Order had kept him on. However, I thought it was time for him to leave. My having to tell him of my decision was an extremely hard and painful experience for both of us. He was very surprised and angered at his dismissal. Sadly, this was followed by the death of Mrs. Flye a few days later.

"He finished out the school year, but did absolutely nothing about moving his things from his campus house before he left for his summer duties in New York. Fr. and Mrs. Flye had a pack rat syndrome. Nothing that came into their house was thrown out: newspapers, magazines, empty oil cans. Among the things that were found was a box, wrapped and labeled 'string too short to use'; another was burnt matches; and still another box with rusty needles. It was amazing how much they had salted away inside their place.

"The fact is that, although we taught together at St. Andrew's for seven years, I did not know Fr. Flye well. Except for an occasional midmorning faculty coffee, he did not socialize with any of us. I had the impression he considered us his inferiors, but that caused no friction until the problem of his retirement arose. I am still convinced that the time had come for him to go."

Father Flye was 70 years old, mourning Grace's death, struggling with being fired at St. Andrew's, and it was plainly too much for him to handle. He suffered from what psychologists call "denial." He could not cope with reality. Spencer had told Flye in February that he had to leave St. Andrew's at the end of the school term, but he failed to remove his belongings from the bungalow ahead of time.

Eleanor Talbert recounted: "After Aunt Grace died, Dorothy and I didn't know what was going to happen to any of us, so we sat tight and waited. We kept our jobs at the Monteagle Court Motel, but we knew something was up. Uncle Hal hadn't told us he had been let go back in February; we didn't learn that until the last minute. I noticed he was getting agitated in April, but didn't know exactly what the problem was.

"Just a few days before commencement in June, he floored us when he announced he was off to St. Luke's for the summer! Without actually saying it in so many words, Dorothy and I were expected to handle the details of emptying his house. That job fell to us by default. My cousin, Mary, couldn't help us; she had a family to raise. Jean Tallec pitched in, and one of the St. Andrew's pupils, Harvey Simmonds, also helped. We were overwhelmed with the enormity of the job.

"Uncle Hal and I had gone over the situation, and he decided he would make a down payment for me on a house in Washington, D.C., somewhere big enough where his books could be stored. Dorothy and I quit our jobs, hired some mountain men, and the big job got underway. Thirty enormous truckloads of tin cans, magazines, bottles, newspapers, you name it, went to the dump. It was June and incredibly hot inside that house. You could have floated a battleship with all the sweat generated. Uncle Hal told me he had saved his letters, and we weren't to throw out any books marked with chalk. We sent 14 tons of his books and papers to Washington!

"I'll be the first to admit there was a lot of gold mixed in with the trash; however, we didn't have the time or the know-how to sort through each book, magazine, copies of the *Congressional Record*. In addition, I think there was every publication put out by the Order of the Holy Cross. I saw complete sets of St. Andrew's textbooks [saved for the proposed school at Birdwood]. The house was really packed from the attic to the basement. Yes, some of the valuable things were thrown out, but we did the best we could. The school made it clear we had one week to empty the place. The top priest at St. Andrew's was disgusted the house had not been emptied earlier. All of us felt the pressure to finish the job quickly.[7]

"Uncle Hal found a marvelous place in Washington for me, a big four-story house on New Hampshire Avenue, and that is where his huge book collection and papers were taken. His book collection was so huge it took up all the shelf space on four floors of the house, except for the kitchen, dining room and pantry. His books were a mixture of old and current, dealing with history, the church, poetry, philosophy, biographies. The ceilings in the house were very high, maybe up to twelve feet, and Uncle Hal's books made it look more like a library than a private home. I loved that great house that was built back in 1870.

"Uncle Hal would visit me about twice a year, and sit for hours, sometimes all alone, going over his old letters, papers, and so on. I have been asked about what happened to all his books and personal papers. Harvey Simmonds and Marnette Trotter split the stuff between them, and Harvey gave the rest to Vanderbilt University."

Father Flye's journals contain little personal introspection. One can only guess at what he thought about personal or intimate matters. He wrote letters on politics, societal values and history, but his journals dealt mostly with policy at St. Andrew's. Insights into his private ups and downs come from interviews and Grace Flye's letters. Some of Flye's journals and letters were deposited at Vanderbilt University; others were edited, lost or misplaced. The journals covering the 1920s and 1930s, for example, are "scattered years" as described by archivists. Flye kept journals all of his adult life, but there are gaps of many years where no journals exist. Flye's belongings were taken from his St. Andrew's bungalow in a frantic atmosphere in 1954, so it is not surprising that valuables were lost in the process. No one has yet explained what happened to most of Grace Flye's paintings and pencil sketches. It is painful to consider that her work may have been discarded or taken to the dump. Father Flye was a constant letter writer. For example, he wrote 18 letters and 47 postcards between June 7 and August 10, 1920; he wrote 44 letters between February and May of 1923. Letters usually stimulate replies. What happened to them? Father Flye did not discard his letters; his St. Andrew's bungalow was crammed with boxes of correspondence. The teacher became nationally famous for saving James Agee's musings, but he also saved letters from countless other people. His correspondence was taken to Eleanor Talbert's home in Washington, but only part of the letters were donated to the archives at Vanderbilt University. This is a sad footnote to an extraordinary life. Arthur Ben Chitty wrote about Father Flye's personality and the final disposition of his personal papers: "He was a gentle man of God with the uncommon capacity to accept other people's shortcomings. But being only human, there was a hidden side to him. He could not forgive the Order of the Holy Cross for what he saw as harsh treatment of the boys at St. Andrew's. This is why he and Mrs. Flye are buried side by side in the Sewanee cemetery; he did not want their final resting place to be on St. Andrew's property. Father Flye's papers ended up at Vanderbilt, instead of Sewanee, where his records would have been infinitely more appreciated. The man was rarely aroused to anger. But, as the story goes, he overheard a Sewanee professor snidely call St. Andrew's a reform school. Deeply offended by the fool's remark, he decided at that moment his papers would not go to the University of the South, therefore denying a great wealth of scholarship to Mountain-based historians."

[1] Many interviewees recalled seeing Grace Flye's canvases rolled up and stuck between boxes or books in the bungalow, even hanging from the ceiling. In all likelihood, these were still-life renderings or pencil sketches. Nearly all of her portraits were given to the person who was painted. An example of Grace Flye's work can be seen at the Headmaster's office at St. Andrew's-Sewanee School: a 1919 portrait of Mary Helen Goodwin, the first female graduate of St. Andrew's.

[2] Steiger later became a prominent artist in the Chicago area.

[3] Warren Eyster, who worked with David McDowell in the publishing business, surprised researchers when he made this observation: "Both David and James Agee loved Mrs. Flye. She had a very strong influence upon them. Their love for her was the foundation for their lasting closeness with Father Flye. Both men called her a living saint." Several months before her death, Mrs. Flye received a tape recording from James Agee. On it, he said: "For many years we have seen each other only very intermittently, and yet with many years between our seeing each other, we have always resumed a conversation as if I had just gone into Sewanee, and that has been one of the delights of my friendship with you."

[4] At the time of her letter, Grace Flye's clothes washer had sat unused, becoming progressively more rusty, for at least 10 years on the bungalow's porch. Grace asked her husband to get the washer repaired when it first became inoperative in the 1940s. Father Flye casually mentioned the problem to a St. Andrew's maintenance man, but he never filed an official repair order. Father Flye's haughty attitude and his wife's stoicism meant that, from then on, clothes washing done inside the bungalow was done by hand. Visitors recalled a clothesline stretched over the bungalow's bathtub, draped with drying garments. How often the Flyes used the school's laundry is unknown.

[5] Researchers tried to verify the tale of the would-be groom dying in an auto accident one week before he would have married Grace Houghton, but were unable to confirm it. If this story has merit, it probably refers to Robert Newbegin, an Ohio attorney, who was mentioned in several of Grace's letters when she was 25 years old. He was also mentioned in Grace's letter to her father in April 1915, shortly before her wedding.

[6] The Flye and Santee marriages were eerily similar. The passions of both the doctor in Pennsylvania and the priest in Tennessee were strictly cerebral. Grace Flye and Elizabeth Santee were reclusive in their latter years. The Flye and Santee households were overrun by pets (in addition to the indoor cats at the Santee residence, at least 20 outdoor cats lived on the premises). Both homes were frequented by numerous guests.

[7] Father Flye wrote in a letter dated May 8, 1943: "Why should one long to preserve in permanent form thoughts, records of incidents, photographs? This seems based on a deep-lying assumption that there will be others to whom such things will mean something. There will be such individuals, no doubt, but how many? Much of what Mrs. Flye or I treasure, is to many people just rubbish."

The history teacher was partially correct; however, some of the material the Flyes saved was invaluable.

CHAPTER 14

After St. Andrew's

He who loses money loses much. He who loses a friend loses much
more. He who loses faith loses all.
—ELEANOR ROOSEVELT (1884-1962)

*T*HE SUMMER OF 1954 was stressful for Father Flye. In June he
traveled to St. Luke's in Greenwich Village for his normal summer
duties, but he was distracted with a host of concerns. He was worried
about his books and papers that had been transported to Eleanor Talbert's
house in Washington, D.C He had no idea what he was going to do when
the summer was over.

He was enormously relieved, and pleasantly surprised, when a friend from his
past, Charles Hugh Blakeslee, came to his rescue in August 1954. Blakeslee, the
Rector of St. James' Episcopal Church in Wichita, Kansas, asked Father Flye to
be his assistant. The two men had met years earlier, when Blakeslee was a college student at Sewanee.[1]

Wichita was a new challenge to Flye, and he responded with vigor to meeting
new people and taking an active part in the church's varied functions. Father
Blakeslee wrote Arthur Ben Chitty in April 1955: "Fr. Flye's presence among us
is a great joy to me." In the same letter, Blakeslee commented on Flye's eccentricity: "Winston Churchill and Mark Twain were eccentric; he is in good company. Charles Gale, a parishioner, says Father Flye is a certified adorable eccentric. I agree."

In 1956, driving his ancient Packard, Father Flye returned to St. Andrew's;
however, his visit was unofficial. The Order of the Holy Cross never knew of his
clandestine return to the campus.

Harold Kennedy, a 1939 St. Andrew's graduate, had been one of Father Flye's
favorite students, and they had kept in touch. Kennedy, a tall redhead, was the
St. Andrew's football coach and a history teacher in 1956. Mary Barnard, Kennedy's

daughter, described the priest's poignant arrival at her campus house: "It was dark, and Father Flye quietly showed up at our back door. We heard this gentle knocking on the door, and I opened the door. There he stood, holding his hat in his hand.

"We lived next to the track and Father Flye had parked his car at the highway, and he had waited for the sun to go down before walking to our house. He said he knew he wasn't welcome at the school. Can you imagine this? This man who taught for so long there, and was adored by so many, believed he wasn't welcome at St. Andrew's! How horrible that he felt this way!

"Daddy was enraged; he always claimed the school should be ashamed for the way the old man was treated. Daddy loved Father Flye, and he often told me how Father Flye took an interest in him when he was student. He was the person who got Daddy first interested in history. He was a tremendous help to Daddy when he wrote his Master's thesis on the Cumberland Plateau at Middle Tennessee State.

"Daddy was a history teacher who tried to emulate Father Flye's techniques. Make it exciting, talk about the personalities, not just dates and names. Daddy had been a bomber crewman in World War II and he took his boys on combat missions in history class. Students would tell me: 'Mr. Kennedy told us about his air raids over Germany, and this made the war real to all of us.' That's good teaching which sticks to the ribs. Betty Speegle, a faculty wife, said Daddy was the kind of teacher who made Father Flye proud."

Barnard continued: "Father Flye looked sad when he visited us, but he had a gentility, a grace under pressure. He had a quality in him that was saintly. Later on, the tide turned and the school had Father Flye back to St. Andrew's to honor him. It was connected to James Agee, which was somewhat fraudulent in my opinion.

"While he was staying with us, he and Daddy toured the campus, but only at night.

"The Headmaster never knew Father Flye was at our house. Daddy corresponded with Father Flye over the years, seeking his advice. Daddy saw him as an older friend, and he wasn't alone. A lot of people thought of Father Flye that way."

During his visit to the Mountain in 1956, Flye drove to Birdwood. Joseph D. McBee, University of the South librarian, remembered: "The buildings were empty shells, the place was abandoned. I was about nine years old, and along with some other boys, we were swinging from the vines, yelling and having a great time. Suddenly we spotted this little priest standing there watching us. We expected to be booted out of there, but all Father Flye said to us was: 'Have a good time, but be careful. Don't get hurt.'"

Following several successful years in Wichita, Flye transferred to the St. Barnabas Church in Omaha, Nebraska, where he was the priest-in-charge during the absence of the Rector. In late 1959, he moved back to resume his duties at St. Luke's in New York City. By now, he was officially retired, but he remained busy.

Spanning 23 years, 1960-1983, Father Flye lived in small apartments in New York City on Perry, Barrow, and Hudson Streets. He celebrated Mass every Friday morning at 7:30 a.m. at St. Luke's, and maintained an informal ministry in his private abode wherever he lived. It has been said that he hosted more than 1,000 private visitations during those years. His visitors ranged from a wheezy bum looking for a handout to a scholar seeking information about James Agee to an ex-St. Andrew's student paying his respects. Except for the panhandlers, Flye was unfailingly cordial.

Ross Spears first met Father Flye when he was producing the film *Agee*. From those original meetings, Spears developed a friendship with the elderly priest, and later he created a one-hour video called *An Afternoon with Father Flye*.

The following is an excerpt from an 1996 interview with Spears: "I visited Father Flye over a period of 10 years. I loved the man, but most of all, I learned from him. He was a born teacher. Meeting his former students was all the confirmation you needed; his students worshiped him at St. Andrew's. He was a man of expansive enthusiasm, the best quality a teacher can have. If you spent any time with him, you saw this immediately. We were once walking in the garden at St. Luke's Chapel and he looked up to the sky and said: 'There are galaxies up there light years away. Isn't it wonderful?' I was astonished that a man his age could still get so excited. He loved to laugh. One of his favorite quotations was from a speech once given by the Bishop of London, in which the Bishop said: 'If you don't have a sense of humor, get down on your knees and pray for one.' Father Flye had a great sense of humor."

Spears continued: "He would look me straight in the eye and act excited about what I was doing. He always acted so glad to see me. One of the nicest things about visiting Father Flye was how he would be so thrilled you were there. He would say: 'I'm so glad to see you. Thank you for coming.' I was overwhelmed by his genuine friendliness. I was just out of film school when I did the Agee piece and Father Flye was the first interview I did. It was a huge project for me to do as a young producer.

"I didn't have any money to rent equipment, so I borrowed the camera from a friend, but the camera kept breaking down. Earlier I had told Father Flye I would be at his apartment two hours, but it took five hours. Looking back on it now, it was a horror story. I was so embarrassed, but he was as gracious as he could be. He never showed impatience with me; Father Flye was so understanding and amenable.

"Once the film was finished, we had a wonderful private screening in 1979 when I rented a little movie theater in New York. I invited friends of mine, and about 40 people showed up. Harvey Simmonds brought Father Flye and they sat down in the second row. While the film was showing he never could sit there quietly. When he saw a shot of the boys at St. Andrew's he would say out loud, 'Oh, oh, look at that.' There are parts of the film which are very sad, it deals with Agee dying, and Father Flye would weep out loud. It was moving to me, and everybody else who was there. The film ends with Father Flye reading prose that Agee wrote. Father Flye had a big role in this film, no question about it. The film's introduction was in Knoxville, and then we later showed it at the Museum of Modern Art in New York.

"Former president Jimmy Carter is in the film. He is a great fan of James Agee's *Let Us Now Praise Famous Men*, and we were showing the film at the Kennedy Center in Washington, D.C., and Jimmy Carter showed up for that. After the film, we had a question-and-answer session with the audience. What was really interesting about it was the fact that Mr. Carter had earlier told me he wouldn't stay for the Q and A, but when it started he stayed rooted to his chair. I was up on the stage answering questions as best I could."

Spears concluded: "At one point, Carter raised his hand and waited for me to recognize him, like a schoolboy. Can you imagine a former president raising his hand to be recognized? That's the way it happened. Anyway, he stood up and asked me: 'Why don't you talk about the real star of this film, Father Flye? And, by the way, why don't you tell the audience that yesterday was Father Flye's birthday?' So I said: 'President Carter wants me to tell you that Father Flye just had a birthday.' I looked over and saw that Father Flye was embarrassed. It was an incredible scene."

Flye's reputation grew with the passing years, but this did not affect his modesty. He urged visitors to express their interests, yet he shied away from remarking on his own accomplishments—he did not think them worthy. He was a magnificent storyteller, willing to reveal himself through recollections and reflections. Because he had so much to offer, his visitors were content to let him be the judge of what was discussed, simply because anything he shared was of interest. He was a shy man, best recalled as someone who had a humming energy that belied his shuffle brought on by old age. Everyone left his company feeling better.

His visitors were invariably shocked by the clutter inside his apartment. There were boxes, crates, reams of both new and yellowed newspaper articles, papers kept inside saltine cracker boxes, Nabisco cartons, and wicker boxes filled with letters dating back to the 1800s. Father Flye moved this assortment off his bed to the bathtub every night before he went to sleep. The next morning, the process was reversed. On his small desk was an old Underwood typewriter on which he attempted to answer his mail. However, his responses to the letters were always late; he never stayed abreast of his enormous correspondence.

Books were everywhere—on the floor, under a chair or bed, tilted against the wall, stacked high. The book titles illustrated his esoteric preoccupations: *Intolerance: Is One Religion As Good As Another?*; *Death Penalty: A Moral Standard Based*

Newspaper photo of author Bowen Ingram with Father Flye, 1977

on What?; Lives of a Cell. Mixed among the scientific literature were books on religion: *The People's Anglican Missal;* the 1928 *Book of Common Prayer;* and the King James version of the Bible. Faithful to his profession, he read his prayers aloud in the morning and evening. If he was involved in a Biblically-heavy dispute, he broke the tension by citing doggerel written by his friend, W. H. Auden:

> The Book of Common Prayer we knew
> Was that of 1662.
> Though with it sermons may be well,
> Liturgical reforms are hell.

Following is a sample of some of the items that people remembered seeing at Father Flye's apartment: an exercise machine, The Greenmeadow Runner, a gift from the inventor John Stroop, who first met the priest when he was a St. Andrew's student; a bottle of holy water from Lourdes; a picture of children at a one-room schoolhouse in Florida; a scroll with the Apostles' Creed written in oriental strokes; a magazine article on the Alexander Hamilton-Aaron Burr duel; a set of James Agee's criticisms, poetry, and prose; *The Communist Manifesto: The Red Limit;* books by Will Percy; and a book of poetry by his friend, Allen Tate, inscribed: "This book is given to Father Flye with deep love, Margaret Brearly."

Father Flye had many autographed books. One read: "To Rev. J. H. Flye—

gratefully, William F. Buckley, Jr." Also *The American Dissent: A Decade of Modern Conservatism*. He had books on the occult. *The Unexplained* (with a foreword by Bishop James A. Pike) was signed by the author: "To Father Flye, great wishes on your spiritual and psychic quest—Alan Spragget." Inside the cover of *The Upward Path*, author James A. B. Haggart wrote: "To Father Flye in gratitude for his life-long help, from one of his former students." *Multitude, Multitude* carried this inscription: "To Father Flye, with my love and best wishes—Amy Clampitt." *The Search for the Edge of the Universe* was signed: "To Father Flye with deep regards—Timothy Ferris."

Other book titles recalled were: *Out of the Silent Planet; Loren Isolates The Night; Cycle Cyberspace 6; The Square and Other Selected Points; The Neurotic's Notebook; Alighieri's Dante; A Way of Seeing*, and countless newspaper and magazine columns on just about every subject imaginable. As a boy in Haines City, Hal Flye had become an avid reader, and he retained this habit for the rest of his life. Oliver Hodge once said: "He had an insatiable appetite for knowledge."

Flye's love of poetry never diminished. He communed every day with Tennyson, Shelley, Blake, Keats, Shakespeare, as well as with the ancient Greek and Roman poets. At a moment's notice, he could recite their treasured verses.

One visitor remembered Father Flye saying: "One contemplates the Big Bang theory. I can't conceive of life as always being here, but, on the other hand, I can't conceive of its beginning. How did oxygen and nitrogen get together to be used by all of us? One can contemplate the processes, but what's behind it? To me, it has a continuing sense of mystery."

Interviews with those who visited him in New York indicate that Father Flye's eating habits were sometimes bizarre. For example, for about a year, it appeared he ate nothing but canned pumpkin, crackers and peanut butter. His visitors knew of his eccentricity, of course, and thought such behavior went with the territory for an exceptional person. Later on, his eating patterns improved after a crew of caretakers was assigned to watch over him.

St. Luke's churchgoer Jeannette Roosevelt remembered one of Father Flye's unusual habits: "He used to wash his money, various bills, lots of times. He would wash and dry them over the gas jet on the stove. I'd come to his apartment and he'd be waving these bills over his stove. I was afraid the money would catch fire."

Thomas Church, a 1950 St. Andrew's graduate: "During my last visit with him in New York, I walked in and spotted him leaning against the wall upside down, with his feet pointed toward the ceiling. I feared he would fall and hurt himself. He was practicing yoga, which he said 'gets rid of the barnacles.' He was amazing."

James Lee, 1948 St. Andrew's graduate, said: "In the world of learning I had many models. One was Father Flye, the finest history teacher I ever saw. He lived for a very long time, which I fear is a commentary on clean living and right thinking. He neither smoked nor ate meat. At the tender age of 70, he still ran wherever he went. I saw him in New York City when he was 90, and his physical state was understandably not good, but his mind was as sharp as ever. He could still recite poems he knew by heart when he was my teacher at St. Andrew's."

Clint Wade, New York City public relations executive, said this about Father Flye: "He honed in on those folks who had an appreciation of literature. I recall him telling me his mother read *The Arabian Nights* to him when he was a child. She was the one who whetted his appetite for reading. Her influence on him was profound.

"Father Flye's memory of poetry was incredible. It didn't matter if you were in some restaurant or walking down the street, something would click in his mind and all the people around him would be enthralled. His poetry was often whimsical."

Wade continued: "I don't see how anyone could have looked into his eyes and not seen spirituality. It makes me think there is some truth to mysticism. If he was alone in a forest, he would be comfortable in his surroundings, because he had his own reality. He was man without any guile whatsoever. It is impossible to describe the man. However, your questions are appropriate, because the best judgment of a man is that of his contemporaries. I'm reminded of what Cicero said: 'The best armor of old age is a life well spent in the practice of good deeds.' This is why Father Flye aged with such poise and civility."

Father Flye quietly continued his good works without fanfare. Walter Chambers wrote: "It was in February of 1974 when I learned I would not be given a contract for the next year at St. Andrew's. I loved the place and was crushed. Father Flye called me from New York City, and told me he had the same experience at St. Andrews. He offered encouragement, assuring me I would be happy in the future. His surprise telephone call helped me keep some perspective. I considered it an honor to have known this remarkable man of God."

St. Luke's parishioner Catherine Maldonado: "I first knew Father Flye when he was living on Hudson Street, next to the Parish House. Some of us went to fix supper for Father Flye. On cold winter nights it was a cozy feeling to be puttering around in the little kitchen finding the mismatched china to serve his supper. Sometimes we shared a glass of wine. Pat Read and Jeannette Roosevelt made martinis for him sometimes.

"When I was there, we concentrated on poetry. I had said to him that poetry gave me great comfort in times of stress, and he was happy in being able to recite poetry. One of his favorite poems was by a minor French poet, Montaneiken:

La vie est breve	Life is short
Un peu d'amour	A little love
Un peu de reve	A little illusion
Et puis bonjour!	And then goodbye!

La vie est vaine	Life is frivolous
Un peu d'espoir	A little hope
Un peu de haine	A little hate
Et puis bonjour!	And then goodbye!

"I would answer with Verlaine's lines where he feels he is losing faith in himself:

J'ai perdu ma force et ma vie	I have lost my energy and my life
Mes amis et ma gaiete	My friends and my mirth
J'ai perdu jusqua la fierte	I have lost even my pride
Qui faisait croire en mon genie	Making me believe in my spirit

"Then Father Flye would remember Shakespeare's sonnet: 'When in disgrace with fortune and men's eyes,' and we would go on to discuss what a feeble thread we cling to when we stake our hopes on ephemeral love.

"We also talked about how important it was for older people to write down what they remembered and because of that, I started gathering my diaries and comparing childhood tales with him. We read together from Robert Coles' *Irony In The Mind's Life* and knew the main thing was to love God and to work at loving one's neighbor.

"His modesty was genuine and touching. One day he looked at me quizzically and said: 'Catherine, isn't it odd that I should have all this acclaim in my later years?' He had become a celebrity, and his name was known far and wide. Down in Virginia, for example, people said to me: 'You go to St. Luke's? That's where Father Flye lives.' I recall how he would sit under the big tree in the garden. Now, I wish he were sitting there under his tree and able to talk to me about his gentle faith."

In November 1974, Father Flye had cataract surgery. From then on, he had to wear thick lenses and get very close to what he was reading.

Rachel Foreman first met Father Flye during "Agee Week" in 1972. She said: "I was a St. Andrew's student, young and extremely shy. One day in the dining hall, a crowd had collected around this older, smiling priest. Curiosity made me get closer. There was something about him that attracted me. I loved him right off. Completely out of character for me, I approached Father Flye and asked him if we could correspond. He wrote down his address on a piece of paper, and I walked out of the dining hall light as a feather."

Flye's letters to Rachel Foreman are intriguing. On the subject of dealing with animals, June 21, 1973: "Logical reasoning, understanding and appreciation, response to beauty, imagination, intellectual tastes and interests, are areas which the animal simply cannot know. Our field of communication with them is narrow. We can be fond of them and show them we care for them. We must make allowances for their nature and limitations. I have sympathetic understanding as to why the dog's barking is upsetting to you; however, remember that he is acting on instinct, not logic as we understand it."

Regarding his travels to Florida, St. Andrew's and Nashville, March 15, 1973: "For the past several years I have been going down each February to see my sister and others at Winter Park, Florida, and this time instead of returning directly I came back by way of Tennessee. At St. Andrew's I spent quite a bit of time talking to Mr. Chambers, a teacher. Then I went to Nashville, where a niece of mine lives. Then I took a plane to Washington for a visit at the home of another niece. Many of my books and papers are there. I then came to New York on a train."[2]

In another letter to Foreman, dated March 10, 1975, Father Flye expounded on the study of Latin: "It is a tough language to master, but the knowledge of it can be worthwhile. I would recommend your putting in the time to get a good grounding in Latin—learning word meanings and the declensions and conjugations so that you know them thoroughly. Don't think of this as a dull task. Remember that it takes a lot of practice to master any skill, in athletics or playing a musical instrument, or mastering any art. There can be a certain amount of pleasure here if one approaches it the right way.

"To notice, for example, how ordinarily in Latin the adjective comes after the noun instead of before it (which seems sensible) and how the order of words in a sentence can be varied more in Latin than in English, because of the case and verb endings which show word relationships. And the interesting derivation of some of our English words from Latin. Investigate the words 'salary' or even 'investigate' itself. Get all the knowledge of Latin that you can. Learning French will also be helpful to you."

In a letter dated July 31, 1979, he mentioned his failing health: "My eyesight has deteriorated considerably. I couldn't manage to read your letter. However, a few days ago, a woman I know came to see me and she read your letter aloud. I am so glad you are taking German. I did take first year German by myself and after passing an exam took second year German at Yale. Latin and Greek certainly have relevance and value for those who are aware of our western civilization. A good teacher helps but a good start in either of these can be made by almost anyone with a good sense of languages. Years ago, I knew a little girl in Florida who by herself began both in April and by September entered school in third year Latin (Cicero) and third year Greek (Homer) and got high grades in both.

"I am noticeably growing older. Hearing, eyesight and memory are failing. Arthritis in my knees, though not painful when resting, is a bother. I now use a 'walker' and have less pain but progress is slow. Using a wheelchair is likely."

In another letter to Foreman, Father Flye wrote about David McDowell: "I'm happy to learn of your going to Kenyon. You know of David McDowell, with whom I have had a good relationship from the time he was a boy at St. Andrew's. Graduating from there (St. Andrew's) in 1936, he attended Vanderbilt University for a year and then (as did John Crowe Ransom) transferred to Kenyon, where he graduated with honors in 1940. I visited him there in the spring of that year and met a number of the faculty. He was in New York City for several years. He is now in Nashville."

In December, 1978, Father Flye sent this Christmas message: "My dear friends, your remembrance of me at Christmas means a great deal to me, and you can be sure that you are in my thoughts with constant affection. If we could meet in person we would talk readily enough, I am sure, but I am regrettably in arrears as to my letters. In my advanced age I am limited in various ways, but I have much to be grateful for."

In June 1979, Father Flye had a crippling stroke. Harvey Simmonds related how he found the priest one morning: "I came to his apartment and found him delirious. I called a nearby hospital; the doctors there kept Father Flye for about a month. His mental processes were affected; he was in and out of lucidity. The stroke changed his ability to fend for himself. He needed care around the clock. What was unavailable was the money to pay for someone to stay with him, well beyond what I could provide."

Simmonds spent most of his childhood at St. Andrew's School. His father was a longtime school employee, and for years Father Flye was a close friend to the entire Simmonds family. After graduating from St. Andrew's in 1956, Harvey stayed in contact with Father Flye, and when he became an editor for Eakins Press in New York City, he frequently visited the priest at his apartment. Father Flye may have died if Simmonds had not discovered the disabled clergyman when he did.

Sociologists frequently say that aging is a time of life spent among strangers. Many old people in our country are housed in an institution where their personal care is handled by employees. They are caring strangers, perhaps, but they are still strangers. The effect on the aged in this scenario can be devastating. Patients in a "nursing home" frequently feel forsaken. Intimate friends are rare for an older man who is unmarried or widowed. Flye was the exception; he had many friends, and they were determined that he stay at St. Luke's. Money for his private care was needed, but where was it to come from?

The priest had built a reservoir of good will over his long lifetime, and now it was time to balance the scales. In the early 1980s, following the stroke, Simmonds created a fund-raising entity known as "The Friends of Father Flye." He explained: "The list of people who became the 'Friends of Father Flye,' the group that provided the money to hire caretakers, came from a list I put together. There were plenty of people who kept in touch with Father Flye, and shared the idea that he shouldn't be forced to live at a nursing home. He loved his independence."

Simmonds continued: "I wrote people asking for help, and the response was excellent. Former-St. Andrew's students who learned of his situation pitched in. Robert Toupal, John Stroop, Spencer Smith and Stanley Hole come to mind. If a

Harvey Simmonds with Father Flye in New York City, 1977

man had once gone to St. Andrew's, he invariably wrote a check. The vault of love Father Flye had accrued was amazing. He was encircled by well-meaning devotees."

In the early 1980s, Simmonds decided to enter a monastery.[3] Before he could become a monk, however, he needed someone to take over the Friends of Father Flye project. He chose a woman with enormous energy. Her name was Marnette Trotter, and she played a critical role in Father Flye's later years

Simmonds explained how he met Trotter: "She was vacationing on the Delta Queen, a paddle wheeler that sailed on the Ohio and Mississippi. At the time, I was a Delta Queen employee. After some conversations, we knew we had mutual academic pursuits, and that is how our friendship began." Harvey's knowledge of literature and art pleased Trotter; she was a fan of the "artistic world." Their rapport developed over several years, as Trotter traveled to New York to shop, see a Broadway play and visit Simmonds. During one of those trips, Simmonds introduced her to Father Flye, and she was thrilled when she discovered the priest also composed poetry. Trotter wrote "Reflecting Pool Prayer" in the 1970s:

> May I be for all those whose lives touch mine
> A reflecting pool, with love, understanding, freedom
> Mirrored in me as the up reaching trees, sky, birds
> Are mirrored in the clear water

She was a taskmaster in managing the Friends of Father Flye crusade. She had a history of strong opinions, of going against societal standards. She caused controversy in the 1940s in Pine Bluff, Arkansas, by paying her domestic help the federal minimum wage and also contributing toward their Social Security. She lobbied the newspapers in Little Rock to use identical courtesy titles for black women as were used for white women in news stories. Not long after the 1957 racial crisis at Central High School in Little Rock, she startled the establishment by hosting a well-publicized integrated dinner at a downtown Little Rock restaurant.

Trotter was a Renaissance woman with many intellectual pursuits. She was one of the few women in the nation who was scholastically authoritative on Robert E. Lee and Thomas Jefferson. The Bryn Mawr graduate met her husband, John F. Trotter, while he was recuperating at a Pine Bluff hospital, after his imprisonment at a German prisoner-of-war camp in Poland.

Trotter was financially secure. She had the time and money to pursue what she called "my causes." When she agreed to take over the Friends of Father Flye campaign, she moved to New York temporarily and began hiring people to oversee Father Flye's daily regimen. Kevin Kennedy was the first caretaker. He was a free-lance artist, poet and playwright. He had earlier met Flye, seeking input regarding a screenplay he was writing about James Agee. Rachel Foreman was the next to join the caretaker team. At that time, she was an art student in New York City.

Another caretaker was Colin Sanderson, who had benefitted from the priest's help in the past. He was joined by David Lyle, a former St. Andrew's student who had the primary job of staying overnight with Flye. The four caretakers did the best they could.

Due to Trotter's behavior, some tensions developed. Kennedy said: "She would burst in, giving orders at the top of her lungs. She was insensitive to the peace and quiet we had in Father Flye's apartment. I recall her once going over to his hearing device and shouting in his ear, and him shuddering with irritation. When she left, he whispered: 'Thank God, blessed silence.' He liked to have a jigger of sherry at supper time. I didn't see any harm in this, and he looked forward to it. But Marnette made a scene over the sherry."

Foreman reported: "I tried to ignore Marnette. She was well-meaning; however, her aggressive personality got on my nerves."

Catherine Maldonado, a St. Luke's parishioner, recalled: "An admirer of Father Flye's showed up and asked Marnette Trotter if he could take Father Flye for a walk in his wheelchair, and she said okay. Marnette didn't know where they'd gone and she got quite excited after an hour or so. She came over to my place, across from St. Luke's, and I stuck my head out the window and asked anyone going by to help us locate our Father Flye. We called the police, but they couldn't help. Finally, along came a very distracted-looking literary-type senior citizen pushing Father Flye in his wheelchair. It was innocent enough. They had gone to Washington Square and had a great time."

❏❏❏

In a loving tribute to Father Flye, Kevin Kennedy wrote: "'To be a child is different from the man of today,' wrote the poet Francis Thompson in his essay on Shelley. In the varied roles that Father Flye played out—as a student, teacher, priest, husband and spiritual father to a countless number of children and adults—he kept housed inside himself the breath of the child-within; the child who sees with the heart the mysterious universe with wonder and awe.

"Father Flye kept alive and buoyant this child-like spirit, and he drew out the same spirit from all who came to know him, regardless of age. He cajoled it, nurtured it with wit, mirth and charm, with an endearing amount of love for beauty and for truth, with understanding and a student's seriousness, with an encompassing warmth and gentleness that took you well into his heart with both friendship and generosity abounding, with prayers and most especially with poetry, in which he reveled.

"Father Flye was nourished by poetry and, in turn, he nourished others with the true recitation of countless poems he had memorized over his lifetime, beginning from the time he was a young boy and first discovered his keen ability to memorize. When Father Flye recited a poem, he became that poem, the very embodiment of its spirit, in tempo, tone, rhythm and phrasing, and with a sensitivity to its resonance as music over water. His repertoire was extensive, flowing down through centuries of poets. Beginning with the authors of the Bible, the Greek and Roman poets, and through Shakespeare, Donne, Milton, Cowper, Blake, Wordsworth, Coleridge, Longfellow, Emerson, Holmes, Whitman, Tennyson, Browning, Dickinson, Field, Cummings, Kipling, Yeats, Millay, Nash, Keats, Shelley, and countless others, some renowned and otherwise. Imagine all these poets sitting in one classroom with Father Flye in their midst; it has the makings for a wonderful imaginary photograph."

❏❏❏

In 1979, Father Flye's life took a turn. Donald Dietz and David Herwaldt had first visited the priest in 1976 out of curiosity about his friendship with James

Agee. That visit led to others. One day in 1979 Dietz and Herwaldt were in Flye's apartment at St. Luke's discussing photography, when Father Flye showed them some photographs he had taken in the 1930s at St. Andrew's.

Both Dietz and Herwaldt were photographers and they immediately recognized the value of the photos—images of an age of innocence. Without knowing it, Father Flye had captured on film with phenomenal clarity the honest realism of boys playing marbles, at a baseball game, dozing in class, swimming in a mountain pond, lounging against a wall, playing tennis. These photos demanded attention. They were compelling, yet had gone unnoticed for a half century.

Dietz and Herwaldt sat mesmerized as Father Flye explained he bought the camera from David McDowell in the mid-1930s, simply because the youngster was eager to get some cash. The St. Andrew's teacher was 50 years old and had never before handled a camera.

Father Flye never thought of himself as a photographer. He took photos casually, with no advance planning, never going out of his way. He rarely showed his photos to other people, believing they were solely of personal value. They probably would have remained inside a dusty box, unknown to the world, had Dietz and Herwaldt not seen them. The priest had no concept of their intrinsic worth.

Herwaldt explained: "Father Flye put his camera to use photographing in the ordinary run of his life. He never mastered the technique required by his camera; but he saw through photography things he would not otherwise see. His photos were as unambitious as any snapshooter, but they were accomplished photographs."

Dietz, Herwaldt, Simmonds, and Erik Wensberg embarked on an ambitious project—to produce a booklet showing Father Flye's photographs. In addition, they planned a multi-city photo exhibition. After receiving a grant from the Lyndhurst Foundation, they achieved their mission.

Their book was titled *Through the Eyes of a Teacher*, and contains 48 pages of description and photographs. Nineteen pages of photographs were taken at St. Andrew's; four pages show children in Harlem; one page shows Will Percy; and two pages show James Agee and his wife, Mia. The foreword is by Harvard Latin professor Robert Coles. *Through the Eyes of a Teacher* has been praised as a noteworthy tribute to Father Flye.

Priscilla Ann Fort, of the Public Relations office at St. Andrew's School, mailed out a press release on September 16, 1980, announcing the school would host the exhibit of Father Flye's photographs, October 10 through November 2.

In addition to St. Andrew's, "Through the Eyes of a Teacher" photo exhibits were held in Sewanee; Boston; New York City; and Charlottesville, Virginia. Stories about the photographs appeared in the *East Side Express* in New York City, the *Boston Globe*, the *Boston Observer*, the *Sewanee Mountain Messenger*, and the *Daily Progress* in Charlottesville. Lincoln Caplan wrote: "Father Flye would

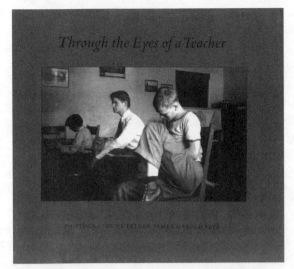

Through the Eyes of a Teacher

PHOTOGRAPHS BY FATHER JAMES HAROLD FLYE

Through the Eyes of a Teacher, *published 1980*

not judge himself in the company of Henri Cartier-Bresson, but the famed Frenchman's eye for humanity comes to mind when I consider the pictures of Father Flye."

The traveling exhibits, which incorporated 75 photos, always drew large crowds. The local newspaper articles were always flattering. Naturally, the feature pieces explained Father Flye's long tenure at St. Andrew's and his friendship with James Agee.

Manhattan book store manager, Thomas Martinez, recalled: "I went to the New York Public Library to see Father Flye's exhibition and I was favorably impressed. None of the photographs was posed, they were all genuine. It was nice to see he was getting the attention he deserved. We can be grateful that his snapshots were luckily spotted by professional photographers. I stayed at the exhibit for a couple of hours and saw how he enjoyed being at the exhibition, and I was happy for him."

❏ ❏ ❏

[1]The Rector at St. James' Church in Wichita was a war hero. In 1946 the *Sewanee Alumni News* reported: "C. H. Blakeslee won the Silver Star for gallantry in Germany. He was separated from his company and with only his tommy gun for any support, captured ten German officers and twenty enlisted men. Charles Blakeslee left the university to enter the Army in 1943. He has now returned to continue his studies."

[2]When Father Flye traveled to Winter Park to stay with his sister, Barbara Chubb, he often met with Gamble Rogers, well-known folk singer and humorist. Rogers was born into a central Florida family of architects, but chose entertainment as his profession. Rogers was posthumously inducted into the Florida Artists Hall of Fame. Flye's nephew, Henry Chubb, said in a 1996 interview: "It was disgraceful how Uncle Hal would go sing and cavort with Gamble Rogers, rather than stay and visit with my mother and the rest of us."

[3]Harvey Simmonds became a Cistercian monk at a Roman Catholic abbey in northern Virginia. He is now called Brother Benedict.

CHAPTER 15

Twilight and Eulogies

The most consummately beautiful thing in the universe is the rightly
fashioned life of a good person.
—GEORGE HERBERT PALMER (1842-1933)

KEVIN EDWARD KENNEDY'S PAINTINGS and pen-and-ink draw-
ings have been published in literary journals in Canada, England, and the
United States. His stage play, *A Man Between Twilights: A Portrait of James
Agee* was presented at the Lincoln Center in New York City. This creative work
introduced him to Father Flye.

Kennedy spent more time with Father Flye than anyone else over the period
following Flye's stroke in 1979 to the time Father Flye was transferred to a
Monteagle, Tennessee, nursing home in 1983. With emotion, Kennedy described
the elderly priest this way: "Poetry was a main artery in his personal makeup. If
each encounter doesn't teach us something, what is the point of this experience
called life? That is why the poet is so important in society, so extremely necessary, as water and light are to living. Father Flye was a man who dreamed dreams
out of which he created realities that were more honest than those who lived by
the rules. This was wisdom acquired by fire. He was a man filled with poetry,
and he turned to it to help heal his battered heart.

"I have vivid recollections of him sitting with his cat, Socrates, on his lap, the
perfect portrayal of love. He used to say: 'Love something or someone, but love.'
He loved everything with a passion, with gusto, and with the great trust and
belief of a child. It was the most extraordinary thing I observed about him.

"Father Flye's view of the world was always one of beauty, whether it was
through the lens of a camera, the naked eye, or what he experienced living day
by day over his life. He always saw the good and beautiful within a human being,
especially children for whom he had more respect than he did for adults, but he
connected with grown-ups who still saw with the eyes of a child.

Kevin Kennedy, 1976

"Most of us are caught up in our own high-octane anxieties, never seeing life with our rapid-eye peripheral vision. We scan but never focus. However, being a poet, Father Flye would see the butterflies in the garden and stand perfectly still. He noticed four butterflies become eight, then twelve, then twenty, harvesting a plot no bigger than a small vase."

Kennedy recounted: "I can still see his ancient face, heavy with the wrinkled skin which vanished when his eyebrows went up in surprise at something that I said made him laugh. In that moment of laughter, as he threw back his head, so far back that every line vanished from his face, with a laughter like the gleeful joy of a child who discovered something wonderful for the first time, he was suddenly a child. It was then that I first fell in love with him. We were like children together.

"I think often of the years I spent caring for Father Flye, and how many times a great despondency came over him, because he didn't have the energy to accomplish much in a single day, other than his daily prayers. He never understood what in the world was keeping him alive so long. He felt his mortality. Not sorrowfully, mind you, but he accepted the fact his longevity was running out.

"When I first began taking care of Father Flye, after his daily prayers at 4 p.m., I sometimes brought him cheese and crackers along with a glass of sherry. The alcohol slowly worked its way through those old veins until a desperately needed energy hit him. From the kitchen I heard him yell out a soft 'yippee' with a genuine joy. I knew how active his life had been, but now he mourned his condition. This was poignantly sad. His brilliant mind was trapped inside a wasting vessel."

Kennedy continued: "He was puzzled by his longevity. He was about to turn 98, and we were about to have breakfast, and we were discussing his age and he said: 'I don't know. I could die next week or next year, but that could be said about any of us.' He had great wisdom, along with a sense of humor. It is difficult to put into words, but there was always a cheerful countenance around him. He found beauty and humor in everything. It was easy to see how children would take to Father Flye.

"One time I left the kitchen to do some typing. When I returned, Father was still seated at the kitchen table. I paused at the door, for he was saying to himself: 'Here I am facing death as my ancestors did. What it will bring I do not know. How worthy I have been I do not know. Almighty God, I commit myself to your care.' He started to recite Macbeth's soliloquy after he had heard of the queen's death:

> Tomorrow, and tomorrow, and tomorrow,
> Creeps in this petty pace from day to day,
> To the last syllable of recorded time;
> And all our yesterdays have lighted fools
> The way to dusty death. Out, out, brief candle!
> Life's but a walking shadow, a poor player
> That struts and frets his hour upon the stage
> And then is heard no more. It is a tale
> Told by an idiot, full of sound and fury,
> Signifying nothing.

"I stood there silently, unseen, deeply moved. This was a time with Father Flye that I remember as a holy moment, a blessing. He knew that art, poetry in particular, gave meaning to reality, and he used it as a point of reflection upon his own life."

Kennedy concluded: "This man lives within me to this day and will for the rest of my life. I will always call on him whenever I am in trouble, and I know, like some angel with very large wings, he will be there to help me through my difficulties. He gave me his harmonica, and it is a treasured keepsake. But this was the gift Father Flye really gave to me—it was more than possessing a silver penknife or having any possession of value that could be lost or stolen; he taught me to forgive, because he had within himself so much love."

Following are excerpts from an interview with Marnette Trotter: "I remember a sweet time when it was his birthday. They were having a meeting of the vestry at St. Luke's, and after they adjourned they stood outside his apartment and sang 'Happy Birthday' to him. He was so loved.

"Even at his advanced age, he was the celebrant for the 7:30 morning Mass. He was given special permission by the Bishop to use the old prayer book. He knew it all by heart. His services were popular with the older parishioners at St. Luke's. He did this into his 90s until he was forced to use a wheelchair.

"I met a man in Oklahoma City who knew Father Flye. His name was Father James Law, the Rector at one of the Episcopal churches there. He knew Father Flye when he was a boy in New York City. He lived close to St. Luke's, and he knew Father Flye when he would come for summer duty. He admired him, as a little boy looking up to this revered priest.

"I remember corresponding with people in Wichita and Omaha. They wrote he'd never walk up the stairs when he could run. Well, he wasn't so young then. I went to visit my son in Twin Falls, Idaho, and I went to church. The priest there had been an acolyte in Omaha and he spoke of how Father Flye had the energy of a man half his age. He would pick up the bottom of his long cassock and sprint everywhere.

"Harvey Simmonds was taking care of Father Flye long before the Friends of Father Flye was formalized. He realized there was this great need. I can't tell you how fine Harvey was with Father Flye, in every way trying to preserve his self-respect. Harvey was his housekeeper, secretary, butler and nurse for a long spell.

"The old man loved Premium crackers, and he would save the boxes, plus shoe boxes, and put his things in them. Harvey would come in and get things straightened up, but when he came back later, Father Flye had his apartment messed up again. It was like a rabbit's nest. The entire floor, the tables, the bed, were covered with Father Flye's items, books, papers, you name it. You could scarcely move around the room, so Harvey would have to start all over again."

Trotter added: "Harvey and Father Flye came to see me in Charlottesville in 1975, on their way to stay with Father Flye's niece, Mary Boorman, in Nashville. A little girl on the airplane had taken up with Father Flye, and the two of them came off the airplane giggling and holding hands. The girl's mother was astonished. Father Flye had this sort of charm that attracted children to him.

"Then in May of 1976, I stayed at Mary Boorman's. Harvey had to rush back to his job in New York, so it was proposed that Father Flye and I should drive back to New York City. So, we did. I remember when I first got into the car, I thought to myself: 'Well, my goodness, what in the world will we talk about all this way?' Of course, we never quit talking for a minute. He loved to quote poetry. I did also, so we got along just fine. Better than fine, we hit it off handsomely. He was such a delight.

"When we started our trip, he was sitting regularly in the car, but he kept scooting closer to me, and by the time we got to Virginia he was sitting right at my shoulder. It was so cute. During our trip, he told me about the first book he remembered his mother reading to him. It was *Diddie, Dumps, and Tot*, a book about children. The title was the nicknames of three little girls. When we got to New York City, Father Flye piloted me through the Holland Tunnel, through which I had never driven.

"I remember he and I once went to the Grolier Club, a somewhat exclusive literary club. Harvey was a member and he was doing the floral arrangements that day. After a while we missed Father Flye. We learned he had gone outside and gotten a cab, and he was going to stop by a drug store and get some vitamin tablets. Thank God, the man who hailed the cab knew where he had gone.

"When I started running Friends of Father Flye, I thought here I am in New York, what will I do? But everybody was so helpful, the Laughlins, Catherine

Maldonado, Jeannette Roosevelt. Harvey had given me a long list of people to contact. We got out of the city once in a while. We went to Woodbury, Connecticut, and had lunch with Clare Leighton. She was a well-known woodblock engraver who had come from England. I have a print of hers, and a number of her books. She and I got to be very good friends. Of course, she just adored Father Flye."

Trotter added: "I recall the only time he received Communion from a woman priest. It was so funny. I was staying at St. Andrew's in 1976, and Father Franklin Martin and his wife were going over to St. Mary's to celebrate Mass, and Father Flye and I tagged along. After the service started, we suddenly realized Father Martin was being helped by a woman priest from Sewanee. Father Flye was a gentleman who wouldn't make a scene, so he just stood there and received the bread from Father Martin and the wine from the woman priest. He gave this awful shudder that went all over him. He was not happy."

Trotter continued: "It was absolutely phenomenal that so many individuals joined hands financially to protect Father Flye in his later years. It is a wonderful story. You don't see that often. At one time, we had close to 200 donors; the number varied. It got down to 100 once, and we were worried. As the money came in, it went out. It never accumulated."[1] The number of contributors generally averaged about 125.

On February 13, 1983, Harvey Simmonds wrote to Henry Chubb, in part: "Over the last year and a half, Father Flye's needs grew and it was necessary to have more assistance. A half dozen friends came together to sustain the James H. Flye Fund by making monthly contributions, ranging from $25 to $300. This is a supplement to Father's pension and Social Security making it possible to meet necessities. With the new conditions, an additional $900 monthly is required. We think you might wish to be part of making it possible for Father Flye to stay at Saint Luke's."

Father Flye suffered a second stroke in June 1983, and the decision was made to move him to the Regency Health Care Center in Monteagle, Tennessee. He was 98 years old and obviously needed 24-hour professional care. His departure from New York City was heart-rending for the St. Luke's parishioners. Catherine Maldonado reported: "We were in shock. Many of us stood around crying and sobbing, because we knew his leaving was the end of an era. He had been inspirational, a delight, for so many of us for so long. We knew his brightness couldn't be replaced."

On August 10, 1983, Trotter wrote a long Friends of Father Flye letter: "Father stood the trip to Tennessee better than anticipated, greeting his wife's niece, Mary Boorman, at the Nashville airport. Susan Core, who teaches English at St. Andrew's-Sewanee School, and her husband, George Core, who is the editor of *The Sewanee Review*, met us and drove us to the nursing home in Monteagle.

"Kevin Kennedy stayed at night with Father, he and I sharing the day care for the first 8 days until we were able with the help of Jan Nunley, St. Andrew's

Left to right: Mary Boorman, Mary Douglas, Bowen Ingram, Howard Boorman with Father Flye, May 1977

Postmistress and daughter of Father's old friend Cecil Knott, to find other helpers. Although the Regency is a fine facility, spotlessly clean with kind workers, it does not have enough staff to provide the personal care that he needs for bathing, dressing, bathroom visits, meals and individual attention.

"Providence brought us Mrs. Frances Sutherland Anderson, whose grandparents and mother had been on the St. Andrew's staff for 50 years. She has a sweet story about her first Easter Egg hunt as a child at St. Andrew's. She was small, too tiny to find any eggs, and was on the verge of tears in frustration when a priest gently tapped her on the shoulder and pointed to his coat pocket. She reached in and discovered an Easter Egg! Of course, it was Father Flye.

"Her nephew, Greg Thorpe, comes in the afternoons and Nadine Stines at night, with fill-ins for the weekend. Frances, besides the usual bathing, dressing, helping with feeding, leads Morning Prayer with Father. Greg plays gospel songs on his guitar before Father retires for the night, and Fathers Rhys and Patten give Communion on Sunday mornings.

"Father seems to have a renewed sense of hope and purpose in life, helped by visits of old friends from Sewanee like the Arthur Ben Chittys and Betty Foreman, and new friends like the St. Andrew's-Sewanee Headmaster, the Reverend William Wade, and Director of Development, Pat Gahan. As always there is this amazing spiritual effect on those whose lives he touches.

"I'm working with the devoted help of Kevin Kennedy to turn Father's apartment back to the Church of St. Luke in the Fields by August 24th. A word of gratitude must go to the Rector, Fr. Leslie Laughlin, Jr., his wife Roxana, the vestry family, and Father Schniepp who celebrated Mass for him, and Catherine Maldonado, Jeannette Roosevelt, Alice LaPrelle, Mary Reath, Elissa Lane, and Robert Costa.

"I'll be continuing as Harvey's stand-in, coming from Little Rock every month or so to see Father Flye and keeping in constant touch through the George Cores who have agreed to be Father's local representatives, and seeing about paying the helpers and meeting needs, coordinating friends' visits. Jan and Roger Nunley have agreed to help out, and also do the bookkeeping."

During a telephone interview, Trotter outlined the general situation after Father Flye arrived back on the Mountain: "I stayed there two weeks to help get him settled. He was still aware of things, but was not fully cognizant. I realized he was going to have more care than the nursing home provided. We raised $3,000 a month for Father Flye's care. It came to that, what with the salaries and such.

"There was a very touching moment. Kevin and I had taken Father Flye to the Lady Chapel at St. Andrew's. We placed his wheelchair in front of the altar. And there's this huge painting there of the Madonna. All of a sudden he looked up, and he saw that painting, and you could just see recognition coming. From then on we felt, or hoped, he was aware he was back on the Mountain, because he had lived and worked for so many years at St. Andrew's. His dreams and aspirations were nurtured among those huge pine trees."

Cynthia Thorpe, a staff employee at the Regency Health Care Center, remembered Father Flye in fond terms: "He was 98 years old when I first met him. He had visitors from time to time, such as Bishop Millsaps, who gave him communion, and other priests from the University and St. Andrew's-Sewanee School. Father Flye got a ton of mail. Either the staff would read it to him, or the sitters would. He so enjoyed hearing what those letters said, often asking us to repeat a word. He dictated his replies; they were usually short. We used up a lot of envelopes and stamps.

"Mr. David McDowell's visits were extremely special to him, you could really tell that. They would pray together. He would sit and hold Father Flye's hand for hours. Their relationship had a special quality. He was the most consistent visitor to Father Flye's room, I'd say five times a week. I think they had known each other for a long time. Mr. McDowell obviously loved Father Flye."

Thorpe continued: "Father Flye had private sitters, but the staff still had to take care of him. The sitters were my husband, Greg Thorpe, and Frances Anderson, Mark Sepulveda, Nadine Stines, Carol Stennett. They were paid by the people who ran Friends of Father Flye. They had eight-hour shifts in his private room. The staff was told to check on him every two hours.

"Greg was good to him. He played his guitar which always brought a smile to Father Flye's face. We'd take him over to Greg's mama's house when he was up to it, and he would enjoy those outings. But, for some reason, Mrs. Trotter didn't approve. She didn't want anyone to take him out except her or Susan Core. I knew how to lift him and all. It wasn't like I didn't know anything, I was a nurse's aide. We did baby him, maybe more than we should have. He'd hold Marshall, my four-year-old son, and talk to him for hours. Marshall was insane about Father Flye. He would just stand beside him and wouldn't move. If we had let him, my boy would have stayed with Father Flye 24 hours a day.

"I loved to talk with Father Flye. I believe his greatest love was for children. He told me about helping boys at St. Andrew's who didn't have stuff, like clothing and shoes, and how he enjoyed that experience. He once chuckled that he would have been a great used shoe salesman. Even though he was very old and failing, he kept his sense of humor. I got the impression he loved life for all it was worth, and this was what made him so adorable.

"Father Flye loved animals, and they loved him. He would hold our rabbits when he came to visit our house, and they would sit in his lap, so still and so quiet, as if in a deep trance. But the most amazing thing was how Greg's mother's dogs responded to him. They were outdoor dogs, nearly wild and always rowdy, but those dogs sat at his feet, totally behaved, and went to sleep. It was incredible.

"He was bad off when he first arrived. Nadine was trained as a therapist, and she really worked with him. She got him so he could write a little. He loved to write notes. They didn't always make sense, but we would agree with him, and he'd say: 'Yes, yes, yes.' He was really a cheerful person. He was angry only one time. Nadine gave him a whirlpool bath. Before that, we had only given him sponge baths. His skin was fragile, and it would tear easily. This happens when you get very old. He would scream in the whirlpool, and it frightened all of us.

"Father Flye was so happy when he was interviewed by someone from the *Grundy County Herald* on his 100th birthday. They had a party for him at the Regency with birthday candles and a cake.[2]

"I knew he was a special person right from the start. He'd put my hand on his hand, and I'd feel better immediately. He once cured my headache in minutes when he said he would pray for me. I have good feelings about him. I remember him with a great amount of affection."

Registered nurse Hallie Bennett worked at the Regency, and she recalled: "I helped the staff move him out of bed. He was feeble, not always aware of his surroundings. His private caretakers treated him gently. I saw that he was a special person. My goodness, look at all the folks who came to see him."

The Episcopal publication the *Living Church* commemorated Father Flye's 100th birthday (October 17, 1984) by printing his 1965 meditation "The Tree." Trotter wrote in a footnote: "Although Fr. Flye no longer is able to write, he maintains his interest in literature. The last time I was with him, I read to him the poems he used to recite from memory—the ones about St. Jerome, St. Anthony, St. Phillip, and "A Ballad of Lost Objects." At one time, Fr. Flye knew reams of poetry, and many books of the Bible by heart." St. Andrew's-Sewanee School also celebrated Father Flye's 100th birthday. On October 17, 1984, a reception was held in the school's Gallery, followed by "Readings and Reflections" by David Herwaldt, and the showing of the film *Agee* in the Refectory.

Donna Dykes wrote in Franklin County's *Herald-Chronicle*: "Realizing his own mortality at the age of 100, the Episcopal priest has given others enough during his lifetime to ensure a place in their memory long after he leaves for his heavenly home."

Herman Green, retired Sewanee bank manager, was a regular visitor to the Regency Health Care Center to see the priest: "I knew Father Flye as far back as 1925, so it was great to be able to see him again in Monteagle. I remember Mrs. Flye's parents coming to town every once in a while, back in the 1920s, to make bank deposits in their joint account with Mrs. Flye. They were sizable too, sometimes up to $500. Mr. and Mrs. Houghton were from Ohio and very educated.

"I wanted to go to St. Andrew's, but my father wouldn't let me. He said the school was too 'Pope-ish' to suit him. Father Flye was often invited down to Otey Memorial Church in Sewanee to preach. He could have been a great missionary.

"My wife started out as a Baptist, but Father Flye convinced her to join the Episcopal church. She thought so much of Father Flye. She idolized him. He would take off his glasses and talk slowly to her. She said he was truly Christian, spiritual without being doctrinal. I also believed he was saintly. There is no question you were with a great person when you were with him.

"I was born in 1908, and even though I wasn't a student at St. Andrew's, Father Flye and Mrs. Flye befriended me when I was a young man. I went to their house many times. They were the ones who got me started reading the newspaper and listening to the radio. At night, if atmospheric conditions were right, Mrs. Flye and I sat together and listened to Ernestine Schumann-Heink, the opera singer, on WLS in Chicago. By the way, she once gave an operatic performance at the Assembly in Monteagle. It was around 1930 that I bought an enormous Attwater-Kent radio console."

During a 1996 interview, Green continued: "Back in the 1930s, I saw Father Flye at EQB Club meetings in Sewanee. Father Flye got excited when William Gorgas spoke at the EQB. He was the military doctor who got rid of malaria and yellow fever at the Canal Zone in Panama. Father Flye wanted to start his own school here on the Mountain, but it never was started. A business acquaintance of mine, L. F. Reid, had a lot of the books that Father Flye had saved for his school. Mr. Reid also had Civil War memorabilia that Father Flye used in his St. Andrew's history classes."

❑ ❑ ❑

James Harold Flye died on April 12, 1985, six months past his 100th birthday. He was buried in the University Cemetery in Sewanee, Tennessee.

❑ ❑ ❑

Cindy Thorpe: "I was not at work the day he died, but they called me at my house, because they knew how much I loved him. I was on maternity leave, but I did not hesitate a second to go be at his side. I washed him before the mortician came to get his body at the Sewanee hospital."

Marnette Trotter: "It was very meaningful. When he died, the priest was there with him, and Frances Anderson was there with him in the hospital. Of course, they had called me when they had taken him to the hospital. The minute after he drew his last breath, they called me. The priest said it was the only time when someone was dying that he had been able to do the whole service, everything the prayer book called for regarding a person who was dying. Father Flye's death had a lot of symbolism around it. I suppose God intended it to be this way. I never knew a man who was so unique, so special, so learned, so humorous. My regret is that I didn't know him years earlier, when he was in his prime, and not so crippled by poor health.

"We asked Father William Wade, the Headmaster at St. Andrew's-Sewanee School, if Father Flye's body could stay in the Lady Chapel at St. Andrew's, and he said yes. He died on a Friday and he was taken to St. Andrew's on Sunday. His body lay in state in the tiny Lady's Chapel, a place so dear to him, until the funeral, which was the following Wednesday."

Father Wade said in a 1998 interview: "I was the celebrant at Father Flye's burial mass, and Father Martin was the preacher. Father Canon Howard Rhys, a theology professor in Sewanee, was present. Another priest who took part was Father George Hart. There were approximately 100 people gathered in the chapel for the mid-afternoon services."

Father Franklin Martin, veteran St. Andrew's Headmaster, said: "Father Flye's death came five years after I left St. Andrew's. I traveled down to the Mountain for his funeral, and it was a moving experience. I recall talking to a man who flew over from England for the occasion, and we agreed that we wouldn't see the likes of him again. His gifts to the world can't be measured. During my many years as Headmaster at St. Andrew's, I was impressed by the number of former students who spoke of him with a special reverence.

"One of Father Flye's recitations—there were hundreds he had memorized—was one by the 16th Century prelate, Jeremy Taylor, that dealt with the commonality of death. He once remarked: 'Father Martin, none of us are going to leave this earth alive.' Father Flye believed death was a doorway to a better place. In the meantime, he hoped his life would be worthwhile. Without question, his prayers were answered. The moment he died a bright new star appeared in the night sky."

Little Rock reporter William Lewis, who wrote Father Flye's obituary for the *Arkansas Gazette*, used these words: "Father Flye worked his own magic on everyone who met him. In one of the many feature articles about him during his lifetime, the *New Yorker* described him as a friendly dynamo of good will, who cast a lasting spell on people. His influence on hundreds of lives and careers is beyond estimation. He was a legend in his own time, a rare phenomenon. Is it possible that the memory of James Harold Flye will be more enduring than that of James Agee?"

Father Flye's demise received more media notice than had James Agee's death. The priest's obituary in the *New York Times*, April 14, 1985, took three times the column space than had Agee's death 30 years earlier.

Father James Harold Flye's death was reported in 32 publications, including the *New York Times, Washington Post, Boston Globe, Anglican Digest, Village Voice, Atlanta Constitution, Rollins College Review, Los Angeles Times, Boston Observer, Chattanooga Free Press, Chattanooga Times, Nashville Tennessean* and other newspapers throughout central Tennessee.

❑ ❑ ❑

St. Andrew's-Sewanee School instructor, William "Andy" Simmonds, wrote in a letter dated July 10, 1985: "Better than anything I can say, Father Flye's own words in 1938 express what he hoped for, and we know he achieved: 'Each person's life is a problem with which we may, to be sure, get help, but which he himself, not someone else, must ultimately work out. I have been helped by the wisdom of others, given either personally or through books. I believe that if certain things can be said to us, considerations presented by wise and trusted friends at the right time, it would help us. I have often wished I might be able thus to help someone in need, some young person perhaps. However, the person in question doesn't know whom to speak with, or is too shy to be frank; or perhaps a wise and trusted counselor is not at hand, or what is said is not heeded. Much that one may know cannot be handed on. Life is easier to live than to understand.'"

Clyde E. Medford, a 1943 St. Andrew's graduate, became chairman of the chapel renovation drive at St. Andrew's-Sewanee School in 1988. In a letter dated August 17, 1988, he wrote: "I want to tell you of our plans to include a memorial for Father Flye to be placed in the Lady Chapel on the south side of the main chapel. As this part of the chapel is associated with James Agee's *The Morning Watch* we felt it appropriate to memorialize Father Flye." A small (6x9-inch) bronze plaque on the wall in the Lady Chapel reads:

In Memory Of
Father James H. Flye
By
Friends Of Father Flye

❑ ❑ ❑

On May 1, 1989, a group of St. Luke's church members met to honor Father Flye by dedicating a plaque in his memory. Part of the printed program reads:

Left to right: Christopher Kennedy, Jeannette Roosevelt, Catherine Maldonado, Kevin Kennedy, Marnette Trotter, Robert Costa, Colin Sanderson (kneeling) at the dedication of the Father Flye plaque at St. Luke's in New York City, May 1989

A Memory of Father Flye	Kevin Edward Kennedy
An excerpt from "Death in the Desert" by Robert Browning	Marnette Trotter
An epigram by Callimachus translated by William Corey	Robert Costa
"The Tree" by Rev. James Harold Flye	Catherine Maldonado
Letter from Fr. Flye to James Agee Nov. 23, 1938	Colin Sanderson
"A Kind of Love Letter to New York" by Phyllis McGinley	Jeannette Roosevelt
A Lullaby—Vocalist	Kathleen McGrath
Memorial Dedication	The Rev. Leslie I. Laughlin

Another tribute to Father Flye was held at St. Luke's on April 12, 1997. Despite a heavy rain, over 50 people attended the re-dedication of the Father Flye plaque.

❏ ❏ ❏

Trotter told of her visit to Father Flye's grave: "I wanted to say a private adieu, so I hired a musician in Chattanooga, and we drove to Sewanee. It was a misty day. We stood at Father Flye's and Mrs. Flye's joint grave site. The musician put on his regalia and played "Amazing Grace" on his Scottish bagpipe. This was the way I said goodbye to Father Flye." Until her death in 1999, Trotter had flowers placed weekly at the Flye tombstone.

❏ ❏ ❏

JAMES HAROLD FLYE
BIOGRAPHICAL SUMMARY

Born in Bangor, Maine	October 17, 1884
Received B.A. Degree from Yale	1910
Received M.A. Degree from University of Virginia	1912
Ordained a Deacon from the General Theological Seminary, New York City, by Bishop of Newark, Rt. Rev. Edwin S. Lines	May 1, 1915
Married Grace Houghton	July 15, 1915
Ordained a priest by Bishop of Atlanta, Rt. Rev. Cleland K. Nelson, at Milledgeville, Georgia	December 21, 1915
Pastor at St. Stephen's Church, Milledgeville	1915-1918
Began teaching at St. Andrew's School	1918
Began summer duty at Saint Luke in the Fields, New York City	1942
Death of Grace Houghton Flye	February 13, 1954
Retired from teaching at St. Andrew's	1954
Assistant Rector, Wichita, Kansas	1954-1958
Assistant Rector, Omaha, Nebraska	1958-1959
Returned to continue long association with St. Luke's	1959
Letters of James Agee to Father Flye published	1962
Through the Eyes of a Teacher published	1980
Moved to Monteagle, Tennessee	1983
Died in Sewanee, Tennessee	April 12, 1985

Acknowledgments

Ken and Ninian Williams, Russell and Maudie Leonard, Dudley and Priscilla Fort—they were there in the early days, giving much-needed support.

This manuscript could not have been completed without the help of Juanita Barry, Don Armentrout, Ann Tate, Rachel Foreman, Larry Meyer, Will Jackson, Kenneth Speegle, Anne Armour-Jones, Thomas Church, Candy Jacobus, Howard Boorman, Phil Cook, Cindy Thorpe, Henry Chubb, Andy Simmonds, Erik Wensberg.

Also: J. Waring McCrady, Andrew Lytle, Betty Matthews, Kathleen Yokley, James Hollingsworth, Dale Doss, George Wilson, Stanley Hole, Ethel Louise Simmonds, Mildred Watts, Charles A. Mark. Robert S. Lancaster, Hartwell Hooper, Russell Wheeler, Clyde Medford, Herman Green, Thomas Martinez, Frank Caldwell, Floyd Garner, Sue Hite, Buck Jackson, Mary Barnard, Claire Friedenberg, David Madden, Clint Wade, Dan Barry, Maurice Wolfe, Ross Spears.

Also: Catherine Maldonado, Jeannette Roosevelt, Ralph Warren, James Lee, Roxanna Laughlin, Marnette Trotter, Hallie Bennett, Parker Lowry, Mara Grodzicki, Beverly McDowell, Vernon Ragland, Warren Eyster, David Madden, Jean Tallec, Margaret Chambers, Leon Sutherland, Charlotte Lorna, Dave Garroway, John Steiger, Amy Clampitt, Anna Zachary, Timothy Barton, Walter Chambers, John Seymour Erwin, Joe David McBee, James Lee, Harvey Simmonds (Brother Benedict).

And these clergymen: Bishop William Millsaps, Father Franklin Martin, Father Leslie Laughlin, Father A. Edward Sellers, Father Julien Gunn, Father Bonnell Spencer.

A special thanks to Brian McDowell, who showed personal courage with his candor about family secrets.

Also to Robert Costa, who gave so generously of his time and expertise about Father Flye's love of classical poetry.

Kevin Kennedy has my gratitude. He told of his private moments with Father Flye with the eloquence only a poet could have.

Eleanor Talbert is to be commended for her honesty about Grace Flye.

Mary Boorman allowed Grace Flye's portraits to be photographed, and made available the treasure chest of her aunt's letters. She made this book possible.

My thanks to Dr. David Lockmiller, whose enthusiasm never diminished.

My gratitude goes to Father William S. Wade, the Headmaster at St. Andrew's-Sewanee School. Also to the following school employees: Margaret Matens, Glenda Hall, Sandra Gabrielle, Elaine Gipson, Tim Graham.

A heartfelt thank-you to Arthur Ben and Elizabeth N. Chitty. They were consistent in their encouragement regarding this project. They spent many hours editing rough drafts, and their professional counsel was invaluable.

A special vote of appreciation goes out to Jill Carpenter. Her editing and advice was superb. She cast a wide net for the author.

I wish to thank the following for their assistance: Franklin County Register of Deeds Office; Vanderbilt University; Rollins College; Louisiana State University; University of the South; Ohio State University; Polk County Historical Society; Orange County Historical Society; Dade County Historical Society; Order of the Holy Cross; Church of Jesus Christ of Latter-Day Saints.

Bill Hampton
Monteagle, Tennessee
2001

INDEX

A

Adkins, Gil 47, 56
Agee, James 60, 64, 72, 129-34, 136-40, 143-5, 186-7, 190, 192, 194-5, 215, 217, 220-2, 224-6, 228, 233, 235-7, 241, 244-5
Agee, Laura 130, 143
Agee, Mia 131, 134, 136
Aiken, Conrad 110
Allen, Austin 160
Allen, Sturges (Rev.) 28, 74
Alligood, Milton 36, 82
Anderson, Frances S. 239-40, 243
Anderson, Roger (Rev.) 51, 74, 117, 120-1
Anderson, Samuel 43
Angermeyer, Charles 136
Auden, W.H. 110, 191, 223

B

Baker, Carlos 110
Baker, George M. 92, 98
Baker, Lloyd 153
Barnard, Mary 219-20
Barry, Juanita 126, 145
Barry, Nina 73
Barton, Timothy 186
Baumgartner, Clyde 120
Bayle, William 36
Beatty, Troy (Rt. Rev.) 113
Bellow, Saul 110
Bennett, Hallie 241
Blakeslee, Charles 219, 233
Boorman, Mary 62, 115, 171, 203, 208, 211, 237-8
Brown, Francis 142
Brown, Georgie 36
Brown, John 83
Brown, Lena 8
Brown, Whiskey John 106
Bryan, William Jennings 63
Buckley, William F. 190, 224
Burke, Kenneth 110
Burns, Ken 92

C

Caldwell, Frank 77
Caldwell, Hugh 106

Campbell, Robert (Rt. Rev.) 67, 69, 74, 107, 116, 136, 165
Camus, Albert 110
Caplan, Lincoln 232
Carter, Jimmy 222
Carter, Sam 120
Cathey, Thomas 151
Chamberlain, Neville 63, 191
Chambers, Margaret 56
Chambers, Walter 54-5, 125, 138, 225, 227
Chambers, Whittaker 131
Chapman, George 62
Chapman, Laura 73
Chapman, Mary 72-3
Chapman, Samuel 73
Charles I 123-5
Cheney, Brainard 136
Cheney, Frances 136
Chenson, Andrew 95-6
Chitty, Arthur Ben 1, 35-6, 76, 92, 98, 106, 129, 136, 171-2, 187, 216, 219, 239
Chitty, Elizabeth 98
Chubb, Barbara 233
Chubb, Henry 233, 238
Chubb, Leland 5, 19
Church, Jack 161
Church, Thomas 82, 85, 224
Claiborne, Alice 49, 60, 98, 166
Claiborne, Wm. S. (Rev) 24-6, 49, 60, 75, 96-8, 166-7, 172, 213
Clampitt, Amy 179, 181, 224
Clay, Henry 86
Coles, Robert 226, 232
Collins, Gertrude 31, 73
Colmore, Robert 25-6
Colson, Rod 69, 125
Compton, Anne 181
Cook, Phillip 85, 89, 154
Core, George 238-9
Core, Susan 238, 240
Costa, Robert 93, 171, 188-9, 197-8, 239, 245
Coughlin, Charles 64
Cowley, Malcolm 110
Crane, Stephen 82
Crankshaw, Joseph 90

D

Darrow, Clarence 63
Davidson, Donald 101
Davis, Jefferson 77

Dewey, John 161-2
Dietz, Donald 231-2
Disraeli, Benjamin 172
Dominic, Brother 42, 68-9, 108, 158-9
Doss, Dale 40, 51-6, 79,202, 214
DuBose, Wm. H. 96-7
DuBose, Wm. P. 97
Dubus, Andre 110
Duveneck, Frank 12
Dykes, Donna 241

E

Eliot, T.S. 110, 194
Eng, Mon "John" 187
Erwin, John S. 200
Evans, James 31
Eyster, Warren 133-4, 136, 141, 217

F

Faulkner, William 110
Ferris, Timothy 224
Fielding, George 131
Finney, Buford 160
Finos, Dale 197
Fitzgerald, Robert 133, 138, 191
Flye, Barbara 4, 8-9, 18-19
Flye, Donald 4, 9, 18-19
Flye, James Tyler 2-4, 7, 19
Flye, Mary 2-5, 7-8, 11, 18-19
Flye, Vondel 3, 6
Foote, Shelby 110
Foreman, Rachel 226-7, 230, 239
Forrest, Nathan 101-2
Fort, Priscilla 232
Foster, Reginald (Rev.) 192
Frazier, James 170
Friedenberg, Claire 141-2

G

Gahan, Pat 239
Gammon, Wirt 152
Garland, Dainty 151
Garner, Art 73
Garner, Floyd 67, 79, 152-3
Garroway, Dave 178
Gibbon, Edward 71
Gipson, Dolly 73
Goodwin, Helen 73
Goodwin, Mary 31, 217
Goodwin, R.E. 70, 166-7

Gordon, Caroline (Mrs. Allen Tate) 102, 110, 133
Gorgas, William 242
Gorman, Thomas 151
Grayson, Cary 85
Green, Alexander 167
Green, Herman 61, 63, 214, 242
Green, Paul 117
Gunn, Julien (Rev.) 74, 107, 115, 125

H

Haggart, James 224
Hampton, William 82, 156, 186
Harris, H.D. 121
Harrison, McVeigh (Rev.) 18-9, 42, 74, 121, 147
Hart, George (Rev.) 243
Hartford, Huntington 136
Hauper, Jack 65
Healy, Josephine "Jo" 143
Herwaldt, David 231-2, 241
Hiss, Alger 131
Hitler, Adolf 62, 64-5, 98, 197
Hodge, Oliver 36, 40, 46-7, 49, 82, 90, 170, 224
Hodgeman, Sam 82
Hole, Stanley 59, 81, 137-8, 200, 228
Hollingsworth, James 51, 83, 91, 100, 103-4, 115, 158, 167, 172, 181
Hooper, Hartwell 79, 106
Hopkins, Thomas L. 155
Houghton, Albert 11, 13, 19, 60, 82, 115, 143, 168, 213, 242
Houghton, Amy 11
Houghton, Charles 12, 62
Houghton, Henry 12
Houghton, Myra 13, 19
Hubbell, Edward 40, 49-51, 56
Hughson, Shirley (Rev.) 28, 74-5
Huntington, James (Rev.) 24
Huntsman, Willie 161
Huske, Joseph (Rev.) 36
Huston, John 136, 144

I

Ingram, Bowen 134, 137

J

Jackson, Buck 102

Jackson, William 106, 185
Jewell, Richard 93
Johannsen, Jean McClane 15
Jones, Madison 136

K

Kelly, George 161
Kennedy, Harold 26, 156, 219-20
Kennedy, Kevin 209, 230-1, 234-6, 238-9, 245
Kennedy, Patrick 150
Kent School 39
Kersey, Raymond 160
Kline, Henry B. 101
Knickerbocker, Wm. 98, 110
Knight, Harry 70
Knott, Cecil 239
Koski, Augustus 70, 74, 121-2
Kroll, Leopold (Fr. Superior) 126
Kronenberger, Louis 136

L

Lackey, Sam 73, 95
Lancaster, Robert 92, 99, 123
Lane, Elissa 239
Lanier, Lyle H. 101
LaPrelle, Alice 239
Laughlin, Leslie (Rev.) 184-5, 188, 237, 239, 245
Laughlin, Roxanna 185
Lautzenheiser, Clarence 147, 150
Lautzenheiser, Ernest 150
LeBaron, Eddie 158
Lee, James 111, 136, 224
Lee, Robert E. 83-4, 102, 161, 230
Lewis, Billy 160
Lewis, William 243
Lindsey, John 164
Lockmiller, David 23, 33, 46, 76-7, 200
Long, Frank 98, 120
Long, Margaret 136
Longstreet, James 81
Lorna, Charlotte 181-2
Lowdenslager, Paul 36, 108
Lowry, Parker "Peanuts" 90, 118
Lyle, David 230
Lytle, Andrew 63, 83, 91, 100-2, 110, 136, 142, 168, 170-1

M

MacDonald, Dwight 136

MacDowell, Malcolm 165-7, 169
Mackleheron, George 169
Madden, David 101, 134, 136-7, 139-41
Maldonado, Catherine 178, 225, 230, 238-9, 245
Manfred, Frederick 136, 141-2
Mann, Arthur 36
Manning, William (Rt. Rev.) 124
Maritain, Jacques 110
Mark, Charles 64
Martin, Franklin (Rev.) 74, 91, 126, 136-7, 145, 238, 243
Martin, Sam 67
Martinez, Thomas 182, 233
Matthews, Betty 51
McBee, Joseph 220
McCadden, William 73
McCarthy, Coleman 1
McCrady, J. Waring 38
McDowell, Alan 132, 141
McDowell, Beverly 140, 143
McDowell, Brian 141-2, 145
McDowell, David 61, 96, 129, 132-4, 136-45, 151, 169, 196-7, 199, 208, 214, 217, 227, 232, 240
McDowell, Madeline "Mara" 132, 139-40, 143, 169, 199, 208
McGinley, Phyllis 178-9, 245
McGrath, Kathleen 245
Medford, Clyde 43, 61, 244
Medford, Ethel 73
Medley, Lee 173
Mencken, H.L. 63
Merriman, Erle (Rev.) 212
Merrit, James 170
Merton, Thomas 110
Meyer, Lawrence 61, 108, 118
Millsaps, Wm. (Rt. Rev.) 127-8, 240
Moffat, John 38
Mooney, Dave 161
Mulligan, Dorothy 210, 214

N

Newbegin, Robert 14, 217
Nixon, Herman C. 101
Nunley, Jan 238, 240

O

Oates, Carol 110
Obolensky, Ivan 133, 139-40, 144

O'Connor, Flannery 110
O'Dear, George 160
Orum, Liston (Rev.) 46, 67, 74-5, 90, 124, 150
Owsley, Lawrence 101

P

Parker, Francis (Rev.) 43-4, 58, 68, 149
Pearce, Nina 41-2
Pennington, Adele 5, 10
Percy, Will 61, 96, 100-2, 223, 232
Perry, Sanford 117
Peyton, William 66, 136, 150
Phillips, Edmund 136
Porter, Katherine 110
Potter, David 95
Pound, Ezra 64, 110, 141
Puffer, Winthrope 73

R

Racine, Colleen 40
Ragland, Vernon 153
Ransom, John 82
Ransom, John Crowe 101, 228
Reath, Mary 239
Reid, Allious 31, 42-4, 73-4, 154
Reid, L.F. 242
Reston, James 188
Rhys, Canon H. (Rev.) 239, 243
Ricketts, "Hawk-Eye" 69
Riggins, Charles 85
Roberson, James 117
Robinson, Bruce 155
Rogers, Gamble 233
Rollins, Jackson 29, 73
Roosevelt, Jeannette 224-5, 238-9, 245
Rosen, Louis 117
Ryan, W. Carson 155

S

Sanderson, Colin 230, 245
Santayana, George 86
Santee, Frederick 37, 141, 189, 196-9, 218
Sappho 98-9, 100, 110
Saudek, Robert 136
Schliemann, Heinrich 80
Schumann-Heink, Ernestine 242
Scopes, John 63
Seidule, James 116, 153

Sellers, A. Edward (Rev.) 17
Sellers, Horace 30
Sharp, William B. 96
Shoemate, Clara 110
Simmonds, Ethel 59, 80, 88, 170, 204
Simmonds, Harvey (Br. Benedict) 204, 209, 215-16, 221, 228-9, 232-3, 237-8
Simmonds, William "Andy" 88, 244
Skidmore, Fletcher 31
Slater, Henry 79
Smith, Claude 32
Smith, Margene 132
Smith, Spencer 228
Spears, Ross 221, 222
Speegle, Betty 220
Speegle, Kenneth 139
Spencer, Bonnell (Rev.) "Bonny" 36-7, 39, 52-3, 74, 89, 107, 113, 123, 149, 156, 171, 207, 214-15
Spragget, Alan 224
Stapleton, Archie (Rev.) 142
Stark, Young 101
Steele, Novice 153
Steiger, John 203, 217
Stein, Gertrude 89
Stevens, Harmon 3
Stewart, John 161
Stewart, Robert 161
Stines, Nadine 239-40
Stott, William 136
Sullivan, Mark 161
Sumers, Dunning 64
Sutherland, Leon 200

T

Taglienti, Maria Luisa 132
Talbert, Eleanor 62, 190, 198, 209, 212, 214-16, 219
Talbert, Henry 178
Tallec, Jean 212-13, 215
Tate, Allen 36, 101-2, 110, 136, 223
Tate, Ann 108, 203-4
Tate, Elisha "Smokey" 151, 158
Tate, Shirley 121
Taylor, Peter 110, 136, 141
Taylor, Sidney 159
Temple, Robert 191
Thomas, Dylan 110, 133
Thorpe, Cynthia "Cindy" 240, 242

Thorpe, Greg 239-40
Tilden, Bill 158-9
Toupal, Robert 228
Towers, Claude 7
Towles, Eugene 36, 156
Trotter, John F. 230
Trotter, Marnette 84, 216, 229-31, 236-8, 240-1, 243, 245-6
Turkington, Wm. (Rev.) "Turk" 36, 39, 70, 74, 116, 153, 156, 158
Turner, Si 47
Twitchell, Amy 11
Twitchell, Myra 12

U
Utley, Edwin 28

W
Wade, Clint 225
Wade, John D. 101
Wade, William (Rev.) 38, 239, 243
Ware, Sedley 92, 98
Warren, Leila 41-2

Warren, Ralph 91, 105
Warren, Robert Penn 101, 110
Watts, Mildred 59, 80, 203
Webster, W.G. (Rev.) 24
Wensberg, Erik 183, 232
Wheeler, Russell "Doug" 89
Whitall, Edwin (Rev.) 67, 74, 116, 166
Williams, Tennessee 133, 136, 143-4, 191
Willis, Sam 161
Wilson, George D. 67
Wilson, Harold 39
Wright, Claude 40, 51
Wright, Erskine (Rev.) 60, 111, 130, 143, 165-7, 170, 200
Wright, Laura 60

Y
Yokley, Edward 40, 42-5, 149, 152
Yokley, Kathleen 45

Z
Zachary, Anna 183-4

ABOUT THE AUTHOR

William I. Hampton is a retired broadcast journalist. After serving as a Strategic Air Command bomber crewman in the U.S. Air Force, he embarked on a career of radio newscasting in Tallahassee, Portland, Cleveland, New York City, Dallas, Miami and Los Angeles. He won numerous citations for his in-depth reporting, including the Golden Mike Award, given by the Los Angeles Press Club, for his documentary about oil drilling off the coast of California. He received national recognition for his Dallas on-the-spot coverage of the assassination of President John F. Kennedy. His report from Parkland Hospital is featured on *Four Days That Shocked the World*, a collector's edition. He ended his broadcasting tenure by owning and operating a radio station in Oregon. He later wrote *The Winning Vote*, a book on how to win a local election.

Bill Hampton during a radio newscast in 1962